CITIZEN

CITIZEN

*Faithful Discipleship
in a Partisan World*

C. ANDREW DOYLE

Foreword by Cynthia Briggs Kittredge

CHURCH
PUBLISHING
INCORPORATED

Unless otherwise noted, the Scripture quotations are from New Revised Standard Version Bible, copyright © 1989 National Council of the Churches of Christ in the United States of America. Used by permission. All rights reserved worldwide.

Church Publishing
19 East 34th Street
New York, NY 10016
www.churchpublishing.org

Cover design by Marc Whitaker, MTWdesign
Typeset by PerfecType, Nashville, Tennessee

Library of Congress Cataloging-in-Publication Data

Names: Doyle, C. Andrew, author.
Title: Citizen : faithful discipleship in a partisan world / C. Andrew
    Doyle ; forward by Cynthia Briggs Kittredge.
Identifiers: LCCN 2019039850 (print) | LCCN 2019039851 (ebook) | ISBN
    9781640652019 (paperback) | ISBN 9781640652026 (ebook)
Subjects: LCSH: Christianity and politics. | Christians--Political
    activity. | Citizenship--Religious aspects--Christianity.
Classification: LCC BR115.P7 D67 2020 (print) | LCC BR115.P7 (ebook) |
    DDC 261.7--dc23
LC record available at https://lccn.loc.gov/2019039850
LC ebook record available at https://lccn.loc.gov/2019039851

The tyranny of a prince in an oligarchy is not so dangerous to the public welfare as the apathy of a citizen in a democracy.
            —Charles de Montesquieu, French philosopher and judge[1]

Contents

Foreword

When good, polite, and well-meaning people of faith, in a sincere effort to get along, avoid the subjects of politics and religion, they abdicate both their civic and their religious responsibility, and they leave the conversation to those who will exploit division. The incisive diagnosis, the call to shared values, and the word of hope offered by the Christian gospel are silent, and the country and the world grow more fractured and more severely damaged. Realizing God's dream for human flourishing recedes, and the church of Christ is weakened.

Those who are commanded to love God and to love neighbor and to be a community to heal the world cannot escape the responsibility of politics. In the chapters that follow, C. Andrew Doyle exhorts Christians to fulfill their vocation as Christian citizens. His passion for this task arises from his theological commitments that have been shaped and sharpened by his particular experience as pastor, preacher, and church leader. Doyle's pastoral identity energizes his project—he has witnessed congregations, anxious about changes in society and the church, paralyzed by apathy or swept up into partisan wrangling. He has listened to their conversations about the separation of church and state and heard echoes of the identification of America with Christianity. To this corporate wrestling, Doyle, the pastor, brings compassion and moral direction. As a preacher, Doyle interprets and proclaims Holy Scripture as it addresses human suffering within a damaged and diminished world community. He brings the vision-creating, rousing music of biblical voices to give hope and awaken communal action. Andrew Doyle is an ordained leader in the church, a bishop, called to a specific ecclesiastical role of oversight, unity, and teaching. He exercises this historic traditional role in the new circumstances that are this moment. As many readers of this book will be, Doyle is also an American nurtured in the culture of patriotism and pride that intersects and interacts with Christianity in this country. He embodies the tensions within many people of faith.

Bishop Doyle is a reader, and he engages the gospel with a wide range of contemporary writers. In dialogue with thinkers in ethics and theology, history, and political science, Doyle draws on the resources of the Christian tradition to offer a model for congregations to engage in politics as Christian citizens. Characterized by conviviality and openness to the voices of others, the model invites people of faith to enter the conversation as Christians first and Americans second. Describing the complex interaction of principles and philosophies in the founding of American democracy and acknowledging the ambiguous history of call and conquest, Doyle tackles the complex challenge of distinguishing Christian faith from American civil religion. To the romantic American individualistic freedom to choose one's own story, Doyle contrasts the compelling Christian story that enfolds and transcends the individual.

It is from the diverse voices of Holy Scripture that theologians, biblical scholars, and preachers have built this Christian story, and it is to scripture that Bishop Doyle turns to critique major ideological pillars of modernity and to play out an alternative Christian vision. The "garden imaginary," Doyle's crystallization of this vision, is an interdependent, organic society, where humans are bound to one another and in partnership with God. Within the garden imaginary sibling rivalry and violence are rejected. From the Pentateuch and the prophets, in the ministry of John the Baptizer, of Jesus and Mary of Galilee, and from the letters of Paul, Doyle amplifies the scriptural voices that critique and resist the forces of domination and the celebration of imperial power, of their time and of ours. Drawing on the beautiful and compelling scriptural imagination Doyle invites Christians to imagine and to create a society of nonviolence and self giving action on behalf of others and for the common good.

In his passionate engagement with the biblical text, Bishop Doyle per-
forms a significant hermeneutical service as a preacher, teacher, and church
leader for our times. He plays confidently in the field of scripture and
does not abandon that pasture to those who would employ a hermeneutic of inerrancy or literalism. He rejects conventional readings of Caesar's
coin and the spiritualization of Jesus's healings and feedings that make the
separation of religion and politics far too easy. He brings the principles
of the garden imaginary—mutuality, partnership, familial faithfulness—
and the life-giving paradox of Jesus's death and resurrection to read the
accounts of Jesus's exorcisms, his parables, and his provision of food for
hungry crowds. He shows how this vision of a just community can speak a
critical and constructive word about gun violence, mass incarceration, mili-
tarism, climate change, and to all the "real" matters with which we wrestle.
With theological commitments to freedom, fairness, and love of neighbor
Doyle presents an inclusive vision for human flourishing, harnessing the
rhetorical potency of the same Bible that has been read to legitimize slavery, patriarchy, violence, and exploitation of the earth.

Bishop Doyle's model of Christian engagement in politics exemplifies the distinctive position and particular charism of the Episcopal
Church as an instrument of God's mission in this American context at
this urgent and fraught moment. Rooted in the ancient Christian traditions, yet deeply shaped by the values of the Enlightenment that made
such an impact on the founding of this country, the Episcopal Church
has nurtured leaders who are able to learn from psychology, sociology,
political science, and contemporary biblical studies and to put them into
conversation with the insights and vision of scripture and tradition. Their
preaching and teaching is shaped by modernity and also able to critique
where it is blind or misguided.

From their location in the Episcopal Church, Christians can and must
engage in "politics" in a way that accepts and values pluralism. In the public square they will speak and act out of fiercely held Christian convictions without seeking to obtain sectarian privilege or achieve Christian
supremacy. Not willing to surrender to the forces of secularism and to die

out, neither do we promote an imperialistic vision of American society with church (with us) at its center. This place is a tricky and precarious one to occupy, but Bishop Doyle shows in this book how it is also a place of potential power, healing, and grace.

Citizen calls us to think, to pray, to act in community. For the sake of the world, for the sake of the church, be not afraid. Live within and work out of that Christian story that has chosen us. Together read scripture with heart, mind, and imagination. Strengthen the church. Till and keep the garden. Realize God's dream.

—Cynthia Briggs Kittredge
Seminary of the Southwest Dean and President
and Professor of New Testament

Introduction: Engaging an Apathetic Christian Citizen

Where you see wrong or inequality or injustice, speak out, because this is
your country. This is your democracy. Make it. Protect it. Pass it on.
    Thurgood Marshall, U.S. Supreme Court justice[1]

The 2016 U.S. election revealed that Christians are divided about what it means to be a citizen[2] in God's kingdom and a citizen of the empire. We have not been forming the baptized for the task of navigating the complex waters of a dual citizenship. This book is about Christian citizenship. What is its framework? What are its originating principles? How does it engage the princes of this world? What is its message? How does it make its way in community? These are just some of the questions I attempt to shed light upon.

Similar to Christian formation, civic formation in America has eroded. Voting percentages are down, there is a malaise among citizens towards their government, and hopelessness pervades political conversation. This malaise is a symptom of the overall crisis of citizenship formation that has taken root in most nations around the world.[3] The church has all but abandoned the conversation about Christian citizenship altogether. When apathy becomes the *modus operandi* of citizenship, and especially Christian citizenship, then we are in trouble. In the vacuum left by a retreating church, the nature of citizenship is being defined by other, less charitable voices.

Very few of the congregations in my diocese speak about voting or the duty of citizenship. Few speak about the importance of being a Christian citizen. Citizenship formation in my tradition is silent at worst, or merely preached from the pulpit, which is not helpful. The church has offered little teaching on the topic of Christian citizenship, so that her people bring their secular politics into their congregations totally unexamined.

I found clergy and lay leadership underprepared for the difficult conversations that emerged in the 2016 political environment. For example, there was widespread confusion about the separation of church and state. Somehow, we started to believe that separation of church and state meant we should not talk politics or religion with friends and family or at church. This is poor advice. Just because we don't do these conversations very well doesn't mean we shouldn't have them. We should be able to speak with skill and nuance about politics and religion. And, if we can't, in the immortal words of Napoleon Dynamite, "We need to get some skillz."

I would argue that schools, political parties, and the corporations that control the media have largely defined what is meant by citizenship. In this way, unchurched people have defined the terms of Christian citizenship for those inside our faith communities. The notion of Christian citizenship fell prey to the wider forces of principalities. The end result was that some Christians found themselves parroting their political party's agenda as Christianity. Others left the church from an inability to speak honestly about their opinions within a Christian framework or to have their opinions heard.

One of my priests related a story about a man who burst into his office barking and cursing, and alleged that the priest was a puppet of the Democratic party. After some conversation, the shocked priest who had done nothing more than invite his church to pray for the children separated from their parents at the U.S. border, responded, "Maybe you are a puppet for the Republican party." In the end the two remained colleagues and recognized that each has an important role to play in the discussion. Other conversations around my diocese were less civil.

Some parishioners came up for air following the election and were confused about the inner congregational conflict. I heard from many that their priest or their church friends weren't who they thought they were. Members' families were divided. One group in a Spanish-speaking congregation explained that as a family they talk about everything, but they were struggling because they could not talk about the election. Elsewhere, many parishioners thought that it was the work of Christians to be good Americans and support the nation-state without question. It wasn't that people didn't want to talk, they didn't want the church to ask critical questions about their government. This sentiment is commonly expressed when a president from your preferred party is in office. It is the rare Christian citizen indeed who manifests the same critical eye towards the government regardless of presidents and parties holding office. It is a rare Christian citizen who sees the issues defined first from the Christian perspective and then as a citizen of the nation.

Our post-9/11 politics have shaped many Christians into an unquestioning group within the wider voting population. Prayers for our soldiers and first responders during the prayers for the people abound, with no prayers for other civil servants. There is no critical conversation about the way the United States participates in armed engagements and occupations around the world. There is no safe space for opposing views. This is true even in our schools where critical space for political discourse is hard to come by. Teachers are struggling to form healthy citizens with critical political skills. Anxious parents, jittery school boards, and a never-ending politically charged news cycle makes this nearly impossible.[4] Churches share all of those same variables, but the way that our life in church intersects with deeply held personal and spiritual values and emotions make the conversation even more charged. My wife even asked, "Are you going to get in trouble for writing this book?"

Our discussions in public, private, and at church are charged with emotion and tribal loyalty to our political party. People feel threatened, anxious, and powerless. And, why not? The massive number of baby boomer retirements is putting pressure on our social services. The economy is good, but healthcare is gradually becoming something only the wealthy can afford.

Demand for skilled and unskilled labor is becoming unbalanced. The state of Texas itself is losing about 1 to 4 percent of its white population a year due to death. It will be a majority Hispanic state by 2020. American cities are quickly becoming majority minority communities. And, there is what some are calling a "death tsunami" coming, because as Deacon Bob Horner likes to say, "People have had too many birthdays." This will speed up the transformation of the country in the next twenty years. All of this threatens an old lifestyle and exacerbates power shifts.[5] There is a lot at stake for people and more than enough anxiety in the nation.

All of this reveals that what must be plumbed is not only what it means to be a Christian citizen, but what does that citizenship look like within the wider geography of local and global relationships *and* what does it look like as a theological concept over and against the powers of this world?

There are biases I need to name here. My first bias is that Christians must be Christians first, and citizens of their country second. This book is not about being an American who happens to be a Christian. This book is very much about what it means to be a Christian citizen in the reign of God who happens to be an American, or a citizen of any other nation-state. I firmly believe that a good citizen in the reign of God is a good citizen in whatever nation one may find oneself. Being a good citizen in the reign of God also requires that we subject the powers and principalities that make up our nation and permeate our government to a healthy degree of critical scrutiny. I understand that we need to have laws, have safe borders, and protect ourselves from threats. But I am not interested in bending the Christian story to justify unchristian means of achieving those things. When we do that we undermine our citizenship in the reign of God and make Jesus into a puppet of the empire. It also makes us poor citizens, because it erodes the critical eye that maintains the health of American democracy.

My second bias is my conviction that Christian citizens in the reign of God must have a global eye. God, the creator and redeemer of all things, is not interested in Americans only. God created all people. God came into the world to save all sinners. God has a global vision of the kingdom and therefore so must Christian citizens. This means that it matters how we treat people who are not Americans. Christian citizens are obligated to care about how our government treats foreigners, our neighbors, and those who are citizens of every other nation. Honoring our global calling will require a much bigger conscientious horizon.[6]

We are entering the conversation about Christian citizenship at a moment of seismic shifts. We can see these shifts clearly by analyzing our relationships and the nature of conversation within our congregations. Presently, the very idea of democracy is being reconsidered and many are questioning the assumed foundations upon which it operates. Anglican scholars John Milbank and Adrian Pabst write in *The Politics of Virtue: Post-liberalism and the Human Future*:

> The sway of both social and economic liberalism is today being quali-fied by the intrusion of political polarities that do not readily fit into a left-right spectrum. These new polarities concern variously the populist *versus* the technocratic, the bio-conservationist *versus* the trans-human, rootedness *versus* mobility, the interpersonal *versus* the anonymous, the virtuous *versus* the amoral, the local *versus* the uni-formly global and, above all, the primacy of society *versus* the primacy of the economy and the polity.[7]

In the Letter to the Ephesians (whose authorship is unknown but tradi-tionally attributed to Paul the apostle) we are reminded that we cannot be "tossed to and fro and blown about by every wind of doctrine, by people's trickery, by their craftiness in deceitful scheming" (Eph. 4:14). Instead we are to put on the person of the Christ. We are put together a community made up of citizens of the reign of God, unified by the work of Jesus upon the cross and by virtue of our baptism. The preface for baptism found in the Episcopal Book of Common Prayer reads, ". . . because in Jesus Christ our Lord you have received us as your sons and daughters, made us citizens of your kingdom, and given us the Holy Spirit to guide us into all truth."[8]

We are at once defined by the one God in Christ Jesus, and at the same time we are the many knit together by his work. The Letter to the Ephesians continues, "We must grow up in every way into him who is the head, into Christ, from whom the whole body, joined and knitted together by every ligament with which it is equipped, as each part is working properly, promotes the body's growth in building itself up in love" (Eph. 4:14–16).

The body of Christ cannot leave its understanding of the polis, the city, the nation, the state, and our place in it as dual citizens, to secular philosophers, politicians, political partisans, or the media. Presently, Christian citizens are being blown this way and that. As we survey the landscape of our churches, our worship looks more like a reaffirmation of our political partisanships than the renewal of our Lord and Savior's body in the world. We are the most politically, racially, and ethnically divided on Sunday morning.[9]

A vacated Christian citizenship means the loss of a critical voice within the wider political discourse. In the U.S. there is more at work here than simply a disagreement between red and blue states. There is a deep work of manipulation underway by the powers that be to manipulate local and global forces towards greater inequality, and income disparity, through wage theft, lack of access to health care, and the reining in of freedoms.[10] Assumptions that Christian citizenship is equal to an American civil religion are over. The church no longer has the luxury of believing that Christian citizenship is synonymous with American citizenship—as if it ever were. The same is true for Christians in every nation.

Outsiders cannot define the work of virtuous citizenship for the Christian. The outsiders who promote a false understanding of the division between church and state in order to manipulate Christians into supporting their unchristian agenda includes but is not limited to politicians, campaign managers, political commentators, and the media. Christianity is not practiced alone. Christianity is not an individual sport. It must be practiced among people in relationship. A practiced Christian citizenship affects various levels of community, in relationship to goods and services, and as part of the wider economy. It cannot be practiced in the church only. Christian citizenship must be lived out in the world, supported by the church.

Christianity is not a spiritual exercise for the individual but a communal expression that, if lived as imagined by God, cannot help but be political. Christianity is about politics. What is interesting here, and of no little importance, is the fact that Americans define politics as oriented around the nation. Politics for most Americans is defined as the work of government, the art of influencing policy, the science of holding control of government. It is political actions, practices, and the political affairs or business of parties. It is professional in nature.[11] Christians define politics as the primary relationship between citizens and systems that govern their community. This book is not interested in a secular American understanding of a political ideology that serves the government and those who work in it. It is concerned with the role and work of Christian citizens in shaping the systems of authority that impact our community, nation, and the world.

As Christian citizens we have a particular way in which we do this. We approach it with a posture of conviviality. When we use the term convivial, we understand that there is a personal interdependence within the broader whole that captures both individual freedom and relationship to God and others.[12] Christian theologian and cultural critic Ivan Illich suggests that conviviality is Christian citizenship lived out in action. For instance, convivial citizens resist only speaking and answering the question in their minds while the other is talking. They practice the art of listening first before speaking. Convivial citizenship requires an active curiosity, a constant looking and watching in order to gain understanding of our context. Convivial citizens practice their virtuosity in relationship with a diverse group of other people. This conviviality generates its own path and is always opposed to oppression because it is so reliant on relationship between citizens who are different. This book will imagine a Christian citizenship that takes a convivial approach to all people, thereby destroying the invasive political notion that *if you are not for us then you are against us.*

I say all of this by way of introduction because this book is not simply offered as another book on citizenship to be read by the like-minded. Instead, I aim for this book to be a guide for conversation and for listening, for thoughtful action, reflection, and prayer; brought forth from God's imagination and generative within the community, polis/city, nation-state and global contexts in which Christians make their home. I hope that this book will offer an engaged, virtuous, habit-forming Christian citizenship that is convivial in manner and works towards a common good.

Chapter One

A Birth Narrative

Neither religion nor liberty can long subsist in the tumult of altercation and amidst the noise and violence of faction.
　　　　　　　　　　　　—Samuel Adams, founding father[1]

Our country was birthed from a unique soup of emerging political philosophy and constructive Protestantism. We need to dust off our old sixth-grade ideas from social studies and remove ourselves from the media and political parties that presently have our ears. We need to try to get some clarity about the birth of our nation. This is our origin story.

When we look at the original texts, correspondence, and writings of English separatist and member of the Mayflower community at Plymouth John Bradford, we cannot doubt his view of the place this new colony would have in God's history. His motives for cross-continental migration were indicative of the Puritan Pilgrims making way towards a new land. They believed they were called by God to create a new society. Looking back when his life was nearing its end, Bradford believed they had survived only by God's providence.

One of my ancestors was aboard that boat. He was John Howland, an indentured servant. He would survive the Mayflower voyage having been washed overboard during a storm and rescued. He then survived the conditions of the strange foreign land. He would later become the private

1

assistant and personal secretary to Governor John Carver. From there his fortunes would grow, as did the family's, until the stock market crash of the 1930s. What the Atlantic could not do to John, the sea of financial change did to my great grandfather and he took his own life. God's providence and fortune lasted for just so long. I am proud of my family and its link to the founding of a nation. I have other relatives who were refugees, immigrants, and the like. I am proud of them, too. Life was harsh for those early colonists just as it has been for most newcomers to America. I am also very aware that the Pilgrims and Puritans were often cruel and harsh people.

The shores of the new land seemed like a blank canvas upon which Protestants could paint their vision of God's kingdom. They were ambitious to prove the political ideas of "constructive Protestantism," which means just what you think. Here in the new colonies they dreamed of moving beyond the ever-present conflict they were in with the more moderate authorities of the old world. They could cease protesting the principalities of the religious wars, and build a new society. There was no monarchy, no religious institutions, and no laws of obedience.[2] President John Adams, reflecting upon this moment in history, wrote, "Soon after the Reformation, a few people came over into this new world for conscience sake. . . . Perhaps this apparently trivial incident may transfer the great seat of empire into America."[3]

The story of this "few people" is rather difficult to parse out when we consider motives. It is clear, for instance, that Bradford and his Pilgrim group came to make a new Godly society. They were not interested in what anyone else was up to. They were intent on their version of constructive Protestantism. Also present were Quakers, Baptists, Moravians, Dunkers, Mennonites who joined the Methodists, and Franciscans or Dominicans who were also shaping and forming colonial society in this new land, not to mention bewildered indigenous people who knew nothing of the years of religious conflict that had beached so many refugees on their shores. In their own ways each of these groups had a vision to build from scratch a church society that was the world.

The chartered Virginia colony is a great example of the many and varied ideas about just what was to take place on this blank slate of a new world. John Smith and John Rolfe, the first leaders of the Virginia colony, believed they were coming to bring Christianity to the ignorant. King James I echoed this in his charter inviting the colonists to do "noble work."[4] The king orders them to take possession of the land, take possession of all natural resources, to search and mine for gold, silver, and copper. Furthermore, they are to protect these new assets of the king's from others. Historian and biographer Jon Meacham points out that of the 3,805 words that make up the charter only 3 percent, or 98 words, have to do with the kingdom of God in America.[5] The colonists had one idea and King James I had another.

The colony was soon in disorder. Thomas Gates arrived on the scene two years into the endeavor and quickly set about creating a theocracy of ordered life which consisted of "Laws Divine, Moral, and Martial" and they were to be kept by the religious and non-religious of the colony alike or suffer "pain of death."[6] This did not however deter the king from his goals.

In his book *The Kingdom of God in America*, historian and theologian H. Richard Niebuhr offers a view of our history that reveals how this constructive Protestantism led to particular ideas about American society that were formative in the nation's earliest moments. You will notice I did not include the Anglican Church as part of the aforementioned group. They, too, came as colonists, but later. I should also mention that in many ways the Anglicans were the people the above group of constructive Protestants were trying to get away from! These new religious people in America sought to get out from under the thumb of an established Anglican Church that was completely enmeshed with the organs of government in the British Isles.

These first colonists strove to create a theocracy with a priesthood of all believers. What they faced was the struggle of creating a land of laws, and the result of this could be "religious anarchy or wild sectarianism in which every group and every individual could claim to speak for God."[7] They had been protesting so long that construction was nearly impossible. In the end they would have a profound impact on American society in its infancy as they brought with them values such as the limitation of human power and moderation, a sense of a sovereign and transcendent God, limits on economic life and work, and the independence of the church.[8] This last value is important. They believed that the church should be free from the entanglements of government, not that the government was free from the criticism and accountability of the church. Finally, and perhaps more importantly, these first colonists believed in the idea of progress. Just as the Pilgrims made their progress in the new land so too was the nation to value and make progress. The sovereignty of God was institutionalized in the laws and so was the idea that we as a nation were progressing towards God's kingdom. This became a national moral sanction and belief in American progress.[9]

Dietrich Bonhoeffer, protestant theologian, wrote that America is "Protestantism without Reformation." Meaning that here in this country there was a Protestant faith that was birthed without the necessity of dissent against existing structures of government. This freedom meant that Protestants have a unique focus upon community, liturgy, and a commitment to a social gospel.[10] An amendment of the 1833 Massachusetts constitution eliminated any established church, and in its place created a civil religion founded in society itself. The amendment reads, "The public worship of God, and the instructions in piety, religion, and morality, promote the happiness and prosperity of a people, and the security of republican government."[11]

Niebuhr's critics today look at his work as the last vestiges of a Constantinian church that once enjoyed a privileged place within the Western structures of community and government. This is no longer so.[12] I do think Niebuhr got it right that constructive Protestantism was an essential part of what brought some folks to the Americas, and what drove them to settle and create societies here. But the mythic Mayflower narrative that everyone came for religious freedom to start a new Protestant society is just that—a myth. The true end result is a hodgepodge of Protestantism, Republican/Democratic political theory, and common sense.[13]

The first colonists were a diverse group, even including nonreligious people. They came with varied public and private ambitions. We also know their strongest critique of making this a Christian nation was born out of the forge of writing our founding documents and congress itself. While it is true that a few early colonists came to tame the savages and bring

Christianity to the natives, we also know that there was more to the colonial enterprise than that.

Take, for instance, the battle over a Christian religious test for office holders. The argument between William Williams and Oliver Ellsworth in 1787 was another turning point in our history. William Williams wanted government office holders to be Christian. Ellsworth's sentiments won the day. He countered that it would be good for the Congregationalists, Presbyterians, Episcopalians, Baptists, or Quakers in our midst, but such a test would leave out over three-fourths of American citizens.[14] This gives us a sense of how Ellsworth saw the American public—three-fourths—as not necessarily religious.

We know that when it came to creating a country, the influence of a sovereign transcendent God was important, and that Jesus Christ was left out of the founding documents intentionally. George Washington and Thomas Jefferson were clear: America would be a country for everyone regardless of place of birth or religious faith. The national motto "In God We Trust" has been challenged as a violation of this principle, but the Supreme Court has ruled that ceremonial deism is not religious in nature.[15]

The government we founded was not solely based upon either the Christian ideals of the Puritans and their friends, nor was it birthed solely out of a reaction to them. Our government and our understanding of the citizen's role in it also emerges out of a relationship with Great Britain. The king of England and eighteenth-century forms of government in Great Britain are important dialogue partners from which our country springs.

The American colonists were reacting to what was normative in Great Britain and across Europe. They were also reading and discussing the most recent thoughts in political philosophy.

Great Britain had a king and after the *Magna Carta* a parliament. The nature of citizenry in England was birthed through one's local town receiving a charter from the king. Local politics were very important and things like administration, crime prevention, regulations, and economy were all run by the local citizenry—those who lived in the chartered town.[16] The colonists in America were not afforded such privileges. This common web of relationship was essential in the British style of government and would become one of the big issues in the new colonies.

It was not until after the Civil War in England (1642–1651) that people started to ask questions about citizenship, property, and representation. The disaster of Cromwell's revolution combined with emerging political thought got people thinking. Real questions like, "Who gets to vote?" were not even considered prior to this moment in British history. During the Restoration a very radical thought occurred—who is a citizen? Who gets to vote?

There is a fascinating conversation, recorded for posterity, between two British army officers inside a Putney church in 1647. Colonel Rainsborough said, "I think that the poorest he that is in England has a life as the greatest of he . . . and I do think that the poorest man in England is not at all bound in a strict sense to that government that he has not had a voice to put himself under." General Ireton, who was present, was not fond of the idea and quickly moved the notion of limiting the franchise to land owning individuals.[17]

What emerges as the American colonies are being founded is a deeper understanding of this political form that is defined and protected by the laws of the land. The word "citizen" and the concept of citizenship are rarely used, if at all. Eighteenth-century principalities did not have much use for the concept of citizenship, so it was relegated to a very broad understanding of relationships. The word citizen itself does not even come into recognized use in the English language and appear in a dictionary until 1910.[18] Historian Robert Roswell Palmer wrote in 1959, "In the English language the word 'citizen' in its modern sense is an Americanism."[19] This is how important our particular notion of participatory government is.

Political philosophers were trying to put some flesh and bones on the ideas of citizenship and participatory government around the same time as the conversation at the Putney church. In an age of monarchies and despotism dependent upon neoplatonic thought, four philosophers influenced by Aristotle take the stage and change the world forever. The impact of their thinking is essential in understanding the shift to a world of enlightened individuals and modern politics. These four philosophers, to whom American politics is deeply indebted, are: Thomas Hobbes (1588–1679), John Locke (1632–1704), Charles-Louis de Secondat, Baron de La Brède et de Montesquieu who was simply referred to as Montesquieu (1689–1755), and Jean-Jacques Rousseau (1712–1778); each is considered a founder of modern political philosophy. In brief here are the basic ideas each contributed.

Thomas Hobbes of Malmesbury, England, began his treatise *Leviathan* by asserting that humanity has had freedoms, such a "state of nature," as to build up a leviathan—a commonwealth.[20] Within this state humanity was naturally equal. The individual was free to do what was needed to live life. However, that life was lived in a perpetual state of "continued fear and danger of violent death; and the life of man [was] solitary, poor, nasty, brutish, and short."[21] Hobbes then used an older idea from contract law to say that the people agreed among themselves to "lay down" their natural rights of equality and freedom and give absolute power to a sovereign for protection. Hobbes's contribution to American politics is the idea that government results from people's willingness to trade their freedom and equality for peace.

It was English philosopher and physician John Locke who took it a step further. He believed all human beings had rights. He argued in his *Second Treatise of Civil Government* that everyone had the right "to preserve . . . life, liberty, and estate."[22] The founders of the United States borrowed this idea but changed the word "estate" to "happiness"; the post-revolutionary French changed "estate" to "security and resistance to oppression."[23] At the time property was as much a problem as citizenship, which is why it is listed in Locke's treatise. He believed everyone deserved representation in the government.

Charles Montesquieu wrote *The Spirit of the Law* in 1748. In it he suggested something radical indeed: the best form of government was one in which a legislative, executive, and judicial power were divided in order to keep each other in line, thereby preventing any one branch from becoming too strong or powerful. Montesquieu sought a power balance in the decision-making for the citizens the government represented. In this way the citizens were protected.[24] If they were going to give up their powers to a centralized government then the people had to be protected from the very force they were creating by sacrificing their liberty and equality.

Jean-Jacques Rousseau is our final contributing philosopher. He was a radical thinker and hoped for a pure democracy. His work entitled *The Social Contract* was truly radical and took the other three philosopher's work to an extreme. The opening words are, "Man is born free, and everywhere he is in chains."[25] Rousseau understood the world and culture in which he found himself. With clear eyes, a bit of Plato, and a whole lot of Aristotle he worked out a new system of politics that included a very healthy understanding and updating of Aristotle's idea of citizenship. In Rousseau's government, every person was an individual citizen who voted directly, with no intermediary, in order to make the laws of the land. He believed that rather than give up one's freedom to a government one did so by giving it up to a collective of individuals. In doing so, a civil state of citizens was created, and law, security, justice, and liberty are enabled. Political power was attached to the majority vote, which was taken to express the general will. All of this was based upon a radical understanding of the individual.[26] The individual and their reasoning faculties governed by voting.

John Witherspoon, long tenured president of Princeton University and signer of the Declaration of Independence, believed that the American system of government with its battling powers would be ruled by a kind of "common sense" philosophy. He based his ideas on the work of British philosopher Thomas Reid (1710–1796), founder of the Scottish School of Common Sense, who was a key philosophical father of the tradition. British philosopher Thomas Paine's book *Common Sense* (1776) picked up the philosophy and ran with it. He applied the tradition to society and politics. The "common sense" tradition is a combination of empiricism and intuitionism—of knowing and gut feelings. Witherspoon believed that humans come with a kind of power of judgment: common sense. In this way we can say, we are created by God with "natural and original" abilities to know and reason, and we might call it reason and it was the primary means by which our founders understood their work.[27] The final gift of our founders is that our rights are God-given and discerned by reason.

The thoughts of our four philosophers became the pillars of American political thought. Alongside the transcendent God and common-sense reason came the idea of the individual search for happiness. The citizen became the highest authority. "We the people" from Rousseau, the balance of power amidst the forms of government (legislative, executive, and judicial) from Montesquieu, "life liberty and the pursuit of happiness" from Locke, and the social contract between the governed and governor from Hobbes found their way into the Declaration of Independence, the American Constitution, the Federalist Papers, the Bill of Rights, and its amendments. Here are the seeds of a different kind of republic—and it all seems quite reasonable.

Patriotism had been understood as a sense of allegiance to whatever kind of society one belongs. One can be patriotic for the land in which one dwells regardless of who rules: despot, monarch, or the elected officials in a republic. But this new nation was different. In American politics, citizenship and patriotism were combined for the first time. The resultant nationalism is a very different concept.[28] Citizenship and national identity had never before been linked. Yet, from this moment on (including the French Revolution), the nation was dependent upon the individual citizen's belief that they are an essential part of the governing of the whole.[29]

The notion that people were citizens of a nation unto themselves, that they were answerable to God and one another alone, was a unique idea at that moment in history. It was prophetic because it offered a very real alternative to the accepted politics of the day. The world was literally turned upside down. The founding Puritan ideals plus the emerging political philosophy inspired the birth of a nation and a violent breaking of colonial ties with Great Britain. When the smoke cleared, these ideas began to create new conflict. Was this fledgling nation going to be Christian?

Patrick "Give me liberty, or give me death!" Henry and others wanted to establish religion (specifically religious school teacher pay) in the 1784 battle over religious freedom in Virginia.[30] Other founders, who were also the third and fourth presidents of the United States, Thomas Jefferson and James Madison, united in order to create a basic understanding of how religion and our government were to relate. Jefferson wrote, "The legitimate powers of government extend to such acts only as are injurious to others."[31] And, "It does me no injury for my neighbor to say there are twenty gods, or no God. It neither picks my pocket nor breaks my leg."[32] Madison wrote, "Whilst we assert for ourselves a freedom to embrace, to profess and to observe the religion which we believe to be of divine origin, we cannot deny an equal freedom to those whose minds have not yet yielded the evidence which has convinced us."[33] There were even attempts to put "Jesus" into the founding documents. These attempts failed and theocrats have been trying to get back in the game ever since. Those who wish to rewrite history and make America's narrative Christian in its telling make wild accusations, dismiss historical evidence, and jump through all kinds of rhetorical hoops so they can say, "They didn't really mean that."

There are indeed many things of importance here. Let us be clear though, America was founded upon a variety of ideals and for a variety of purposes and not as a Christian nation on purpose. Established religion was to be rejected.[34] George Washington perhaps said it best when he wrote to the Jewish congregation of Newport. After his inauguration the new president wrote three hundred and forty amazing words to the congregation who at that time was concerned about religious tolerance in the new nation. Washington believed that religious "toleration" would create a nation of religious liberty. The government would not interfere with individuals in matters of conscience and belief. He then quoted 2 Kings 18:31: "Every one shall sit in safety under his own vine and figtree, and there shall be none to make him afraid." He went on to say that the best America would be one that "gives to bigotry no sanction, to persecution no assistance, requires only that they who live under its protection should demean themselves as good citizens, in giving it on all occasions their effectual support."[35]

Part of what the founders did so well is bring a disunified people together for the sake of a new kind of union. Christianity that is bigoted, that supports unjust punishments, that persecutes, that is intolerant, that pays no attention to the least and lost has no parallel in our best national values. What the American founders accomplished was nothing less than prophetic and continues to shape the world and its emerging democracies.[36]

The American form of democracy is still unique in the wider system of global political powers today. It remains a witness to ideals birthed in the conflict over individual and communal freedoms.

Our particular theology of dominion that drove the first Christian colonists here continued well into the nineteenth century. There is a clear yet creative tension between democracy and dominion present in our DNA from the start. The newcomers to the American shores were looking for freedom and they were also colonists who came to dominate. We must always be careful not to perpetuate a Eurocentrism as we look back. There were people here long before Europeans arrived and exploited their advantage to displace and annihilate whole populations of people. The government formed in the occupied new territories needed apologists. In large part demythologizing this is an essential part of the maturation process our country now faces. Will we continue to perpetuate a revisionist history of the Americas with a European-centric voice or will we find reconciliation and forgiveness through an honest narrative of the conquest of a land that belonged to others?

Nevertheless, as America increased its westward expansion it required a philosopher, and John L. O'Sullivan writing for *The United States Democratic Review* stepped into the vacuum. In his first article published in 1839 he made the case that America was destined for greatness. Rooted in the virtue of progress, O'Sullivan made the case that we were a nation that exhibited humanity's great ability to use common sense for the betterment of the whole. While turning a blind eye to slavery and the oppression of the indigenous people, he made the case that America itself was the shining example of humanity's future, having undone the powers of monarchies, oligarchs, and emperors. Our "liberty, civilization, and refinement" leads us not to replicate the past injustices and cruelties.

> Our annals describe no scenes of horrid carnage, where men were led on by hundreds of thousands to slay one another, dupes and victims to emperors, kings, nobles, demons in the human form called heroes. We have had patriots to defend our homes, our liberties, but no aspirants to crowns or thrones; nor have the American people ever

suffered themselves to be led on by wicked ambition to depopulate the land, to spread desolation far and wide, that a human being might be placed on a seat of supremacy.[37]

Such is the blindness of those who believe in an American destiny that knows no boundaries. O'Sullivan envisioned an America that exhibited, "freedom of conscience, freedom of person, freedom of trade and business pursuits, universality of freedom and equality" regardless of the costs to those without power.[38] His essay was challenged by those who thought American "futurity" needed to have its freedom checked by some measure of moral accountability. This led O'Sullivan to write a second article in 1845 giving voice to America's "manifest destiny." He believed it was our work to lead the whole world to democracy, and this is why we should add Texas to our nation.[39] He wrote that it was our manifest destiny to inhabit the whole of the continent in order to secure not only our democracy and growth but also to fulfill God's providence. California was to be next in our destiny's annexation.

The expansion happened because of the influx of immigrants from across the world armed with plows and rifles. America was unstoppable. A nation would gather under the vision of manifest destiny because of a deeply held belief that God's will for America was not just a human enterprise but that America was created by God to bring about the subjugation of these lands (and the native peoples). O'Sullivan's words pushed America forward, leaning on Thomas Jefferson's acquisition of the Louisiana territory, to Texas, Oregon, and California so that we would be a country united by land from sea to shining sea. It led to setting our boundary with Canada in 1842. James Polk won the presidency in 1845 with the slogan "54° 40' or fight" (a reference to the potential northern boundary of Oregon as latitude 54° 40'). Polk called American claims to Oregon "clear and unquestionable" in his inaugural address.[40]

Manifest Destiny made rivals of siblings; it made Americans covet the western territories for their wealth and natural resources; it led to violence with Mexico; and it secured America's boundaries. I live in Texas. I love to visit Colorado, California, and Oregon. I am a proud American.

Without the doctrine of Manifest Destiny many of my family's ancestors, who were immigrants and eventually naturalized as citizens, would not have found a home in America. Economy and geography made room for them to find a home. Through this expansion greater diversity was brought to America through the culture of the west, as well as the influx of global cultures. And, Manifest Destiny further rooted the value of progress as an American value. These are all good things but they came at great cost to the native peoples of North America.

Manifest Destiny used the notion of dominion as its operating philosophy and its cost was great both in human life and the loss of culture. It led to American imperialism and colonialism: the occupation of Mexico, and colonial occupations of Hawaii, Guam, the Philippines, and Puerto Rico. It allowed for the expansion of slavery and the continued oppression and displacement of the First Peoples. As many as fifty million Native Americans died because of westward expansion that resulted in resettlement, war, and disease.[41] Critics argued that the values of freedom and liberty in our Constitution did not give us the right to violate the rights of other people who held property, to expand slavery, or to continue the breaking of treaties that oppressed the freedom of others. In the end, moral integrity was sacrificed on the altar of the American vision of empire.

The religious philosopher Charles Taylor suggests that compromise is still evident in how American power is wielded today. We are not only a global power, we are the global power.[42] Stanley Hauerwas points out that the reality that we are constantly at war ensures that power. It also ensures a particular kind of religiosity that is part of the public civil religion. Our American civil religion sees war and violence as part of the sacrificial act of maintaining our unique place in the wider family of nations, which creates a particular kind of understanding that sacrifice for the good of American ideals is noble. Professor of history Richard Gamble, in *The War for Righteousness: Progressive Christianity, the Great War, and the Rise of the Messianic Nation*, writes that we have a common enemy that unites us: those who stand against our particular and unique difference in the pantheon of nations. We assume, as part of our civil religion, that we go to war to protect the moral enterprise that is our inheritance.[43]

Jon Meacham believes our country does indeed have good news at its core. It has a special American way that shapes the life of our nation without strangling it. This legacy was created in its founding and is rooted in a sensible center created by Thomas Jefferson and others. Meacham writes, "This victory over excessive religious influence and excessive secularism is often lost in the clatter of contemporary cultural and political strife."[44] This is the American difference that has led to a particular American civil religion.

Chapter Two

Our Beloved Civil Religion

*I believe in one God, creator of the universe. That he governs it by his
Providence. That he ought to be worshiped. That the most acceptable service
we can render to him is doing good to his other children. That the soul of
man is immortal, and will be treated with justice in another life respecting
its conduct in this. These I take to be the fundamental principles of all sound
religion, and I regard them as you do, in whatever sect I meet with them.*
—Benjamin Franklin[1]

While it was not set in stone at the start and has become more
defined across time, American civil religion is a part of American
citizenship. But, in the immortal words of Inigo Montoya from
the movie *The Princess Bride*, "I don't think it means what you think it
means." American Christians are devoted to an American civil religion
and not the Christian Gospel. They steward an American faith in a different god than the God of scripture.

I love my country and believe that democracy is a vital political means
to structure government. I fear that we have taken our love for our country
and its own civil religion too far. It has, in recent years, taken on a nationalistic fervor that concerns me. Moreover, my love for the country, its form
of government, and its civil religion is no substitute for Christianity. I do
have concerns for my nation at this hour but my greater concern is for
my faith and the faith of the church. We must endeavor as Christians to

remind ourselves that there is a difference between the the civil religion of any state and the faith of God in Jesus Christ informed through the power of the Holy Spirit. We have become too infatuated I fear with our beloved civil religion.

Robert Bellah, an Episcopalian and sociologist, spoke often about civil religion. He believed that every nation-state, America especially, comes to a religious understanding of itself and grounds its civic practices in this religion. Civic religion is the self-understanding of a nation manifested in word and deed.[2] Bellah's vision of civil religion is a continuation of pioneering sociologist Émile Durkheim's study of a type of social consciousness that emerges whenever individuals band together to form an institution.[3] Bellah adapts Durkheim's method to American society to reveal a strong religious dimension to American civic life.[4] In presidential inaugural addresses God serves as a frame for the presidential vision of the future. In John F. Kennedy's inaugural address from January 20, 1961, for example, God is mentioned three times.[5] This amounts to far more than a "sentimental nod" to God.[6]

Durkheim's method of analysis makes clear that such references to God are rituals. In fact, all inaugural events and other occasions like the Gettysburg Address by Lincoln[7] are national liturgies with form, prescribed words at times, and timing. Bellah observes that references to specific religious traditions (Jewish, Christian, Muslim) are omitted, but there is clear religious piety associated with the state. The nation has a religious, though not *particularly* religious, dimension. We are reminded that President Dwight D. Eisenhower said, "Our government makes no sense unless it is founded in a deeply felt religious faith—and I don't care what it is."[8]

Despite eschewing any allegiance to a specific church or religious creed, American civil religion does have a particular set of beliefs: The government and the president of the United States have a duty to the people and to God. In Kennedy's inaugural address, this charge of spiritual responsibility clearly originates from an authority beyond America's founding documents. Bellah writes,

Beyond the Constitution, then, the president's obligation extends not only to the people but to God. In American political theory, sovereignty rests, of course, with the people, but implicitly, and often explicitly, the ultimate sovereignty has been attributed to God. This is the meaning of the motto, "In God we trust," as well as the inclusion of the phrase "under God" in the pledge to the flag.[9]

The second time Kennedy uses "God" he is stressing the same point, that an obligation to a higher authority exists. He is saying that human rights emerge from the relationship between individuals and God. This lofty, religious evocation is rooted deep in our American civil religious psyche.[10] In the opening remarks of *The Soul of America*, Jon Meacham argues that presidents remind us of our better selves, of our highest virtues. What Kennedy does, like those before and after him, is remind the Americans that no political power, no group, no party can claim a legitimate absolutism because God is above all of them.

There is a governing transcendence in American civil religion. A god who is beyond any specific denominational or ecclesial specificity stands above all else, judging the work of the nation and its people. Furthermore, Kennedy reiterates that this American god is concerned with those who are oppressed by "tyranny, poverty, disease, and war."[11] There is a higher power other than the president, our national documents like the Constitution, our branches of federal government, the governors, and those governed. This higher power longs for a world free from oppression, according to Kennedy. This same transcendent god favors American success as a means of achieving this aim. And yet this American god sends people to war, oppresses people to serve American interests, and drives out those who have fallen afoul of an American Manifest Destiny. This god serves the United States through his providence. We have referenced this god in our speeches for good and for ill. This American god also requires of its citizens to make virtuous sacrifices on behalf of the state. These sacrifices define our obligation as a nation in relationship to the global family.[12]

Jean-Jacques Rousseau, the founders, the Civil War, Abraham Lincoln, John F. Kennedy, and Lyndon Baines Johnson—all of these people and

events have shaped the American civil religion. Abraham Lincoln referenced the American god repeatedly in calling us to a higher moral ground.
Christian theologian Reinhold Niebuhr has this to say of Lincoln:

> An analysis of the religion of Abraham Lincoln in the context of the
> traditional religion of his time and place and of its polemical use on
> the slavery issue, which corrupted religious life in the days before
> and during the Civil War, must lead to the conclusion that Lincoln's
> religious convictions were superior in depth and purity to those, not
> only of the political leaders of his day, but of the religious leaders of
> the era.[13]

Meacham points out in *American Gospel* that Christianity had a significant
impact on the faith of the founders, but American civil religion was more
transcendent than any one specific religious tradition would allow. The
American civil religion and Christianity are not the same. Meacham writes,

> The Republic is not a church, but it is a Republic filled with churches.
> Let the religious speak but encourage them not to shout; let them
> argue, but encourage them not to brawl. The system the Founders
> built allows for religious considerations to play a role in politics in the
> same measure—no greater, no smaller—as any other consideration,
> whether geographical, economic, or cultural.[14]

American civil religion is characterized by belief in a transcendent god
who invites grace, civility, and charity when we are at our best.

American civil religion has adapted ancient religious archetypes
like "the Exodus, Chosen People, Promised Land, New Jerusalem, and
Sacrificial Death and Rebirth."[15] Americans have their own saints and sinners, heroes and martyrs; speeches are made and life given to the symbols
that place the United States and her people in the center stage. American
civil religion is uniquely ours. It belongs to our nation. It is not Christianity,
though it sometimes resembles it, nor does our civil religion belong to
any other faith or denomination. The American god declares that making war is a holy act of religious observance. Shedding blood to protect
an American way of life is a virtuous duty that should not be questioned.

Some Christians call American civil religion a heresy. I am not sure about that. I think Christian citizens can work congruently within such a civil religion, though we should not confuse the two.

Bellah's conclusions about the American civil religion have been empirically supported by further study. In 1976, sociologist Ronald Wimberley concluded that Americans, regardless of denominational/non-denominational/agnostic tendencies, believe that the United States is God's chosen nation. A president's authority is from God. Social justice cannot only be based on laws; it must also come from religion. God can be known through the experiences of the American people. Holidays like the Fourth of July are religious as well as patriotic.[16] A 1978 study by Wimberley and fellow researcher James Christensen found that civil religiosity is shared across denominations. Protestants, Catholics, the Mormons, Adventists, and Pentecostals, have the highest civil religiosity. Jews, Unitarians, and those with no religious preference have the lowest. Christensen and Wimberley found they all shared the religious beliefs Bellah identified.[17]

When Wimberley again undertook the work some four years later the loyalties had shifted to civil religion from the professed religious preferences. Two years later the professed religious identity mattered less to people than their vocational or professional identities, but the American civil religion remained the number one influence on their behaviors.[18] As their study evolved they found strong civil religious support for the following statements:

"We should respect a president's authority since it comes from God."

"God can be known through the experience of the American people."

"The founding fathers created a blessed and unique republic when they gave us the Constitution."

"To me, the flag of the United States is sacred."

"In this country, people have equal, divinely given rights to life, freedom, and a search for happiness."

"In America, freedom comes from God through our system of government by the people."[19]

Civil religion is not always a unifying force. During hotly contested political periods over the last fifty years, sometimes different views of this civil religion have been at odds in determining the desired future for our country. And yet, what remains is the belief in America's divine future.[20]

American civil religion is a variant of *moral therapeutic deism*. In fact, our civil religion may have even helped to bring *moral therapeutic deism* into being. In the 2009 book *Soul Searching*, Christian Smith and Melinda Lundquist Denton conducted three thousand interviews with teenagers, and highlight commonalities emerging in this generation of spiritual pilgrims.[21] The authors identify five concepts that make up this generation's faith foundation. Smith and Denton call this set of beliefs *moralistic therapeutic deism*. These young deists believe that God created and ordered the world and watches over human life and the earth. They believe that God wants people to be good, nice, and fair to each other as taught in the Bible and by most world religions. They believe that the central goal of life is to be happy and to feel good about oneself. They think that God does not need to be particularly involved in one's life except when God is needed to resolve problems. They also believe that good people go to heaven when they die.

What I find interesting is that the creed of this emerging moral therapeutic deism is identical to the creed of the American civil religion, where a transcendent God creates and orders the world and the nation of America especially. This God supports an American ethic of freedom and common-sense reason that results in the American virtues of goodness, niceness, and fairness. For instance, God wants us to be good to our neighbor—our American neighbor. God wants us to be good to the poor—our American poor.[22] Our country exists to encourage the individual American's happiness. We call on God as a nation to help us in our times of need and against our enemies foreign and domestic.

American Christians are constantly tempted to merge our Christian citizenship into national citizenship. We leave the specificity of our Christian story behind, and subscribe to a moral therapeutic deism that supports the nation. We become non-critical citizens. As a result, we find ourselves uncritically subscribed to a political theology that legitimizes violence for the sake of the nation's policies and laws that do not mesh with the Christian narrative.

American political philosopher Mark Lilla wrote *The Stillborn God: Religion, Politics, and the Modern West*. He suggests that the political theology of American civil religion allows Christians to continue to believe they are Christians while leaving much of their theology at the door when it comes to engaging politics. Being in the world but not of it (John 17:6–19) serves as scriptural cover for a religious partitioning. It is as if Christians in America have forgotten that they are political by nature.[23] This partition limits our Christian identity to church and and the private sphere. Lilla concludes that by undertaking citizenship in this manner we ensure that our political life remains "unilluminated by the light of revelation." He says, "If our experiment is to work, we must rely on our own lucidity."[24]

Alexis de Tocqueville, sociologist and political theorist, visited America in 1831 and returned to France to write, "I do not know if all Americans have faith in their religion—for who can read to the bottom of hearts? But I am sure that they believe it necessary to the maintenance of republican institutions. This opinion does not belong to one class of citizens or to one party, but to the entire nation; one finds it in all ranks."[25] De Tocqueville knew, even in the beginning, that we were a society that would be dependent upon every faith and denomination buying into a civil religion that supports the republic.

We are left with a powerful religious narrative that can motivate people to give their lives for the sacrificial cause of America's civil religion and its god. Historian Mark Noll is interested in this American god and how its theology has greater influential power than the God of Christianity. In his book *America's God: From Jonathan Edwards to Abraham Lincoln* he concludes that the American god does not require worship in a church or any other faith community. The American god is revealed through the structures that protect and govern the free people of the country. He writes that Americans of every political and religious persuasion presume that America itself is the church.[26] Theologian Stanley Hauerwas writes, "More Americans may go to church than their counterparts in Europe, but the churches to which they go do little to challenge the secular presumptions that form their perusal and communal lives."[27] Constructive Protestantism in America may be at its zenith.

I agree with Hauerwas when he suggests that American constructive Protestantism without Reformation is coming to an end. It is so completely enmeshed with civil religion that it cannot pull away or out. He writes, "It is dying of its own success."[28] Evangelical and mainline Protestantism are closely linked to our civil religion, its ideas of freedom, and the ability of the individual through common sense to self-determine what is best for themselves—and thereby the rest of the country. Church is no longer needed. American Christianity is so enmeshed with the civil religion that it no longer provides an alternative vision to the powers and principalities of America or any nation. Protestantism today is difficult to pull apart from nationalism and patriotism, ensuring that the faith handed to the next generations is not Christian faith at all but the kind of ceremonial deism that tolerates a silenced and sidelined church.

All divisions should be set aside, all strong opinions should be shelved, in order that we can remain #Americastrong. This go-along-to-get-along common-sense patriotism is not devastating to churches if they will simply adopt this manner of being and their chosen political party's policies. Stanley Hauerwas is fond of saying that Americans believe we have no narrative until we chose one.[29] The narrative of choice is moral therapeutic deism in support of our nation's civil religion. It is devastating to any church that attempts to uphold a Christian citizenship that offers a different narrative than the one parroted by the supporters of the empire. It is destructive to any church that chooses to hold a Christian narrative over and against that of any American political party. Americans believe we can only be accountable when we act freely—and to act in this way means to know what we are doing and what may happen as a consequence to our actions.[30] We bear little to no responsibility otherwise.

Many years ago, the Episcopal Church was trying out new liturgical prayers. One of them was a new confession. We have a corporate confession in our regular Sunday services. In this new prayer we confessed those things done and left undone. But the prayer added a seemingly new area of responsibility. We confessed our lament for the sins committed by others on our behalf. Oh my gosh! The people in the congregation lined up after church to explain to me how they had no responsibility for those things done that may have been a benefit to them but they did not know about. What we are struggling with as Christian citizens is responsibility for our nation as a whole. We are the people of this government and we are responsible for what it does or does not do. We are responsible on its good days and bad days—whether we know about it or not.

Christian citizens cannot turn a blind eye to corporate guilt. When G. K. Chesterton, theologian and author, reflected on American politics, he wrote that America thinks of itself as "a nation with a soul of a church. . . . I am ordinary in the correct sense of the term, which means the acceptance of an order: a Creator and the Creation, the common sense of gratitude for Creation, life and love as gifts permanently good, marriage and chivalry as laws rightly controlling them."[31] Chesterton's idea is a good one. The Christian citizen must always be mindful of living within both the reign of God and the American narrative; both have claims upon the Christian citizen. We live within the context of America's civil religion, with a notion of God's transcendence, and a moral therapeutic deism. Yet this is not our true Christian narrative.

As we consider how to live out this dual citizenship we would do well to hear Jon Meacham's warning. Christian citizens must be careful when "putting faith into action" so that we keep our mind both upon our soul and upon the work. It is all too easy to lose our way. Meacham suggests that "faith-in-action" must not be about dominance but instead participatory citizenship for the good of the whole.[32]

Our founding fathers could have created a Protestant Christian nation but they did not. They could have used the models of Jamestown; Plymouth, Massachusetts; or Virginia's laws divine. Many a new Christian in the new world attempted to do just that.[33] But the authors of our founding documents rejected this. They intended that many backgrounds of faith would be welcomed. They believed this diversity was essential to the health of the emerging nation. President George Washington wrote, "The bosom of America," was to be "open to receive . . . the oppressed and persecuted of all nations and relations; whom we shall welcome to a participation of all our rights and privileges. . . . They may be [Muslims], Jews or Christians of any sect, or they may be atheists." Thomas Jefferson wrote, "Our country has been the first to prove to the world two truths the most salutary to human society, that man can govern himself, and that religious freedom is the most effective anodyne against religious dissension: the maxims of civil government being reversed in that of religion, where its true form is divided we stand united we fall."[34]

It is important for us to remember that our Christian citizenship was seen and is seen as an important ingredient in what makes America the nation it is, but it is not the sole ingredient. We fail our American citizenship when we do not bring our Christianity to our nationalism, our understanding of scripture's narrative, our understanding of community, our understanding of covenant, compassion, and faithfulness.

Chapter Three

A Frame for Christian Citizenship

Modern systematic politics, whether liberal, conservative, radical or social-ist, simply has to be rejected from a standpoint that owes genuine allegiance to the tradition of the virtues; for modern politics itself expresses in its institutional forms a systematic rejection of that tradition.
> —Alasdair MacIntyre, Scottish political philosopher[1]

Americans believe we are free to choose our story and that we have no story until we have chosen one.[2] In this way, our common-sense reason determines our destiny. Such an understanding of person-hood makes Americans weird.

In 2010, Steve Heine, Joe Henrich, and Ara Norenzayan published a paper entitled "The Weirdest People in the World?" Their goal was to show that most psychological research is done among small groups of people living within societies that are Western, Educated, Industrialized, Rich, and Democratic. These people are WEIRD. Furthermore, Americans as a subset of global citizens are the weirdest of the WEIRD.[3]

In the book *Righteous Minds*, psychologist Jonathan Haidt breaks down this fascinating paper. He notes that WEIRD people and non-WEIRD people perceive the world differently. Haidt writes, "The WEIRDer you are the more you see a world full of separate objects, rather than relation-ships."[4] WEIRD Americans are more likely to finish the statement "I am" with words that are related to the self. For instance: I am interested in

25

classic rock. I am a bishop. I am an artist and author. People who live in non-WEIRD cultures are more likely to finish the statement with words that show relationship. For instance: I am a father. I am a son. I am a husband. Every aspect of our encounter with the world is influenced by this distinction. Most human beings think holistically, while WEIRD people see a series of objects to be juxtaposed according to individual whim.[5]

In a brilliant twist, Haidt also connects this WEIRD science to citizenship, politics, and philosophy. Our unique perspective was both responsible for and formed by political philosophies such as Immanuel Kant's, which is completely focused on individual decision-making.[6] Societies filled with discrete, unbounded individuals require political and moral structures that are highly individualistic, rule based, and universalist. In other words, we have a tendency as WEIRD people to see freedoms that must be safeguarded. This makes our WEIRD society humano-centric. For other holistic societies that privilege relational forms of knowing and being, there is a greater dependence upon socio-centric structures.[7]

Haidt also indicates that our WEIRD perspective is misleading. Scientific research has shown that emotions are the elephant and reason is simply the rider. Our brains make decisions about what we like and don't like even before we know it. Our emotional reaction is immediate and drives everything else we do. According to research by Robert Zajonc, our feelings come first. This is a ground-breaking discovery.[8] Reason is always reactionary, a mental process occurring in relation to the feelings an individual already experiences. Social and political judgments are particularly intuitive.[9] In other words, politics is an emotional function explained by reason.

Heine, Henrich, Norenzayan, and Haidt are not the only ones writing along these lines. In 1995 I read an amazing book entitled *Sources of the Self* by Charles Taylor. Published in 1989, it traces the development of selfhood in the modern age. Taylor details how the West turned away from holistic ways of thinking towards a humano-centric and subjective perspective. He argues that unsaturated reason is an illusion.[10] The privileging of reason was a covert means of separating the processes of Western society from the moral/spiritual foundations of the medieval world, in a movement towards monistic materialism.[11] In lieu of more corporate considerations, pain and pleasure became crucial determining factors in terms of behavior. We are freed from tradition and stand on the raw human desires that shape our political and social systems.[12] This new orientation is premised upon the primacy of reason, the hope that reason can glimpse a universal good beyond mere self-interest, and that we want to achieve such a good. In this way of thinking dignity, reciprocity, justice, and healthy relationships depend upon the benevolence of reason. Reducing human motivation to this pleasure principle means there is no space for us to consider how particular goals make "incommensurable" claims upon us, placing us in an agnostic tension about where the universal good actually lies.[13] Taylor's conclusion is this agnostic tension leaves us grappling with a muddled subjectivism at best and soulless nihilism at its most extreme.

It's important to note the difference between modern thought and postmodern thought here. American society is premised upon the assumption, as the U.S. Declaration of Independence states, "these truths are self-evident"—still external to the self and apprehensible to the self by reason without the intervention of revelation. We as Americans depend upon our common-sense reason. Postmodern thought reveals such a perspective to have been subjectivist, because the subject/object relation can be problematized so that nothing is ever really "self-evident." What I am pointing out here is that the American narrative and civil religion is epistemologically naïve, trusting in a reason that doesn't operate the way the founders thought it did. The unintended result of this naïveté is a society mired in inescapable subjectivity. Charles Taylor argues that subjectivism will inevitably lead to nihilism, which is a form of subjectivism that is self-consciously hopeless. In other words, confronted with the lack of any self-evident truth from which to build a perspective, the nihilist assumes that there are no truths, and no means of knowing anything; existence is just meaningless void and flux. What we are left with is power. American civil religion and moral therapeutic deism are underwritten by this subjectivism and, while not covertly nihilistic, are in and of themselves dead ends. They offer their narratives of "self-evident truths" disingenuously and serve to control the nationalistic demigods of power and control. American civil religion and the modern self and nihilistic despair are interconnected. The latter emerges from the former as an unintended consequence.

There are some good things that have come out of this Western way of navigating the world. Western societies birthed the notion that all individuals are free, and that there can be universal systems of justice and democracy. The worship of the modern self and its capacity to reason fueled the belief in American Manifest Destiny and undergirds the belief in American exceptionalism.[14] All of these changes came from seeking the good for the individual. Taylor demonstrates this good faith by tracing the movement from a holistic cultural view through Augustine, Montaigne, Luther, Hume, Rousseau, and many more to arrive at the understanding of the "self," solitary and alone.

Taylor also notes that postmodern collapse of meaning in the West has caused us more to depend upon epiphanic (revelatory and transcendent) art, poetry, and texts. We rely upon an imaginary frame to provide relief from the lonely selfhood upon which our present WEIRD America depends. Brigitte Nerlich, a professor of science specializing in language and society defines a social imaginary as "the way a given people imagine their collective social life which enables and at the same time legitimises sense making processes and practices."[15] Taylor's social imaginaries are made up of "images, stories and legends, and incorporate both facts about how we usually conduct our social existence, but also norms about how this existence ought to be played out."[16] Within our particular American social imaginary, indeed the Western imaginary, the *self* rules as an increasingly despotic and lonely king. This shift is partly to blame for the compartmentalization of American politics.

Americans are making up their own stories according to their emotions. We are then creating arguments to support our emotional narratives and fleeing into tribal groups that affirm our beliefs. Once organized in this way, citizens are vulnerable to manipulation by power-oriented principalities who sell victorious visions of American progress that are specifically tailored to make their tribe happy.[17] The public square has fractured into fairytale realms controlled by political parties and media, spinning disingenuous yarns that will never come true.

I am certainly not the only one who reacts strongly to the failure of modernity. In his seminal work *After Virtue*, Alasdair MacIntyre argues that humans are story telling animals. Essential to that story is their connection to others and to tradition.[18] There is no time at which we are not part of a narrative. I always begin my own spiritual autobiography by saying, "Everyone's life begins as part of another person's story." All life is a tangle of stories. Not only is there no time when there is no story, there is no communal story that is not part of other communal stories. There is no story about America without the First Peoples, the Puritans, the Muslims, the Jews, the enslaved Africans, and so many others. There is no American melting pot into one single story. The American story itself is part of a tangle of global stories. There is no common-sense reason apart from a person's story and their community's story. The challenge is not only how to collect and tell all these stories, the challenge is to be honest about the limiting particularity of the stories we know how to tell.[19]

The American narrative pretends we are self-made, self-actualized, disconnected, independent human beings. We choose and author our story. When this is our viewpoint, MacIntyre suggests, "The unity of a human life becomes invisible to us when a sharp separation is made . . . between the individual and the roles that he or she plays."[20] In this WEIRD society surrounded by our national narrative and civil religion, and with our theology of moral therapeutic deism, we have come to believe (incorrectly) that we exist in a fragmented deconstructed world. MacIntyre writes, "Work is divided from leisure, private life from public, the corporate from the personal . . . childhood and old age have been wrenched away from the rest of human life and made over into distinct realms."[21]

In the midst of this deconstructed world, virtue is dislodged from the narratives that inculcate it and isolated within one small part of a larger compartmentalization. The virtue ethics of the school teacher, policeman, politician, or citizen engaging government float free, disconnected from any other narrative tradition. We freely choose the narrative of the Republican or Democratic party, and choose the narrative of the school teacher, or the narrative of the father or mother, or the churchgoer without ever having these narratives meet. This is a modernist and Western construct. It is what makes us WEIRD. It is not real.

MacIntyre wants to restore the idea of life as a unified whole. He wants to restore a sense of context to people's lives.[22] Events, stories, and life lived are not separate fragmented moments but part of a great web of narrative that stretches backward and forward. Meaning only happens when particular moments are fit into a larger narrative web.[23] This is not limited to the telling of the story, but that the story itself has context and exists within time and place.[24]

Modernity strips away context. Daniel T. Rodgers describes "the age of fracture" as a context of hostile meta narratives and a fracturing of individual and social life. MacIntyre's take on the "age of fracture" is that we pull meaning from the context, turn the context into playful metaphors, and twist them with cynicism and irony so as to make them all interchangeable.[25] Welcome to the 1980s and the disintegration of shared values. We are trained to be suspicious of a unified narrative especially if it is attached to context. Rodgers suggests that the postmodern aesthetic is "indifferent to consistency and continuity." It is no wonder moral therapeutic deism became a unifying narrative. There is nothing left.[26]

But we are always and everywhere embedded in multiple contexts that are different. We are part of a narrative that is interlocked with other narratives. I am never alone, my story does not exist unto itself, it is always and everywhere in relationship to others. My story—my narrative—is embedded in the community from which I derive my identity.[27] We are "born with a past," MacIntyre reminds us, "and to try to cut [ourselves] from that past in the individualist mode, is to deform [our] present relationships. The possession of an historical identity and the possession of a social identity coincide."[28] Without this our understanding of ourselves and our roles is "unintelligible."[29]

In conversation with other critics of modernity such as Hans Frei, George Lindbeck, John Howard Yoder, James McClendon, and Stanley Hauerwas, I want to reiterate my point here. Citizenship and politics in present-day America fail because they perpetuate incommensurable, fragmented narratives. American political parties seek to deny that we are connected and always and everywhere embedded in each other's lives. The political powers of this present "fractured age" deny our interlocking narratives leaving us feeling alone and forced to seek the good for ourselves alone. They use media to carefully craft a story that is disconnected from the embedded community from which we derive our identity. In so doing they do not create unity out of disunity; they create, instead, various tribes of individuals sometimes at war with one another and sometimes united for temporary gains.

Christian citizenship has a frame, a story, and a context. Christian citizenship makes a particular claim that God invites us into God's story. We claim that we as Christians are invited to be faithful to the life and narrative of Jesus of Nazareth. Our citizenship is embedded as part of the reign of God. Our story is not lived privately in church on Sunday. Our story is not lived privately in our homes. Our story does not obey the boundaries of the postmodern fragmented age where politics, workplace, friends, and family are incoherent individuated narratives. Our narrative is not first formed in these places. In other words, if we are to understand the narrative of Christian citizenship we cannot start with American history. We cannot start in a political party. Our Christian narrative has no other place to ground our practice citizenship except in our origin stories, the life of Jesus, and forward beyond our life to the Resurrection, the ingathering of time. Christian citizenship begins within a narrative that began a long time ago. We begin, as Stanley Hauerwas likes to quip, "in the middle."

Christian citizenship does not have a methodological beginning in the political philosophies of Plato or Aristotle. It does not begin with what kind of Christians our founders were. Christian citizenship finds its roots in the ancient story of God who invites us to be part of God's story by virtue of our own creation. Christian citizenship recognizes that we are always and everywhere a member of God's created realm. We are in relationship to God and to others. Our narrative begins with God and is forever interwoven with others. Moreover, it takes place in a particular context—God's kingdom.

It is the work of this book to remind Christians of the story of their citizenship in the reign of God. We are undertaking to tell the story of

God in relationship to powers, principalities, politicians, and the politics of this world.[30] In so doing we see clearly then that our Christian citizenship is tied to the life of our faith ancestors. It is intimately tied to the citizenship of Jesus and his Lordship. Our Christian citizenship is linked to the "activities of adoration, proclamation, obedience, promise-hearing, and promise-keeping which shape individuals and communities into conformity to the mind of Christ" as theologian George Lindbeck puts it.[31] Christian citizenship is always connected to the wider Christian community in context, as it tries to faithfully live out the biblical narrative.

Now, let us say a word about this narrative. The Christian narrative that I am invoking here is not a fundamentalist narrative. It is not the product of any specific critical historic, literary, or linguistic approach. I am imagining an intertextual mixture of narrative along the lines MacIntyre describes. For instance, Jesus's story is not without intertextual connection to the origin story—Abraham, Moses, or the prophets, for instance—just as they are not without connection to the Incarnation, the Christ. Our work of placing Christian citizenship in America within the context of the biblical narrative is not a matter of finding quotations, allusions, or story lines that fit. It is about discovering all of the ways that the biblical narrative and the American narrative can lie with one another, in agreement and in tension.

We are seeking a kind of relationship that Lindbeck calls "narrative coherence,"[32] which occurs as we connect biblical narrative that proclaims God as creator, partner of Abraham and Sarah, encourager of Moses, and Living Word proclaimed by the prophets to Christian citizenship. As we will see, the Christian citizen is part of this story. We live lives that are intertwined with God and the biblical narrative, and we must reject the "fractured age."

Here is an important and distinguishing characteristic of our frame for Christian citizenship: we are not trying to do what Jesus did. Our story is no mere mimicry of the life of Jesus. We are not trying to go back to some former time when the church was perfect. We are not attempting find the moralist rule of life that we can strive towards as citizens. Our work here is to adopt a frame for Christian citizenship that helps us to see our lived stories as being shaped by the biblical narrative such that they provide a counter-witness, an interruption to the emptiness of modernity, postmodernity, consumerism, and empire.

We, as Christians, have a different way of thinking. We do not believe that we have no narrative until we choose one. Instead Christianity rooted deep in our faith ancestry has an origin story. We categorically reject the idea that we get to choose our story.[33] We believe instead that God invites us into God's story. God chooses us. We are not trying to live out our own rags to riches story or America's story. We as Christian citizens are struggling to live as part of God's narrative that began with creation and continues in our world today and happens to include America. So, get your Bibles out, open to the beginning, and let us wade into the waters of scripture and citizenship.

Chapter Four

A Garden Social Imaginary

From whence are these "rights of individuals" derived, and why should we care? Unless we presume the existence of some greater power that determines what is good, isn't it arbitrary to posit that human survival is more important than private property rights, an equally artificially construed concept? Isn't it arbitrary to assume that some sort of equality is preferable to a system where, say, the poor are assumed to have bad karma? If these "rights of individuals" are derived only from shared humanity, then do "individuals" (a thoroughly meaningless term, by the way), begin to lose them when they act inhumanely? And isn't it totally arbitrary to grant rights to humans rather than other creatures anyway?

—Cornel West, philosopher[1]

We begin with the two creation stories in Genesis. In Genesis 1, God creates the world and then makes humankind in God's image—in God's likeness. God creates both male and female in God's image (Gen. 1:26–28). The whole of Genesis 2 is the second story that uses the imagery of a garden to talk about creation. God takes a man and puts him in this garden. God sees that this man is lonely and God creates a woman. The two partner in the work of keeping the garden. These two creation stories reveal how the organization and politic of the people of Israel were different from neighboring tribes, confederacies, and kingdoms.[2]

In opposition to other ways of understanding creation, our Christian (and Abrahamic) faith reveals that God is first. God's story precedes our creation. God invites us to be part of God's story. We humans are made after God's creative beginning and are placed in the midst of God's garden. God has a "garden social imaginary" and brings it into being. God as the Trinity, as divine community, imagines (reflects) a created community. God imagines the garden as a society of human beings living together, and then God creates what God imagines. God imagined a community and brought it forth. This is as radical a proposition today as it was for the Israelites so many centuries ago.

Moreover, God's story of creation continues. God's narrative does not end with Genesis. God continues to create, through God's Living Word, incarnating God's social imaginary. Theologians speak of this first act of creating out of nothing as *creatio ex nihilo* (creation out of nothing) and this second creative act as *creatio continua* (continuing creation).[3] But it is important to note that there is no continuity between God's substance and creation. God and creation are different. God is infinite and creation is not. God "is" in an entirely different way than created things "are." Creation is unique from God and has a form and substance all its own.[4] In this way God is transcendent and at the same time inaugurates the unraveling of the creation story through time—an emergence of God's social imaginary in the cosmos.

All societies have a way of being, a birth narrative, and a functional social imaginary that evolves through history. Societies have a way of imagining themselves. Theologian Walter Brueggemann points out that we all too often live uncritically within our society's imagination of us. If we were to take ourselves seriously as citizens of God's reign, we would live within a different narrative: God's garden narrative. "Clearly, human transformative activity depends upon a transformed imagination."[5] Brueggemann suggests that we tap into God's narrative so we can live in "God's imagination."[6]

The garden social imaginary begins by making it clear that humans are never alone. There is no *self* alone. God is first and humanity is created within community. God creates two together not one alone. God even says it is not good for one to be alone with God but that others are needed. In

Genesis 1, the first story of creation, God makes all of humanity in one action, versus the story of Genesis 2:18, when God makes humans one at a time. For the Christian, and especially the Christian citizen, there is no humano-centric view of creation. God is the center of the creative act. God is at the center of the garden's social imaginary. God creates and is not alone. God makes humanity and it is not alone. So, there is, as far as the human goes, always community. And, in case you missed it, God has made all humanity as an image of God's incomprehensible self.

The garden social imaginary also makes it clear that God is not gendered. We Christians have for a very long time understood that God is neither male nor female. This is not new theology. The translators of scripture have long been imprisoned by the pronoun. However, both Jewish and Christian theologians have for ages reminded us that God has no image and to make an image (in word or art) that seeks to manifest God as *this* or *that* is actually a transgression of the Ten Commandments. So be wary you pronoun police! Even Moses emphasized this at Sinai, "You heard the sound of words but saw no form" (Deut. 4:12). God is not made of flesh though God makes flesh. God is untethered by the binary constructions of human bodies. And, while we are made in God's image, we do not have a physical form in common with God. God is free and so we who are made in God's image are free. God is free and so we are made free. We are free to be in community one with the other.[7] All humans have this calling to freedom, and by virtue of their very creation they are made part of a community of relationships. The Christian scriptures do not promote a WEIRD story of the individual's creation *a la* Michelangelo's fresco of the *Creation of Adam* in the Sistine Chapel. The Christian scriptures tell a creation story of God making a specifically human community.

The story of God's social imaginary set the people of Israel on a different path from their neighbors who imagined a society benefiting the few who governed. They told stories about gods who birthed their rulers/demigods and gave them power. The hierarchical structures that governed those societies were representations of the gods, dependent upon violence that brings forth creation, and used violence to maintain order. The image of god was reserved for the few: the kings, the nobility, and the tribal leaders.

Genesis twists the stories of neighboring tribes to indicate that all humanity, male and female, are created in God's image. There is no hierarchy here.[8]

It is true that there are parts of the very oldest pieces of our creation story that resemble *The Epic of Gilgamesh* that dates to circa 1800 BCE.[9] But they are nothing alike. The creation myth found in Gilgamesh is a violent one. In it the god Marduk creates the world by cutting up the defeated body of the god Tiamat. Like many other creation stories from this time period and dating into the first century CE, creation is a battleground for the gods. As philosopher René Girard puts it, we see mimetic (repetitive) violence legitimized throughout these creation myths. This violence is visible in the cultures of Mesopotamia, but such originating violence is not part of the creation narrative we receive from Israel. For the Christian citizen, society must practice an ethic of peace by rejecting cycles of violence.

This freedom image without hierarchy is essential in our understanding of human relationships. In governing systems with hierarchy, the use of violence from the god-like leaders to subdue the other is essential.[10] The power differential that exists within the structures of community in neighboring societies is to be turned on its head by the creation story that is part of our Christian citizenship DNA.[11] The original storytellers of Genesis, those who would later edit it, and those who would finally weave it into the wider biblical narrative were making a very clear choice to differentiate this story from all other creation myths. The God of Israel is different from the lesser gods of violence.

Jonathan Sacks points out that the creation story not only dismisses the violence of the mythic age of Mesopotamia but also dismisses the present violent age of science.

> Central to both the ancient world of myth and the modern world of science is the idea of power, force, energy. That is what is significantly absent from Genesis 1. God says, "Let there be," and there is. There is nothing here about power, resistance, conquest or the play of forces. Instead, the key word of the narrative, appearing seven times, is utterly unexpected. It is the word *tov*, good. . . . This is the Torah's most significant paradigm-shift. The universe God made and we

inhabit is not about power or dominance but about *tov* and *ra*, good and evil. For the first time, religion was ethicized. God cares about justice, compassion, faithfulness, loving-kindness, the dignity of the individual and the sanctity of life.[12]

This differentiates our beginning point, as well as our unique perspective apart from all other social, psychological, philosophical, and scientific narratives of beginning.

The origin of God's narrative in which Christian citizens participate begins with God's social imaginary bringing forth human community. This community is centered around a transcendent God who is also in the midst of humans. From this paradoxical position above and within, God continues the creative act. God partners with humanity in continuing the creative act. And the work of community that humans and God do together is *tov*, good.

The community of God furthers God's creative vision by creating and sustaining good society, good community, and good relationships with all people. This was radical in a day when power exercised through violence ruled and subdued people. It is as radical today as it was then. This story of creation, the one upon which all Christian citizenship is based, is a protest against any society that makes a hierarchy of government out of power and violence. It is a protest against societies that relegate people to classes and castes—ascribing to them lesser or greater freedoms and governing powers. It is a protest against any community or nation that denies people the dignity of freedom for reasons of faith, race, gender, or heritage.[13] The root of our faith is a peaceful, communal citizenship where all are equal because of the terms of our creation. We are equal because of our communal createdness, not because we are individuals.

Driving home the egalitarian nature of God's social imaginary in the essay "The Genesis of Justice," Jonathan Sacks reiterates that God did not give humanity dominion over other humans. Not only is there no difference between humans because of their created origin, there is no right given to them to have dominion over one another. We can draw from Jewish Midrash and poet John Milton's *Paradise Lost* to say that to subdue another human and have dominion over them is the sin of Nimrod. Nimrod's sin was "arrogate dominion undeserved."[14] John Milton wrote,

> Authority usurped, from God not given:
> He gave us only over beast, fish, fowl
> Dominion absolute; that right we hold
> By his donation; but man over men
> He made not lord; such title to himself
> Reserving, human left from human free.[15]

The idea that a ruler could not subordinate another human being would have been unheard of at the time of this narrative's first telling. The practice of dominion was legitimized by every other creation myth, which inaugurated a hierarchy of gods and rulers and established the divine rights of despots. Here, in the words of Rabbi Sacks, is the Torah's "deep ambivalence . . . toward[s] the very institution of kingship, the rule of 'man over men.'"[16] What this means is that while the Christian citizen may very well follow the laws of the land, the Christian citizen must be wary when laws establish the dominion of some by others. Laws that dehumanize and lift up some at the expense of others are out of step with the scripture.

God imagined a garden and spoke a community into being. Humanity is the result of that word, and we share in the work of peaceful creation-making. Jesus, the Word made flesh, offers an invitation to practice Christian citizenship and live as a blessing in the middle of this narrative. He does so with pristine clarity in the Beatitudes—literally "the blessings"—where he reminds us that God's intention is for the community of *shalom*, of peace, to witness against the systems of domination by reversing them.[17] Theologian Walter Wink calls this inversion a "domination free order."[18] Jesus's words are not only a past echo. Christ as the living word speaks the same word across time that gave shape to God's social imaginary in the first place. Christian citizens have an obligation by virtue of their own creation story to hold all forms of governments, and all nations, accountable when people are dehumanized.

The creation story is also about partnership. God invites humanity to be partners in the caring of the creation—both the community and the created cosmos. The narrator tells the story of this partnership this way: "The Lord God took the man and put him in the garden of Eden to till it and keep it" (Gen. 2:15). God intended humanity to work the garden. We are told that in fact that God *needs* humanity to till and work the garden. No shrubs appeared until the gardeners had appeared (Gen. 2:5). We are created to be partners in the work of the reign of God. This means engagement.

This notion that humanity is part of the work of building the reign of God is profound. We find it throughout the New Testament as well. It makes its way into our hymns. We work with our shoulder to the Gospel plow. Jesus prays that we might be workers in the vineyard (Matt. 9:37). In Colossians 3:23–24, Paul writes that we are called to build the reign of God. We are to live out the Lord's work when we are living out our Christian citizenship. God expects us to be partners with God, with each other (of every tribe and creed), and with all of society to labor for God's purposes. We are not to labor for dominion, but for a garden where all may dwell—a garden with resources to feed all, clothe all, and shelter all.

Political convictions and the virtues of communities and nation-states never stand alone. Such passions are deeply connected to our underlying view of humankind. Plato argues that humanity, the individual, presupposes community. There is no such notion in the creation story. Humanity is always in community from the standpoint of the Christian citizen. We work together as partners building up the polis, the city. In doing so we are tending the garden.

Rabbi Jonathan Sacks writes,

> Momentous ideas made the West what it is: human rights, the abolition of slavery, the equal worth of all, and justice based on the principle that right is sovereign over might. All ultimately derived from the statement in the first chapter of the Torah that we are made in God's image and likeness. No other text has had a greater influence on moral thought, nor has any other civilization ever held a higher vision of what we are called on to be.[19]

In John F. Kennedy's inaugural address he spoke of the "revolutionary beliefs for which our forebears fought," that "the rights of man come not

from the generosity of the state, but from the hand of God."[20] But let us
be clear, the Christian citizen must add context to this statement. Kennedy
stays within the boundaries of American civil religion. The story of creation
adds to this understanding by transforming the very nature of humanity,
the nature of humanity's relationship one to another, and the nature of
our human work. Our freedom is from God but, for the Christian citizen,
there is much left unsaid in Kennedy's remarks. For the Christian citizen,
the story of God's creation and God's creation of humanity is more than
the dispensation of "inalienable rights."[21] It is the creation of communal
responsibility. We have rights and freedoms, and we also understand from
our creation story that these freedoms exist for the work of community
making. In other words, Christian citizens understand that our freedoms
come with duties and responsibilities to one another.

Christian citizenship is deeply rooted in the story of creation. Without
it we are just another group of WEIRD American citizens. The idea that we
are the image of God in the world, given freedom, responsibility, and work
within a human community, gives us a unique beginning point in any discussion about politics, a beginning point that is not violence and dominion.

Chapter Five

A Rejection of Dominion Politics

A central function of thought is making sure that one acts in ways that can be persuasively justified or excused to others. Indeed, the process of considering the justifiability of one's choices may be so prevalent that decision makers not only search for convincing reasons to make a choice when they must explain that choice to others, they search for reasons to convince themselves that they have made the "right" choice.
—from "The Psychology of the Unthinkable"[1]

There are a number of important parts of the creation story that help us understand the shadow side of the human character. The first is that God makes humanity in God's image, giving them freedom. This means that God does not control human free will—it is free. God creates and invites humanity to work and till creation. Humanity can co-create and bring forth further life. Humanity can also choose not to co-create and bring forth life, but can actually bring creation into ruin. Humanity has the freedom to reject God. Humanity is free to reject community with one another and life together. Humanity is given great responsibility and it can reject that responsibility.

The story of Adam and Eve is important because they decide together to do what God has invited them not to do. I think you know the story (Gen. 3:8–13). God comes to walk with them in the evening and cool of the day and they are nowhere to be found. They are hiding. They are hiding because they are not taking responsibility for their actions. When God does find them they eschew their responsibility. The man blames the woman, and the woman blames the snake. Having done something wrong, they want to get away with it and so they blame others. They scapegoat one another and the snake. Scapegoating is what humans do when they are shirking their God-given responsibilities (Lev. 16). The sins of the individual or group are placed upon another person, group, or object.

A bit later in Genesis, sibling rivalry enters the picture as well, as one of the forces that cause human beings not to take responsibility for their co-creative work. Eve bears siblings Cain and Abel (Gen. 4). Adam and Eve see this as continuing God's invitation to work, and give thanks for God's participation in blessing the provision of children. The brothers are different and enter into rivalry with each other, a theme that will continue across the Old Testament. There will be rivalry between Jacob and Esau, Joseph and his brothers; even Saul and David's relationship appears as sibling rivalry. Key to the rivalry are difference, jealousy, and violence. Cain is first born to Eve, then comes Abel. Abel is a keeper of sheep and Cain a farmer. Cain brings God an offering of grain and Abel the first born of the flock. The narrator tells us God likes Abel's offering and pays no regard for Cain. Cain then gets angry and his jealousy overwhelms him. He invites Abel out into the field and kills him.

We Christians like to think that sin enters into the Garden of Eden through the story of Adam and Eve. That is not true. Sin enters creation with Cain and Abel. Before Cain takes Abel's life, God warns him that if the sibling rivalry gets the better of him he will sin (Gen. 4:7). We might pause here and ask, what is the sin? The sin is not simply the murder out of jealousy. The sin is the taking of a life instead of multiplying life. Cain takes dominion over Abel by destroying his life.

Later God asks where Abel is, and Cain does not answer for his actions. He attempts, instead, to hide the murder from God. Cain hedges the truth with God. He does not actually reject responsibility. He "denies moral responsibility," points out Jonathan Sacks.[2] Cain gives an answer like Glaucon's, who not only argues for self-interest but also argues in Plato's *Republic* for might makes right. Again, Sacks:

Glaucon argues that justice is whatever is in the interest of the stronger party. . . . If life is a Darwinian struggle to survive, why should we restrain ourselves for the sake of others if we are more powerful than they are? If there is no morality in nature then I am responsible only to myself. That is the voice of Cain throughout the ages.[3]

The second aspect of sin, then, is to deny responsibility or to leave such responsibility unconfessed. It is to know and yet not tell the whole of it. Jonathan Haidt's research in his book *Righteous Minds* reminds us that we are truly Glauconian. Our emotions drive our choices and those emotions are completely self-interested.

We are left with a bit of awkward silence as Cain avoids the question. Cain's comeback is, "Am I my brother's keeper?" (Gen. 4:9) This is important because the creation story tells us we are born into community. We have a relationship with God and with each other. We are to be partners. Though the scripture does not say it, the response is clear. "Yes," we are to be our sibling's keeper instead of our sibling's rival. God says, "Abel's blood is crying to me from the ground." Cain is not alone. He may have gone to a deserted place and killed his brother so that he could have dominion in relationship. God rejects such dominion and along with it such individualism. God is in relationship with Cain and God is present in Abel's death. Abel's blood—his murder and death—is known to God. Here is the final aspect of sin, that it seeks to undo community and is focused upon the individual. Sin is selfish.

The story of Cain and Abel is a creation story, an origin story, in that it offers us an understanding of ourselves. We are told that while we are created with freedom, to live with God and each other in community, we naturally become rivals to one another and will seek to undo it. It is not so much that Glaucon is right about the cosmos, as it is that he is right about our nature. Sibling rivalry is a key ingredient to how we function within community.

If we look towards the work of philosopher René Girard, we will see that the creation story is telling us that violence is a key component of sibling rivalry. Sibling rivalry is a key component of community. Cain is the founder of culture, or civilization, of greater community. And, in this founding rivalry and violence are introduced into the structures of society. Notice that Cain's response to God is that now "anyone who meets me may kill me." God responds, "Whoever kills Cain will suffer a sevenfold vengeance." Abel's murder facilitates the multiplication of violence instead of the multiplication of blessing. Cain, as an archetypal citizen, requires more and more blood.[4] Within six generations Lamech, a descendant of Cain, laments:

> I have killed a man for wounding me,
>> a young man for striking me.
> If Cain is avenged sevenfold,
>> truly Lamech seventy-sevenfold.

Genesis 4:23–24

What began in the garden with a lack of responsibility has grown into sibling rivalry and a society of scapegoating. The story of the blood of Abel is unique, especially if we consider the origin stories of other civilizations. Take Rome, for example. The story begins with two brothers who wish to create a sacred city. They argue over where it should be and how high the wall should be. Remus makes fun of Romulus's wall, and jumps over it. By doing so Remus desacralizes Romulus's offering and defames the city's founding. So, Romulus kills his brother Remus to restore Rome's sacred character.[5] The two stories share the nature of sibling rivalry. The story of Romulus and Remus justifies the killing, however, and is a foreshadowing of Rome's dominion over the world. Rome has a sacred mission of death. God hears the innocent blood of Abel and rejects Cain's actions. The origin story of Rome, on the other hand, reveals how sacred violence is an essential ingredient in constituting society.[6]

Cain killed Abel, Lamech, still others, and so it continues. But in God's social imaginary the violence is not justified. God rejects Cain's offering of Abel as a sacrifice for his rivalry. God rejects Cain's scapegoating of Abel. God ultimately will reject Lamech's and all of society's multiplication of death by washing the sin away in a flood. God's rejection of violence as an acceptable solution to rivalry is radical when we consider the origin story of Rome. And, it is a radical way of understanding human community even now as Christian citizens.

For the Christian citizen, God's narrative reminds us that humanity will seek dominion over one another, and that such rivalry will lead to violence. Human societies are mimetic: they repeat sibling rivalry and its violence naturally. Like Rome, societies will justify some violence as sacred and necessary to ensure longevity and domination of enemy nations. The Christian citizen is necessarily suspicious of the means of power in governing systems. The Christian citizen rejects "might makes right" as a governing principle. The Christian citizen understands community to be co-creative rather than dominative. The Christian citizen takes responsibility for the work of making co-creative community and ending cycles of domination. This is the final lesson learned from the origin stories: Christian citizenship rejects individual and corporate self-preservation and selfish violence.

On Sunday, March 31, 1968, theologian Dr. Martin Luther King climbed into the pulpit of Washington National Cathedral and preached,

> We are tied together in the single garment of destiny, caught in an inescapable network of mutuality, and whatever affects one directly affects all indirectly. For some strange reason, I can never be what I ought to be until you are what you ought to be. And you can never be what you ought to be until I am what I ought to be. This is the way God's universe is made; this is the way it is structured. . . . Ultimately a great nation is a compassionate nation. America has not met its obligations and its responsibilities to the poor.

King's sermon reminded America we are not alone.

> One day we will have to stand before the God of history, and we will take in terms of things we've done. . . . Yes, we will be able to say we built gargantuan bridges to span the seas. We built gigantic buildings to kiss the skies. Yes, we made our submarines to penetrate oceanic depths. We brought into being many other things with our scientific and technological power. . . . It seems that I can hear the God of history saying, "That was not enough! But I was hungry, and ye fed

me not. I was naked, and ye clothed me not. I was devoid of a decent
sanitary house to live in, and ye provided no shelter for me. And, consequently, you cannot enter the kingdom of greatness. If ye do it unto
the least of these, my brethren, ye do it unto me." That's the question
facing America today.[7]

Christian citizenship rooted deep within these creation stories understands
that America's origin does not find its root in the gospel of the founding
fathers alone. Our best leaders have called us to the higher responsibility of
citizenship prophesized by Dr. King. They remind us that America is only
as prosperous as its poorest citizens. This is not a calling to make America
a Christian theocracy (though there have been many people over the years
who have tried to do so). No, Christian citizenship invites our nation to
achieve the "promissory note" of the founder's desire to make America
great not by dominion, but by ending sibling rivalry. Through acts of peace
we will fulfill our "sacred heritage."[8]

Genesis gives us another perspective on God's relationship with
humanity. This is lived out in the narrative of Abraham and Sarah's journey
with God. God's creation is a place of shalom—peace. Later in Genesis,
re-creation is the story of Abraham and his wife, Sarah. They are called
to leave the city of Ur of the Chaldeans, which is a sign or symbol of
how Christian citizens understand themselves in the wider body politic.
Abraham and Sarah will live in Ur, Egypt, Sodom, and the land of Canaan.
In each place, they will live as members of a community but always outside
of it. They are always prophets of God's peace in a strange land. They are
citizens of a different kingdom first. They will make their life within these
communities and they will even plead for them out of their own care and
compassion for their neighbors (Gen. 18:16–33). God calls Abraham and
Sarah, just as I believe God calls all Christian citizens, to leave the land
of comfort and journey into unmapped terrain where they are forced to
depend upon God in ever more radical ways. We are constantly invited
into the discomfort of a journey with God.[9] God's work happens beyond
the boundaries of nation-states. To redeem the whole world is God's mission. God calls people into community for the purpose of redemption:

the inauguration of the kingdom of God. God continuously calls us into unfamiliar places to recreate God's garden social imaginary. This emerging kingdom causes friction and is always in conflict with the cultures of humanity. We can see this throughout the circumstances of biblical history and in the words of prophets like Martin Luther King Jr.

In many ways the story of Abraham and Sarah's calling begins the narrative of God's people. Abraham and Sarah were frequently cited by the early church as examples of God's expansive promise to all people. God said, "Go," and all of their worldly plans were set aside as they left their homeland for God's wilderness. Their lives were disrupted by God's invitation. They were called to live as we were created to be—in a relationship with God that echoes the social imaginary of God's garden. Theologian Walter Brueggemann says Abraham

> is caught up in a world of discourse and possibility about which he knew nothing until addressed, a world of discourse and possibility totally saturated with God's good promises for him and for the world through him. (Gen 12:1) By this call Abraham is propelled into an orbit of reality that removes him completely from any purpose or agenda he may have entertained for himself before that moment.[10]

Abraham and Sarah offered themselves faithfully to the journey and became a blessing to the world. This is the work of Christian citizenship: to live and work within the wider society as a blessing to those with whom we live.

God called Abraham and Sarah to become a people that bless the world, which is a habit of God's throughout all of scripture. Faithfulness is the act of accepting the invitation and opening oneself to becoming the blessing. Those whom God invites, God also blesses, in order that they might bless others. God said to Abraham and Sarah, "In you all the families of the earth shall be blessed" (Gen. 12:3). Their promised family would outnumber the stars of Abraham's counting and be a blessing to the world. Brueggemann ponders the meaning of this blessing and says, " 'Blessing' is not a religious or moral phenomenon in the world," it is a "characteristic feature of creation that is fruitful and productive."[11] Blessing, therefore, becomes an archetypal part of life as a Christian citizen.

Abraham and Sarah were called to show how human community could differ from the mimetic and archetypal violence found in the Cain and Abel story. This is clear in God's call to them both and the promise that they will be a blessing throughout all creation. But in case you missed it, it is brought home in the story often called "the sacrifice of Isaac"—which it isn't (Gen. 22). The story not only undoes the sibling rivalry of Cain and Abel perpetuated throughout all creation, but also undoes the work of the powers and false gods (like governments, dictators, and oligarchs) that seek dominion over others.

Child sacrifice, indeed human sacrifice, was the norm in the cultures in which Abraham and Sarah found themselves. This is shocking in our own context, but was not to Abraham and Sarah. What was shocking was God's rejection of ritual sacrifice that is the theme of the story.[12] God rejects the sacrifice and Abraham does not go through with it, though his contemporaries would have completed the task. Governments today continue to sacrifice sons and daughters for the sake of civil religion. This is out of step with God's story and the peace, or shalom, it intends to make a central virtue of God's community. Christian citizens may find themselves out of step with their fellow Americans, when it comes to sacrificing Isaacs for the good of the nation. While Christian citizens might find themselves compelled to serve, defend, and even die for the cause of America, our scriptural narrative robs such violence of any nobility. We are forced to acknowledge that we have chosen to participate in the ritual blood sacrifice that animates the nations of the world.

The God of creation who desires a peaceable kingdom is the true God: the God of shalom and blessing. Consequently, any gods that require sacrifice, execution, or murder for the sake of protecting dominion are not the true gods. Girardian and pastor Paul Nuechterlein preached, "Abraham passed the test of faith not by listening to the voice of the false gods of sacred violence at the story's opening, but by listening to the voice of Yahweh, 'the LORD,' at the story's close."[13]

If we look at the text in Hebrew it appears that a later text is being written over an earlier one. The God that rejects the sacrifice is a very different God from the one who orders it. The God that rejects Isaac is the

God that rejects the religious sacrifice of Christ as well. It the same God that sees Christ crucified by the religious governing powers and authorities of this world, the false gods, and redeems the sacrifice through the act of resurrection. It is not substitutionary atonement.[14] The governing forces, like those that date back to Abraham's neighbors, require Jesus's death. God rejects that as the final word and instead transforms the offering into eternal life.[15]

Healthy systems of law work to discipline outbreaks of sibling rivalry that naturally occur. Good political systems can break cycles of vengeance. They actually take on the work of reforming the lust for vengeance that ails all societies. By giving up individual authority to these wider systems of disciplinary power, we limit ourselves, suppressing our own need for vengeance and allowing the authority to rule in our stead.[16] This is what healthy systems are prepared to do. However, some states still sentence people to death on our behalf. It may be a state law but it affects the virtue of America at large.

Moreover, the criminal system that we have today is a complex system of economic development (prisons for profit) and structural racism. New research reveals that sometimes the body politic fails us because of our Glauconian desire to protect ourselves. Michelle Alexander reveals such undergirding racism in America's own system in her book *The New Jim Crow*. She connects votes against civil rights and for crime bills, points out the discrimination of sentencing, and highlights the difficulties of achieving justice in a society steeped in racism. She identifies the unjust school-to-prison pipeline and the long-lasting effects of separate systems in the 1940/50s. While Woodrow Wilson and others bet on the white advance, his policies ensured generational poverty for the non-white working poor. Today, the majority of those imprisoned in a system that is supposed to help us with sibling rivalry are the victims of sibling rivalry itself.[17]

God made a point of rejecting religious violence by refusing Abraham's offer of Isaac as a sacrifice. God undid the human drive to sanctify murder. God was interested in a shalom that broke the cycle inaugurated by the blood of Abel. Abraham and Sarah's call was to heal the violent estrangements that separated humanity from God. Yet, the feud continues, and so does the division between God and humanity.

Christian citizens are invited to work with others to create forms of governing that break the cycle of mimetic violence and subjugation. When a country tells a soldier who has enlisted to escape desperate poverty that killing someone else is okay because it is for the nation—that is a different story. When the state tells a prison guard it is okay to kill a human being because the law says it is right—that is a different story. When the state tells citizens it is okay to discriminate against each other because the law protects the individual's freedom—that is a different story. When the state says it is okay to deny rights to other human beings because they are not Americans—that is a different story. The story that governments tell is a different story than God's garden social imaginary.

When we accept governments' stories as our primary story, we accept sibling rivalry, the mimetic desire that leads to violence, as <u>the</u> story. We reject the reign of God and we reject our role as Christian citizens. Only when we accept that killing another human being destroys God's creation can we find redemption from the cross. Only when we see that our discriminatory actions lead to generational poverty do we discover forgiveness for our sinfulness, and a path towards amendment of life and society. It is true that nothing can separate us from the love of God; principalities and powers cannot even separate us from God's love (Rom. 8:38–39). The apostle Paul writes this powerful theological truth: God's action upon the cross puts an end to sibling rivalry in God's narrative. In the end God will be victorious. Yet, we must be clear that such an utterance by Paul fits within a different social imaginary than the one given to us by the nations, princes, and powers of this world.

The narrative of civil religion persuades us that the pursuit of God's social imaginary is a private affair. It persuades us that salvation is not only an individual act but a private one that has no bearing on our life as citizens. Christians do not believe we are unnarrated until we choose a story, or that our religious identity is a private concern. Christian citizens reject the fractured fairy tale offered by the nation and instead accept their place in God's narrative arc. N. T. Wright suggests that every act within God's social imaginary done by a Christian citizen will continue as the reign of God. Only when we live within God's social imaginary and reject sibling rivalry does the garden take root. Only then do we live in a world where once again the sacrifice of Isaac is rejected.

The relationship between Abraham and God is typological of God's relationship with all whom God invites into community. Abraham and Sarah were invited to take their community with God into other cities and lands where they pitched their tent. Abraham was not a self-defined human being. His life with Sarah was lived out of his understanding of their relationship with God. Abraham was always in community with others as well. He encountered himself through his relationship to his neighbors. Rabbi Sacks reminds us that our invitation to journey with God means confessing and rejecting the notion that "For there to be an 'us' there must be a 'them,' the people not like us. Humanity is divided into friends and strangers, brothers and others. The people not like us become the screen onto which we project our fears. They are seen as threatening, hostile, demonic. Identity involves exclusion which leads to violence."[18] Abraham and Sarah welcome visitors by the oak of Mamre (Gen. 18) and Abraham argues with God on behalf of Sodom (Gen. 19).

To journey as Abraham and Sarah did means rejecting our inclination to protect ourselves by force. In their going—in our going—we embrace our vulnerability and forsake our tribe in order to journey with God and God's tribe, pronouncing God's blessing upon the world. Brueggemann says, "Abraham is called to exist so that the general condition of curse in the world is turned to a general condition of blessing, life, and well-being. Israel's mission is to mend the world in all its parts." God's people are to be a blessing in the world. God intends the world to be "generous, abundant, and fruitful, effecting generative fertility, material abundance, and this-worldly prosperity—*shalom* in the broadest scope."[19]

Paul used God's call to Abraham and Sarah and their blessing as a paradigm of expanding the work of God in the midst of wider Roman citizenship. Paul read the blessing and invitation of God as being fulfilled in the great expansion of grace to all people regardless of ethnicity, gender, and social class. (Gal. 3:8) God will not be limited to a religious or ethnic "us vs. them," but instead imagines a kingdom where we are all beloved of God. This kingdom is founded upon the rejection of violence for the sake of nation, and in favor of shalom for God. The origin stories of creation, Cain and Abel, and our faith ancestors Abraham and Sarah provide for us the characteristics of the new social imaginary. We are rooted in it by our very nature. The mission is not about nation-states, or making people members of religious institutions. The mission is a journey into a new community of being. The mission is Christian citizenship in the reign of God and how it is lived out.

God's people have lived out their dual citizenship since the time of Abraham and Sarah. Ours is a particular call where we stand shoulder to shoulder with our Abrahamic siblings in the work of government. We work to bring about peace and blessing in the world. We live our garden-lives boldly, through the rejection of mimetic violence and the embrace of healthy communal structures that foster peaceful co-existence.

Chapter Six

Prophetic Citizenship

No man . . . can be so stupid to deny that all men naturally were born free, being the image and resemblance of God himself.
—John Milton, poet and civil servant[1]

Freedom is not always the reality of God's people and when it is not, God takes an interest. To understand Christian citizenship and the garden social imaginary of a free society that informs it, we must not merely ponder the work of Jesus on the cross, but also understand that the work of the cross has deep theology roots grounded in the freedom of the people of Israel. God raised Jesus, but only after raising the people of Israel out of Egypt.[2] We understand then that the work of God's social imaginary has a prophetic quality to it. Just as it was prophetic to proclaim a nonviolent garden narrative of creation amidst societies with violent narratives that empowered despots, it is also prophetic to challenge the despots who use violence to write their own narratives. In this chapter we examine the prophetic quality of Christian citizenship and how it formed by the relationship between God's people, Moses, and the monarchs of Egypt.

Walter Brueggemann argues that, in our present age, prophecy is reduced to "righteous indignation" and translated into "social action."[3] This is *not* the kind of prophecy that characterized the ministry of Moses. Brueggemann argues that the task of Mosaic prophecy is "to nurture, nourish, and evoke a consciousness and perception alternative to the consciousness and perception of the dominant culture."[4] This definition raises the calling of the prophetic citizen above any particular social crisis and fixes our gaze on the bigger picture, the actual dominion politic perpetuated by the powers and principalities of the world. Christian citizenship is prophetic because it is an alternative to a citizenship in thrall to the powers of the world. This difference is clearest in the narrative of Moses, the people of Israel, and Pharaoh.

Of course, the story began out of sibling rivalry. Joseph, son of Jacob, was sold into slavery because his brothers were jealous of his father's attentions. He was taken to Egypt where he did very well for himself. After a great adventure, encountering the wife of Pharaoh, becoming a servant, and a bit of dreaming, Joseph ended up advising the Pharaoh and saving the land of Egypt from famine. Jacob and the family traveled to Egypt where he, the brothers, and Joseph are reunited in dramatic fashion. The Bible says, "Thus Israel settled in the land of Egypt, in the region of Goshen; and they gained possessions in it, and were fruitful and multiplied exceedingly" (Gen. 47:27). In a strange land, they lived out their social imaginary and are a prophetic blessing to the people with whom they lived. The whole story is a sweeping epic that lands the people of Israel in Egypt doing quite well for themselves (Gen. 37–50). Generations came and went and the people grew in number. A time came when the new Pharaoh didn't have a favorable disposition to the Israelites, and he put them to work. This migration into Egyptian bondage is the beginning of the story of Moses (Exod. 1:8–14).

Moses grew up, was nearly killed, ended up committing a murder, and escaped from the land of Egypt to marry and watch over sheep. Moses is a shepherd—a key metaphor of the leaders of Israel in scripture from this time forward. God appeared to Moses in a burning bush (Exod. 1–3). God invited Moses, just as God invited Abraham and Sarah, to go on God's behalf and be God's blessing of peace in the world. God invited Moses onto holy ground and challenged him to accept the mission of freeing God's people. Accepting the invitation meant that Moses would leave his past life behind: his journey in Egypt, the murder he committed, his fleeing into the pasturelands, and his long exile shepherding sheep.

God invited Moses to join in the long line of ancestors on God's mission of shalom. Brueggemann says that Moses's call was "an abrupt act that displaces Moses for a world of conflict propelled by God's holiness."[5] Moses was oblivious to the long history of God's mission until he stood on that holy ground and was invited to "go" on God's behalf. Like Abraham and Sarah, his *going* blesses the world. Vocation is broader than being called into community. Vocation is also about acceding to God's disruptive mission—saying, "Yes," and then going. Christian citizenship is enmeshed in this vocation. Moses lived out his vocation. He was called into a new community and into the work of God. His relationship with the powers will be defined by his obligation to God and his new community. In a single epiphanic moment Moses discovered that he was not alone, he was in a relationship with the divine, and this relationship brought him into relationship with others—his new family and his family of origin, God's people and family.[6] We have heard the story so many times we forget the radical nature of what God is doing through the prophetic work of Moses. We are so desensitized by our sixth-grade reading of the story that we completely miss the "radical and revolutionary social realty" that is birthed out of this moment.[7]

While God sent Abraham and Sarah as a blessing to the whole world, God sent Moses as a blessing of peace and a means of deliverance for God's people. Egypt had become an intolerably ugly place for master and slave alike, and God intervened in this evil course of affairs by sending Moses. Egypt was supported by slave labor long before the Israelites ever arrived. The pyramid of Giza was built before the birth of Abraham. Moreover, these were immigrants in the land. They had even been naturalized into Pharaoh's court. The people of Israel had been citizens and part of the structures of government, but in time this was forgotten and, for the purposes of the mighty, they were enslaved.

When life becomes cheap and people are seen as a means not an end, when the worst excesses are excused in the name of tradition and rulers have absolute power, then conscience is eroded and freedom lost because the culture has created an insulated space in which the cry of the oppressed can no longer be heard.[8] We already know that enslaving one another is part of the cycle of violence. The enslavement of God's people in Egypt was even prophesied to Abraham when he began his journey. Abraham and Sarah's people were destined to be strangers in a strange land[9] (Gen. 15:13). Regardless of his plan to live out his days shepherding with his father-in-law, Jethro, Moses was sent to bring shalom to the people in Egypt.

Moses was a prophet citizen in a strange land. God said, "I have observed the misery of my people who are in Egypt; I have heard their cry on account of their taskmasters. Indeed, I know their sufferings, and I have come down to deliver them from the Egyptians. . . . The cry of the Israelites has now come to me; I have also seen how the Egyptians oppress them" (Exod. 3:7–9). Brueggemann points out that God often goes and does this or that. However, in the call stories, God sends someone as an envoy. Christian citizens are sent as envoys—as prophets in a strange land. In the case of the people in Egypt, God sent Moses.[10] God said to Moses, "So come, I will send you to Pharaoh to bring my people, the Israelites, out of Egypt" (v. 10).

Here is an important part of God's shalom-making. Throughout scripture, we see God at work, reconciling the world to God's self. God builds and recreates the world into the kingdom of peace or shalom: the realm of God. God has special solidarity not only with the poor and oppressed, but also with all the people who dwell in God's creation. God makes peace by inverting the violence that undergirds human interaction. God invites us to aid in engineering this inversion; that is work that humans must do by God's invitation. We might say it this way: God could come down and free God's people alone. Instead, God acts in community with humanity. God acted with Moses to deliver a new state of being to Egypt and the Israelites. Of course, the Egyptians were not able to live within this new relationship without paying a considerable cost in terms of life and wealth. God sent Moses into a real political world. He went into a real context bisected by powers, authorities, and human-made kingdoms of violence.[11] As Stanley Hauerwas is fond of saying, "Faith is not a private matter." To live into God's call, Moses could not hide in the mountains where his sheep grazed. The God who spoke from the fiery bush sends those whom God calls into the world of violent enslaving powers.

Moses offers Pharaoh a vision of a completely different reality. Moses's presence in the court reveals to Pharaoh that there is a different way of making community born in freedom. This is in stark contrast to the Egyptian way of imagining community. The lesser gods of the powerful are always interested in supporting the orders and structures that keep them in place. In the world ordered by the Egyptian gods, Pharaoh and his court were given power to oversee the appropriate sacrifices. Everything in Egypt kept the power exactly where it was. When Moses challenged Pharaoh he did so by suggesting that people are free. He suggested there was an alternative narrative to the narrative of the empire. Moses's vocation as a prophetic citizen was to offer a vision of life lived freely under God, a life that contrasted with the imperial religious order of powers and principalities. Moses also offers a prophetic imaginary that is built on compassion and justice instead of power politics and oppression. As a prophetic citizen, Moses models a different way of being in the world that delegitimizes the politics of empire.[12]

Beyond mere criticism, Moses reveals a God who is free to act in the world—and does act. This is not a god at the beck and call of human sacrifices or liturgies. He also offers a prophetic vision of a people who are free. He invites Pharaoh and the people of God into writing a new history for themselves. Pharoah's failure to heed Moses's invitation is paradigmatic of imperial powers that do not hear the cries of the people and do not answer because they think it is not in their best interest to do so. Moses is at work not merely in the court of Pharaoh but amongst the people to "dismantle helplessness."[13]

The model of prophetic citizenship we receive through the story of Moses and the people of Israel is rooted in an acknowledgement that the powers of empire are not disposed to change and so a free people must take responsibility for creating a free society of compassion and justice in spite of them. Moses's vocation as a prophetic citizen reveals a kind of active criticism. He doesn't wait on passive powers and is not stymied by their inaction; instead Moses navigates the structures of Egyptian governance and identifies the pressure points of Egyptian society focused solely on the freedom required to create and make community.

Imperial society is rooted in the myth of scarcity. It sees no future beyond the old ordered powers. But the prophetic citizen sees that darkness will not have the last word. Along with others, Moses stands up to the darkness and hopelessness that holds Egypt in place. Both Israel and the Egyptian king see the future as more of the same. This hopeless resignation is how imperial powers oppress. Moses breaks into that with the proclamation of freedom, and injects energy into the despair by saying, "Let God's people go."

Imperial society is disinterested in the cries of oppressed people, and very focused in its own expansion. There is an economy to running monarchies and governments and that economy has a hunger and must be fed. The gods of empires legitimize this feeding frenzy. It isn't that people support governments that won't do them any good; it is that governments are not interested in doing the citizen any good unless it profits the power structure and people in charge. This is the lesson learned in Egypt. Moses makes clear that the ignored people are God's people. God is interested in the people themselves. This is a radical notion far more threatening to the rulers of Egypt than some vague notion of what it means to be God's chosen people.[14] God is interested in how the people are being oppressed. God is interested in the least and the lost. God makes his motives clear. God stands with the poor and the slaves against the empire. Theologian James Cone wrote, in *God of the Oppressed*, "The scandal is that the gospel means liberation, that this liberation comes to the poor, and that it gives them the strength and the courage to break the conditions of servitude."[15] God is not a disinterested party. God's solidarity is energizing to a free people.

It is easy to apply everything we have said to the particular case of American exceptionalism. Political pundits have long been in the habit of declaring that citizens are not patriotic if they do not believe that America was chosen by God to be a great country. This propaganda is often rooted in the Exodus story. The suggestion is that America is the new Israel. However, nothing could be further from the truth when one reviews our founding fathers' debate and language. The God that is present in our American origin documents is not a god who shows favor to one nation and curses another. Thomas Jefferson simply wanted the founding

Declaration to "assume among the powers of the earth the separate and equal station to which the laws of Nature and of Nature's God entitle them." We are not a nation founded upon an idea that America is uniquely exalted, only that we are founded as equal among nations.[16] I would suggest that when American exceptionalism arises it is the lesser gods of the empire speaking. God is interested, but not in how empires build up power; God is interested in how that same empire can be made to serve the least of its citizens. American exceptionalism suggests that in an empire, god is not working on behalf of the individual, but instead works for the nation state. Such gods do not warrant our worship. But nonetheless, the gods of Egypt are always reappearing in ever-new shapes and clothing.

The final aspect of the prophetic work of Moses and the people, is doxology. After all of the prophetic work of Moses, Pharaoh lets the people go. The people are grateful and they sing a song of thanksgiving. Miriam, Moses's sister, is foregrounded in this celebration. My professor of Old Testament Theology, the Rev. Dr. Murray Newman, drilled her song into us as first year seminarians. Miriam was a prophet who leads the people in giving thanks for their freedom. Gratitude is an energizing means of remembering. She sings, "Sing to the Lord, for he has triumphed gloriously" (Exod. 15:21a). Miriam's song speaks of God as a bringer of freedom, who cares for the lowly, and hears the cries of the poor and enslaved. This God has a name: Yahweh. Yahweh is no god of Egypt or the lands nearby. Yahweh loves and Yahweh reigns forever and ever she sings (Exod. 15:1–18). Miriam and Moses make it clear that this God wants all of us to rethink how we are ordered as a community, because of our relationship to God. Miriam and Moses, in dancing to this song, reveal their people's own physical freedom from violence and oppression. They are free, and their bodies are free. Finally, there is another reign and it is not the reign of empire but of God, and we are citizens in it. These citizen prophets claim for themselves a holy origin, that nullifies the ancient claims of the empire.[17] The prophetic citizen belongs to God's reign of shalom.

We are part of this history. This is our narrative. We are to be "a sign that God has not abandoned the world."[18] God's "work"—God's "vocation"— is beyond the scope of the world's powers, and God's reign is achieved differently from how the powers of empire are secured. Moreover, God's shalom can only be enacted in person, in community between human beings. Prophetic citizenship and its new social imaginary is required.

Our society, like other empires, stands against this notion of God's "sending" work—this community of shalom. The invitation to Moses was not bumper-sticker political activism. God invites us into a real community with real values. There are political implications to shalom, but for those who accept God's invitation, the journey quickly becomes about a community and a narrative that resonates far more deeply than any political tribalism. God's paradigmatic way of inviting and sending does not mesh with any single empire's exceptionalism.[19]

God invites God's people to create a new community of shalom. A kind of community that is birthed with a dance and a song. We must take care not to simply make God's mission into a social ethic or universal morality. God's call is also not merely a means for achieving better wages and working conditions for the enslaved. It cannot be narrowly defined as a sociopolitical intervention or strategy. Shalom community is not limited to "strategies to ensure just distribution of resources, or the theories of justice presupposed by such policies."[20] God did not give Moses a theory of justice so much as God invited Moses to make a prophetic witness to a God who births a different kind of community. It is not moral therapeutic deism. God fosters real, transformed, and renewed relationships among the people of Israel and the people of Egypt. Remember, the story of Israel in the land of Egypt began with friendship between a lost son and a ruler, Pharaoh and Joseph. What is broken by Israel's oppression into slavery is that original relationship. The relationship between Israel and Egypt devolves into sibling rivalry. A time came when people did not remember the blessings they had been for one another. Shalom, peace, is not a political "symbol" or "myth," but a real state of connectedness that is a different kingdom from the reign of humanity.[21]

Christian citizenship founded upon the social imaginary in our creation stories and lived out in the prophetic work of Moses is a different posture toward the local and global sociopolitical institutions that depend on violence, power, and authority. Stanley Hauerwas says:

Put as directly as I can, it is not the task of the church to try to develop social theories or strategies to make America work; rather the task of the church in this country is to become a polity that has the character necessary to survive as a truthful society. That task carried out would represent a distinctive contribution to the body politic we call America.[22]

I would simply add that these sociopolitical forces have globalized. Christianity has an opportunity to bear the same witness globally and not simply within the confines of local communities. We know that working towards God's shalom community as Christian citizens will be deadly and costly to the Christian citizen because of the stubbornness of Pharaoh and all of Pharaoh's present-day analogues. Nevertheless, the work of Moses was to be a prophetic citizen, a messenger of shalom, to the power of Egypt. Moses was the face of God in the world of violence and oppression. He was the face of God to Pharaoh. Through Moses, God intervened in the world of humans and came into conflict with political power.

God offers presence, power, wisdom, and comfort, and does mighty acts to aid those engaged in the work of shalom making. Brueggemann says that such acts of God can only be "available in the midst of alternative human action."[23] God used these patriarchs and matriarchs, and many more like them, to inaugurate new ways of governance by their very presence in the body politic.

This new way of being is God's peaceable kingdom. Moses is suggesting a community grounded in something deeper than violence. Since the beginning of Genesis, God has been undoing humanity's endless sibling rivalries and inviting us into a community of peace. These sibling rivalries, and the institutions they have birthed, are at the core of human violence.[24] Being called and sent as a prophetic citizen is about participating in a virtuous community of peace.

The prophetic citizen participates in the wider structures of government without sacrificing others to satisfy their own wants and desires. Such a peace is at the heart of the community Jesus imagined. Such peace is at the heart of eternal communion with God. This peace and its community are the means by which all other communities, nations, and politics are to be compared and judged. It is true that we have not always been at our best as the church, but the fact of our own brokenness should not discourage us from pursuing the kingdom of peace, nor does it excuse us from our holy vocation. The church, after all, is supposed to be the practice field for Christian citizenship. As Hauerwas says, "The fact that we have often been less than we were meant to be should never be used as an excuse for shirking the task of being the people of God."[25]

God invites and God sends all of God's people. We are meant to be citizens of God's reign first and then to work and find our place in the wider body politic. God's call to ordinary people, to ordinary citizens, undergirds all other work done in God's name. The core is peaceful human interconnectivity. The call to be a Christian citizen, like Moses's call, is a calling that finds its first home in ordinary people living ordinary lives. After all, Moses was not trained to speak to the rulers of their world. Creating the community of shalom is not a professional exercise to be left to politicians, pundits, and lobbyists. There is no financial or economic benefit to any of those whom God calls. God calls the ordinary, unprepared, and often tentative to be God's voice and to create a new world in God's name. There is certainly no safety guaranteed in this work. Heeding God's call is not the start of an economic exchange. There is no room for the prosperity gospel here.[26] The God of Sinai invites God's people to share the burden of this new shalom society equally amongst all members (Exod. 18:13–27). Everyone is a citizen, everyone is free, and has a share in the peaceable kingdom. James Cone wrote, "The acceptance of the gift of freedom transforms our perception of our social and political existence."[27]

The powers and authorities of this world are "alien" to God's desired kingdom of shalom.[28] We are invited to risk the walk with God, and to relate to each other in ways that transform the present moments we experience. The faithful who say yes to God's invitation to be kingdom citizens first set aside their plans and die to self so God can undertake mighty works through their relationships. The words to Isaiah echo for us, "Whom will I send? Who will go on my behalf? Who will be my messenger?" It is a not a call to professionals or specialists. God calls all siblings into new relationships, and a new kingdom of shalom as citizens. Who will answer the invitation to go? Who will be willing to be the one sent with a different social imaginary for the dismantling of empire theology and sociology? We are intended to be prophetic citizens in the strange lands in which we find ourselves.

Chapter Seven

A Differentiated Wilderness Society

The great temptation many of us face today is to leave the mess of the public square and find another way to be faithful, a way that may be less costly though maybe less spiritually valuable. To yield to such a temptation is to develop amnesia about our first commandment and commission.

—Vincent Bacote, theologian and ethicist[1]

oses's prophetic alternative community exemplifies citizenship as a foreigner in a strange land. However, Moses's prophetic work does not end when the people are led out of Egypt. There is a wilderness period where the people learn to depend on God and claim God as their diety. The wilderness is a place of formation. God is in relationship with God's people by guiding them in forming a particular kind of community. Christian citizens understand this wilderness community as the bedrock upon which the reign of God in this world is founded. When Dr. Martin Luther King Jr. says, "The arc of the moral universe is long, but it bends toward justice," he has in mind the community that Moses builds with God in the desert.[2] This wilderness community starts with ten *d'varim* or הַדְּבָרִים or words. Exodus 20:1 says, "God spoke all these words."

These "Ten Commandments" come with a lot of cultural baggage in America. They are all tangled up in court battles, culture wars, and statuary. Our idea of the "Ten Commandments" in American culture and civil religion doesn't come from the book of Exodus. It also doesn't come from our founders.[3] Instead, our idea of the "Ten Commandments" comes from a movie. Interesting factoid: in the 1950s there was a group called the Fraternal Order of Eagles. The F.O.E. was an international fraternal organization founded on February 6, 1898, in Seattle, Washington, by a group of six theater owners including brothers John W. Cort and Tim J. Cort, along with Harry Considine. "People helping people" was their motto. Wiki tells me that "touring theater troupes are credited with much of the Eagles' rapid growth. Most early members were actors, stagehands and playwrights, who carried the Eagles story as they toured across the United States and Canada. The organization's success is also attributed to its funeral benefits." They also claim responsibility for "Mother's Day," which is not true, though they helped popularize it. The F.O.E. met with director Cecil B. DeMille and funded a promotion in 1956. They donated monuments of the Ten Commandments (which was DeMille's new movie) across the country. It was the same decade when "In God we Trust" was placed on our money and the Pledge of Allegiance was amended to include "under God."[4] Grappling with the aftereffects of World War II and enmired in anti-communist paranoia, Americans longed for a transcendent God. Cecil B. DeMille aimed to give America that vision. The American obsession with the Ten Commandments began as a movie promotion.

American moral theater aside, Rabbi Jonathan Sacks writes, "Thirty-three centuries after they were first given, [these ten words] remain the simplest, shortest guide to the creation of a good society."[5] The founding of the covenant begins like an ancient suzerainty treaty.[6] These types of treaties had a preamble, and then the rules, followed by blessings or a kind of doxology.[7] The commandments follow this form. In the preamble God declares God's self to be the suzerain for Moses and the people. Then God reminds them of God's work raising Israel to freedom after Egypt.

Next come the rules of the game—the basic "principles" of relation between God the Suzerain, and Israel, God's vassal state. There are two sets of five commandments in this section of the treaty. The first words remind the citizen of their relationship with God, while the second group of words sets out relational boundaries with others (Exod. 20:1–20). According to these ten words, the work for the people of Israel (and for the people who claim to follow Jesus today) is to learn to "love as God loved and loves," writes Stanley Hauerwas in *The Peaceable Kingdom*.[8]

Christian citizens must lean into the depth of Hauerwas's summary. We must be careful to reject the Constantinian and Enlightenment/Reformed diversions from the original story. Constantinian Christianity is rooted in "the conviction that Christianity is about being religious in a general and diffuse sense." Meanwhile the Enlightenment/Reformation "makes Christians into apologists to and for the modern world."[9] Moreover, we mustn't make these commandments about "advice" on how to live in particular "circumstances." These commandments are not an ethical prescription to be filled by a loyal disciple; instead they evoke a community living into the blessings and grace of God.

Christians living between Constantine and the Reformation were sorely tempted to embrace the scripture as a list of individual moral imperatives—biblical laws that function for the person like natural laws function for Newtonian physics.[10] Treating the commandments like this is a clever way of honoring them while evading their meaning. Our response to the commandments is not merely individual. As Christians, we read the biblical story in the context of a network of faithful people that stretches forwards and backwards across all of time. From this perspective, scripture becomes "revealed reality" instead of "revealed morality."[11] The next step is arriving at a series of virtues that are faithful to the commandments. We live the commandments through a virtuous common life.

Reading the commandments in this way, we hear them differently. Instead of hearing a list of laws, we hear virtues expounded. Pursuing these virtues is how we learn to love as God loves. In the first set of five commandments, we learn that God is the author of and authority over relationships between citizens. God transcends all other loyalties and laws. To return to a point made earlier, Christians are called to a higher citizenship than any nation's laws can engender, based on a relationship with a God who transcends the laws of humanity. God is a living, active, and involved force, not an abstract distant deistic manifestation of power. Operating in the world with God's nearness in mind suggests that, when the demands of our heavenly citizenship conflict with our earthly obligations, reverence towards God should trump everything else.[12]

The next three commandments address our relationships with each other, and are rooted in God's creation of life. A day of worship helps us reorient our world towards God's purposes. Then we have our relationship with parents and others. The commandment that speaks of murder is debated of course, as it is our natural inclination to rationalize and justify shedding blood in the name of the sibling rivalries that animate our culture. Humans legitimize the taking of life in all manner of ways, employing an infinite number of genteel and rational arguments for rejecting God's desire that we not take life from each other,[13] but God continues to call us to a higher form of relationship than rivalry.[14]

The next group of three commandments has to do with neighborliness. They are the ones about adultery, theft, and false witness. Respecting other people's marriage and our own is key, because marital fidelity is a symbol of God's bond with humanity. People's claim to ownership of property is to be respected, which we talked about in chapter two and included John Locke's treatise as being the key to ordering society. And honesty is the key ingredient to justice.[15] Remembering well and speaking honestly are essential ingredients to a society of trust, and these virtues aid in dealing with pain and suffering when they arise. Truth telling is crucial for reconciliation.[16] All of these combined are a bedrock principle for family groups to live together.

The last word is on envy. We are to refrain from envy of others. René Girard believes, as I do, that the prohibition against covetousness is the core of the whole set of commandments. To go back to Cain and Abel and the garden, envy is the root of mimetic desire. Envy sows chaos in our relationships with our siblings, neighbors, neighboring states, and nations. The repeated struggle in human society is with individual and corporate envy that threatens to unravel all the other commandments. Rabbi Sacks says, "It led Cain to murder Abel, made Abraham and Isaac fear for their life because they were married to beautiful women, and led Joseph's brothers to hate him and sell him into slavery. It was envy of their neighbors that led the Israelites often to imitate their religious practices and worship their gods."[17] Sacks is quick to point out that living with the other nine commandments can help us honor the tenth. Remembering our createdness, God's presence, and image frees us to live differently.[18]

The New Testament refers back to the commandments in a very particular way. In Mark it appears that God in Christ Jesus is the God of the first commandment. Jesus is the Living Word. Jesus also lives out of these commandments as God comes into contact with the people and powers of the time, through Jesus.[19] Jesus is the incarnation and vision of the virtuous citizen. Luke picks up the theme of Exodus 20 by using the language of community. He understands that the commandments are woven into life through virtuous discipleship. In chapter 18 of Luke's Gospel, Jesus stresses the importance of the Ten Commandments, and highlights five out of the ten. Jesus extends the prohibition against covetousness into an emphatic call to share what we have.[20] Luke also makes it clear that the Sabbath is a time when God is working, and we are to echo God's industriousness by joining Christ and the Creator in releasing those bound by the religious and the powerful.[21]

Again, our work is not to live in isolation over and against the world, but to be in the world to free others from the powers that bind them. This is the proclamation of jubilee. We are free to live differently and those bound are to be freed, those who hunger are to be fed, those in debt are to be released, and the field hands are to rest from their labors. Through this expanded vision of the Ten Commandments, all creation is restored.

Rabbi Sacks, in the 2011 *Ebor Lectures*, reminds us that these ten words are a principled foundation for healthy society: there is a difference between a social and political contract and a covenant. The ten commandments are covenant words, not social and political contract words. Contracts outline the boundaries of "advantage," while these words establish a relationship of loyalty and precedence. The contract becomes a higher authority to which I am bound to settle any future disputes. The covenant rests upon the relationship of a higher authority that transforms all other relationships in my life. The nation state and its citizens are governed by a social contract. The covenant established in the ten commandments orients people to each other and to God at a deeper level than that.[22]

The Christian citizen is a member of a higher society than their nation state. The commandments remind us that we are not merely Americans. We cannot simply be patriots. We are citizens of a higher kingdom. We relate to God in such a way that we are marked and the way we live in our particular society is transformed. I can be a dual citizen as long as I remember and return often to the character of my relationship rooted in God.

We are to be virtuous citizens of God's kingdom not only on Sundays, not only within the walls of our homes, but also in the political and social spaces of our community. Global and national society only works if we have character enough to care for one another across the boundaries of states or beyond the scope of our individual rights. I may have the legal right to leave you out in the cold, but as a person in a covenant with God, I have a different responsibility. Society is judged by a people who live according to a higher rule, who live differently within its midst.

God, at Mount Sinai with neighboring tribal powers and monarchial principalities all around, created a wilderness society that forms and reforms as it makes its way in the world. However, the creation of that first new wilderness society got off to a rocky start. After the revelation of the commandments in Exodus, God invited Moses back up the mountain (Exod. 32). Moses was delayed in coming back down because he got lost with God for a while. He was gone for a very long time. In fact, some translations imply it was an excruciatingly long time. In the absence of leadership and their conduit to God, they made an idol. God got upset at their idolatry. Moses got angry and smashed the tablets with the Ten Commandments. Aaron offered a lame excuse and blamed the people, scapegoating them for his failure of judgment. I have always assumed that this story is about totems for idol worship, maybe because I was so affected by the Cecil B. DeMille movie *The Ten Commandments*. I assumed that the Israelites chose another god, the golden calf. After all, Aaron does say, "Here is your god!"

The eleventh-century rabbi Abraham Ben Meir Ibn Ezra anticipated my confusion. He taught that the idol was not made to take God's place, but Moses's. Furthermore, that God was interested in having a direct relationship with God's people. What we know is that everyone has access to God, with or without a leader. The idol was to be the means by which people could commune with God, in the absence of a leader. Sometimes we get into trouble because we think very highly of ourselves. In the case of the Israelites, their idolatry sprung from feeling very small in the shadow of Sinai.[23] Rabbi Sacks puts it eloquently, "Every Jew is an equal citizen of the republic of faith because every Jew has access to its constitutional document, the Torah."[24] In this golden calf moment, the people did not understand that God was personally in relationship with them. God brought them out of Egypt in order that they might be free and continue to be a blessed people and a blessing to the world around them. God did not need any go-betweens, not Moses and not golden calves. They were to be this kind of society together.

The story of the golden calf is about the human tendency to believe that human-made items can mediate our fear, anxiety, sense of lost-ness, despair, and hopelessness by settling our disputes and bringing about right judgments. We hope golden calves will bring about right government and care for the poor and needy. Humans put their trust in just about every kind of political golden calf you can think of. The golden calf is a way of ditching our responsibility. We create institutions and governments to be our go-betweens. This moves our responsibility to the golden calf organization(s) and removes our responsibility for the outcomes. This is how we are able to say the government did this or that—as if we are not our government.

The laws and politics of America and of any nation are a golden calf. Humanity's understanding of truth by means of reason, our best attempts to create just law, political parties, presidents, and even nations come and go. There will always be golden calves to believe in and put our trust in. The Christian citizen is called to a different kind of relational politics that suggest very different outcomes. While we are obligated to obey the laws of our society, Christian citizenship is really the only means to a different sort of world. Reliance on golden calves will not be enough.

Golden calf organizations always function by means of a social contract,[25] which serve as the foundation for a network of formal and informal laws, statutes, constitutions, and treaties. These forms of social contracts help to protect, build commerce, enable travel, and order life when large groups of people live together. Most people talk about the need for social virtues in each of these types of contracted nation-states in order to bring about the very best societies possible.[26] When we discuss Christian citizenship within the sphere of the nation, we are speaking primarily about a different posture towards the social contractual relationships of the wider community. I want to be clear here. Our Christian belief and practice should have a real impact on how we conduct ourselves as Americans. Our covenanted relationship as Christian citizens impacts our contractual relationships with the state and the informal relationships with our fellow citizens and neighbors.

The difference between Christian and non-Christian ways of being American ought to come down to compassion. Compassion is a fundamental virtue, rooted throughout the scripture, and especially in the Old Testament as *hesed*.[27] As Christian citizens in a covenant relationship with God, we receive compassion from God, and we are to have compassion and live compassionate lives with kin, strangers, and neighbors alike. This is not a contract. For the Christian citizen *compassion is a governing virtue of life* lived by citizens in God's reign.[28] All relationships are read through a cruciform lens. The passion of Christ is compassion incarnated and enacted for all people.

Our work of covenanted compassion is entangled with another word: *emunah,* or faithfulness. For the Christian citizen, the work of governing is about living out a commitment to relationships with others. Our faithfulness or *emunah* propels compassion forward and gives all of our public relations a quality of familial faithfulness. *Familial faithfulness is the second governing virtue of Christian citizenship.* Rabbi Sacks describes it as an "internalized sense of identity, kinship, loyalty, obligation, responsibility, and reciprocity."[29] The sole purpose of government is to make us into a society that works. The Christian citizen has a greater vocation. The Christian citizen understands the tradition of familial faithfulness as a unity and relational obligation between kin, neighbor, and stranger. It has a universal quality to it. The Christian citizen is drawn into compassionate relationships outside of the natural and even governed boundaries because the compassion of Christ unites all people—family, friends, neighbors, and strangers—into one faithful familial relationship.

We as Christians are baptized into the reign of God and we are made citizens by Christ's work. Christ is doing what God has been doing all along, making us God's people. We are unified by a God who desires relationship with us, and we are people who believe God makes a covenant with us. The scripture is filled with these covenants. All of them are really of one kind in which God invites us to be a community of blessing to the world rooted in both *hesed* and *emunah*—in both compassion and faithfulness.

To fully grasp the meaning of the commandments given to Moses in order to actualize God's garden social imaginary we must hold together the active words of compassion and faithfulness as we engage the other ten words. As we speak about Christian citizenship in the reign of God, we are speaking about covenant, compassion, and faithfulness to our kin, our neighbor, and the stranger.

Chapter Eight

The Rise of King and Prophet

The country has to awaken every now and then to the fact that the people are responsible for the government they get . . .

—Harry S. Truman, U.S. president[1]

In 1 Samuel 8, the leaders of Israel speak to the prophet Samuel about their future and potential death of their society. They believe that the nations around them have a leg up because they have kings. This is the crucial moment in Israel's history when the people cry out for a king to rule them. There are two reasons for their plea. The first is fear of Samuel's absence in the future, on account of his age and eventual death. The second is a desire to mimic the monarchies all around them. Of course, Samuel is not happy. He believed the relationship between the people and God was most important—moderated from time to time by a good prophet, leader, judge. God was the Lord with whom their covenant was made, so God was their king.

God surprises Samuel and says,

> Listen to the voice of the people in all that they say to you; for they have not rejected you, but they have rejected me from being king over them. Just as they have done to me, from the day I brought them up out of Egypt to this day, forsaking me and serving other gods, so also they are doing to you. Now then, listen to their voice; only—you shall

solemnly warn them, and show them the ways of the king who shall reign over them.

1 Samuel 8:7–9

The point God is making is that the people are eager to have rulers over them. People believe that the principalities of the world can secure great riches and prosperity. God tells Samuel to warn Israel that this will not be so. It is also clear that God is tired of Israel's complaints and has had enough. God reminds Samuel they have been like this since Egypt and they had the same complaints with Moses. People long to have a part in earthly kingdoms that amass great power. People always forget that the powers and principalities of this world serve themselves most of all. "It is good to be the king," Mel Brooks once quipped. Their desire for a king is not a rejection of Samuel, just as it was not a rejection of Moses. It is a rejection of God and God's invitation to imagine a new kind of society.

There was a very real political problem that was plaguing Israel. The tribal confederation was simply not strong enough to hold its own against the growing complexity of neighboring powers (1 Sam. 8:1). The last line of the book of Judges reads, "In those days there was no king in Israel; all the people did what was right in their own eyes" (Judg. 21:25). Judges invokes the horrific anarchy described by political philosopher Thomas Hobbes, who said that such existence was "continual fear, and danger of violent death; and the life of man solitary, poor, nasty, brutish and short."[2]

In order to ameliorate the chaos, the leaders of Israel simply want to emulate the only model of governance available to them, as the writings of Plato and Greek democracy were not yet known. So, the people of Israel transfer control over their bodies and property to a king. They become assets of the king; they are his subjects. Just as Samuel will warn, the king may not be to their liking. Yet, in the face of anarchy or annihilation by rival kings, a bad king seemed a small price to pay. The scriptural narrative understands clearly that the people are rejecting the imagined community of God, and putting in its place a monarchy with a social contract. God gives the people what they want: they wish to have a king, and Samuel gives them one,[3] but it in no way sets aside the characteristics, virtue, or words that describe citizenship based upon the covenant.

Following God's instruction, Samuel warns the people of the danger of their choice.

> These will be the ways of the king who will reign over you: he will take your sons and appoint them to his chariots and to be his horse-men, and to run before his chariots; and he will appoint for himself commanders of thousands and commanders of fifties, and some to plow his ground and to reap his harvest, and to make his implements of war and the equipment of his chariots. He will take your daughters to be perfumers and cooks and bakers. He will take the best of your fields and vineyards and olive orchards and give them to his court-iers. He will take one-tenth of your grain and of your vineyards and give it to his officers and his courtiers. He will take your male and female slaves, and the best of your cattle and donkeys, and put them to his work. He will take one-tenth of your flocks, and you shall be his slaves. And in that day you will cry out because of your king, whom you have chosen for yourselves; but the Lord will not answer you in that day.
>
> 1 Samuel 8:11–18

In other words, kings and principalities take from you and they make war on your behalf and with your assets. They will support themselves and their court with the people's wealth. There is a high cost for having a king.

By the time of Jesus's birth, Israel is suffering the plight that Samuel foretold. Kingship is a deliverance of prosperity under David and Solomon—though the price the people pay is substantial. But then Israel falls into bondage as a vassal state within wider empires, the Roman Empire being the last before Jesus. Jesus comes to reign, but on the original terms of God's garden social imaginary. He is not the sort of king the people want. The rejection of Jesus reenacts the rejection of God in 1 Samuel. We do not long for citizenship in the reign of God and we choose instead to live within the realms of other worldly powers. It is a decision that has real consequences—even if we cannot imagine them. It is a decision we are continuously responsible for.

What this narrative makes obvious is that, if we wish to participate in the reign of God, we must reject the notion that humans are created to rule over each other. The revelation of Jesus is a new expression of the ancient invitation to create such a community. God invites us in Jesus Christ to something more than monarchical slavery. The scripture is not interested in a theocracy. We must reject practices of economic enslavement. Our faith tradition is invested in God-given freedom for all God's creatures, beginning when God explains to Cain that sin is part of choice and that there is nothing in the created order that forces us to do anything.[4] Renowned psychologist and Holocaust survivor Viktor Frankl believed that when every other conceivable freedom is removed from a human being, there is left one. The basic freedom from which all other choices flow is the freedom to choose how one reacts to their context. It is this freedom that roots us to our first ancestors. It is this freedom that takes us to God himself. It is this freedom that reflects God's image and likeness.[5] The God-given freedom cannot be removed, even by a despotic king.

With this freedom in mind, God invites us to create a society founded upon a covenant of compassion and faithfulness. The scripture imagines a society where God is the only sovereign. The garden social imagery is meant to take root in a very real world, where no one owns anyone else, or abuses power; but instead where society is collaborative and diverse under the watchful eye of God. Synagogues, churches, and mosques are supposed to be the mini-models of such harmony. But in the end human sinfulness breaks down those structures too—but that is different book.[6]

When we live under the governing powers and principalities of this world we will be enslaved as Samuel promises: the powers will take our sons and daughters and make them wage war and support the war machine. The powers will make us migrate to places and harvest this or that, and they will feast while we make less than a just wage that would be enough to put food on our table. The powers will make us work in machine shops, in bakeries, and we will become the maker of things while others enjoy them.

We will be taxed to pay for the machine of government itself. We will be the subjects and we will be enslaved to the system we choose.

Human beings ruling over others was "anathema" to God, to Moses, and to Samuel. In some very real way the shift to a monarchy was a rejection of the Sinai covenant for a new model of relationship—a Mount Zion oriented one. Of course, the kingdom that came to Israel was at once fantastic and a disaster. Under a centralized rule that unified the northern and southern tribes, a dynastic reign was created. The Davidic legacy united the literary and cultural history of the people into one story. The kingdom became a center of trade and commerce for the region.

The monarchy continued the narrative of mimetic sibling rivalry in scripture. First was the rivalry of Saul and David, as the two lived out the brotherly relationship of Cain and Abel and all the others who came before them. David's very presence, and true belovedness, enraged Saul. He wanted what David had and desired to be who David was. This desire to usurp David and all he stood for as future king created a deep anger in Saul that resulted in murderous intent (1 Sam. 19:9–10, 19–23). René Girard reveals that it is David himself—his very being, his relationships, what the people said and sang about him—that intensified Saul's desire.[7] Not unlike God's enjoyment of Abel's sacrifice or Jacob's love of Joseph, the people's love of David increased the sibling rivalry. Saul's death on the battlefield finally put an end to this part of the broken history of Israel's kings.

If we are to understand the power of corruption in governments that lose sight of the people and of God we might well take a look at a few of the kings of Israel. Saul was the first of the kings and is credited with bringing about a new stability and unity amongst the tribes. He had a spirit that plagued him and caused him torment far beyond David's mimetic rivalry (1 Sam. 16:14–23; 18:10). Saul actually got into big trouble when he did not follow God's command. (1 Sam. 15:1, 19, 20, 22). Samuel confronted Saul about not dealing with the Amalekites, their king Agag, and all their livestock as God desired. Saul, as in the origin stories, deflected the responsibility to the people (1 Sam. 15:24). Samuel in turn challenged Saul on the lie, because Saul coveted the wealth of Agag's household. Not only was Saul embroiled in personal conflict with David, but he also did not take responsibility for his kingship and actions. He rejected accountability to God and to the people, and he scapegoated the people for his wrongdoing, out of greed.

David is hailed as the great king who brings Israel into a new age of beauty, liturgy, and commerce. But he also had a downfall. He desired Bathsheba, a married woman (2 Sam. 11). He impregnated her and then attempted to have Uriah, her husband, come home from battle to have sex with her so he could deflect blame for the infidelity and resulting pregnancy. Eventually, David had Uriah killed by putting him in direct danger on the battlefield so he could have Bathsheba for himself. They were married after Uriah's death and she bore a son—Solomon. The story of David's crime marked the end of his rise to prominence and the beginning of his downfall. The house of David was also brought low because his elder sons were angered by Solomon's choice to be king.

Solomon was wise and successful as a ruler. Part of what becomes clear from the outset was that Solomon imagined a different reign than those that came before him. (1 Kings 2:46b; 3:1–3). He married a daughter of Pharaoh thereby placing himself in relationship with those who had imprisoned and enslaved the people of Israel. This suspicious connection is not helped by the fact that Solomon himself brought about a great building program on the financial and physical backs of his own people. He built the great Solomonic temple, but we also know that he worshiped the local gods in the high places. He was unfaithful to the Sinai tradition.

When it was all over and Solomon was dead, the elders came to his son Rehoboam and said, "Your father made our yoke heavy. Now therefore lighten the hard service of your father and his heavy yoke that he placed on us, and we will serve you." Rehoboam replied, "My father made your yoke heavy, but I will add to your yoke; my father disciplined you with whips, but I will discipline you with scorpions" (1 Kings 12:14).

Ahab is another king whose misdeeds grab our attention. He is credited for doing everything the others did but to an extreme. He was not liked at all. He was most famous for stealing Naboth's vineyard. According to 1 Kings 21, Naboth owned a vineyard. Ahab wanted it to increase the footprint of his palace, but the land was Naboth's inheritance. Ahab's wife, Jezebel, charged Naboth with blasphemy and had him killed. Ahab then took the vineyard for himself.

We could talk about Amnon, Adonijah, and Absalom, but I think you get the point. Each of these stories reveals, as only the biblical narrative can, the failings of rulers who do not honor the origin stories' lessons, the covenant with God, and their responsibility to the people. They are all stories about not taking responsibility, about desire, violence, and dominion. They repeat the mimetic themes of murderous desire, violence, and scapegoating. The history offered in the books of *Kings* and *Chronicles* gives us a bird's eye view of the results of the Israelites' desire for a king. It reveals human frailty and the continued and repeated failure of humanity to honor God's garden dream for creation.

This period of Israel's history also gives rise to the citizen prophet. Just as the kings surely repeat the lost way of Pharaoh, this prophetic tradition repeats the work of Moses. The government and kingdom of Israel was not immune to the prophetic call to return to the garden work invited by God. This is starkly highlighted by the Sinai prophets who continue to offer a vision of a people united by their relationship to God and one another.

The prophets of the Sinai tradition viewed the centralization of state and religious power in Jerusalem as a kind of detestable suzerainty treaty. While the relationship with God was understood and shaped in a positive way, the Sinai prophets saw this Israel's kings as an occupying power to whom the people were unjustly subservient. The Sinai perspective was that the centralized government propped up a different king in the place of God, and organized a dubious, novel set of disciplines around the Mosaic faith received in the desert. It is clear that this institution-creep was perpetual.

While the vast majority of the Old Testament reveals the priorities of the institution-phobic Sinai tradition, later editors attempted to answer Sinai critics with their own redactions. The edited text allows for the suzerainty of a Davidic monarchy under the power of God. But even so, Deuteronomy 17–18 makes it clear that the Mosaic covenant, the Sinai prophetic tradition, and the rule of God will continue. The redactors hold that the king will be accountable to God, to Sinai, and to Sinai's prophets.[8]

The prophets Elijah and Elisha undertook exactly this work of accountability. Steeped in the Sinai tradition, both of these illustrious prophets maintained a passionate focus on the relationship between the people and their God. In 1 Kings 21, Elisha powerfully reminds the king and the centralized religion that they are answerable to a higher power.[9] Like an episode of *Scandal* or *House of Cards*, King Ahab killed a man for his wife and vineyard. So, God sent Elisha to remind Ahab that God's justice would prevail:

> Then the word of the LORD came to Elijah the Tishbite, saying: Go down to meet King Ahab of Israel, who rules in Samaria; he is now in the vineyard of Naboth, where he has gone to take possession. You shall say to him, "Thus says the LORD: Have you killed, and also taken possession?" You shall say to him, "Thus says the LORD: In the place where dogs licked up the blood of Naboth, dogs will also lick up your blood." Ahab said to Elijah, "Have you found me, O my enemy?" He answered, "I have found you. Because you have sold yourself to do what is evil in the sight of the LORD. . . ."
>
> 1 Kings 21:17–21

The prophet Hosea also worked in the shadow of Sinai. His singular calling was to reform and renew the local shrines that dotted the Israelite landscape. Hosea warned, "In Gilead there is iniquity, they shall surely come to nothing. In Gilgal they sacrifice bulls, so their altars shall be like stone heaps on the furrows of the field" (Hos. 12:11).[10] The worship of the God of Sinai is important in a just society.

Perhaps it is the prophet Micah who outlined the Sinai covenant in the clearest terms. In Micah 6 the prophet called the people to plead their case to God:

> "For I brought you up from the land of Egypt, and redeemed you from the house of slavery; and I sent before you Moses, Aaron, and

Miriam. O my people, remember now what King Balak of Moab devised, what Balaam son of Beor answered him, and what happened from Shittim to Gilgal, that you may know the saving acts of the LORD."

Micah 6:4–5

Micah declared that God acted in history for God's people. In light of that, God suggested what the proper response to God's action was *not*:

"With what shall I come before the LORD, and bow myself before God on high? Shall I come before him with burnt-offerings, with calves a year old? Will the LORD be pleased with thousands of rams, with ten thousands of rivers of oil? Shall I give my firstborn for my transgression, the fruit of my body for the sin of my soul?"

Micah 6:6–7

Micah crafted a direct attack on the centralized kingdom and temple tradition, a bold critique of the religion of Zion and its unfaithfulness. The proper response to God's salvific action is summed up succinctly in the famous passage from Micah 6:8: "He has told you, O mortal, what is good; and what does the LORD require of you but to do justice, and to love kindness, and to walk humbly with your God?"[11]

The sixth chapter of the book of Micah outlines the foundation of the Sinai tradition. God is the God of the holy mountain of Sinai. The desert is the place where God dwells. God does not dwell in the cities of men, in temples, or even in shrines. God is not interested in offerings but in faithfulness. This God—whether upset at kings, angry because of his people's idolatry, or concerned with the tension between religion and faith—is a God who is in relationship with God's people.

Jon Levenson writes, "The mountain of God is a beacon to the slaves of Egypt, a symbol of a new kind of master and radically different relationship of people to state. Sinai is not the final goal of the Exodus, but lying between Egypt and Canaan, it does represent YHWH's unchallengeable mastery over both."[12] It is in the desert that the people learned dependence upon God and how to respond faithfully to God. It is in the wilderness where they learned compassion for one another and their leaders. It is through the Sinai tradition that they began to live in accordance to the garden imagination of God. It was an emerging social imaginary different from kingdom dominion philosophies.

The God of the Sinai covenant is a God who is angered with the temple religion and the religious authorities who collude to reorient the faith toward the state. The prophets of the God of the Sinai see this as nothing more than Egypt remade. Centralized religion, especially when it is connected to the power and authority of this world, will inevitably recreate a system of slavery. God is the Lord and the King—there shall be no others in God's place. In this way, Israel was not a state, a theocracy, or a religious kingdom. Israel was forever a people in relationship with God. The people were to renew their relationship every day and every night. This is the power of the *Shema*, one of the oldest prayers in Judaism. "Hear, O Israel: the Lord our God, the Lord is one" (Hebrew: שְׁמַע יִשְׂרָאֵל ה'ֱלֹהֵינוּ ה' אֶחָד)—found in Deuteronomy 6:4. God is God and will forever undertake the work of freedom. God has acted by raising the people out of Egypt. This abounding grace at Sinai brings faithfulness and compassion as just offerings, and trumps Israel's centralized temple and government.[13]

The prophets certainly saw the rejection of the Sinai tradition, along with the sibling rivalry, violence and scapegoating of neighbors, and the abuse of power to be problematic. What they witnessed was how a society led by princes and powers was very different from the society of shalom that was to be a blessing to the world. They witnessed, prophesied, and held accountable those in power. They saw that kingship was toxic—even when the rule of the king benefited the kingdom overall when it came to building programs, relationships with neighboring kingdoms, and the economy. The prophets were also clear that the community of God's people was to take care of the least, the poor, and the migrant. God had a social imaginary that ensured that all people were cared for even if they could not care for themselves. They were all kin. This was not social welfare; it was an expectation that the prosperity of society in general benefited every-one specifically. From the king to the pauper, from the land owner to the widow and the orphan, from the tribal member who inhabited the land to

Left page (partially cut off at margin):

...ent upon the backs of the poor. Whenever the leaders, gov-
...ials, or society forgot their responsibility, the citizen prophets
...emselves and disrupted the totalization of kingly storytelling.[15]
...prophets were regular citizens with big callings. They were
...nown prior to their emergence on the scene. Most came from
...ruling order—from the countryside. They rejected the myth of
...iolence and decried common disregard for the poor, orphans,
...s by the empire. "They have a very vigorous notion of the gov-
...God. But along with that sense of tradition, they have an acute
...cial reality."[16]
...ork of prophetic citizenship is holding the powers and principal-
...ions to the high standards of the garden social imaginary. When
...y does not take responsibility for its own actions, or uses violence
...oating for the sake of dominion, then the Christian citizen who
...marily within God's garden social imaginary must engage and
...overnment to accountability. Furthermore, the Christian citizen
...a society that reverses the dominion principles when they take
...of the poor for the benefit of the rich. The Bible is clear that the
...cial imaginary foregrounds the needs of the widow, the orphan,
...nd the foreigner—the stranger in a strange land. In our context,
...o add the homeless, the addicted, the generationally poor, the
...he prisoner, and those who work three jobs and can't make ends
...ur own context, Christian citizens might fight to end the prac-
...yday lending, wage theft, the deprivation of justice for foreigners,
...ard for migrants and refugees, and regressive practices and poli-
...eave the poor in perpetual servitude to the wealthy.
...conomy of empire does not have to do these things. The empire
...act without compassion and familial faithfulness. It is free to
...Sinai covenant. All societies are free to turn their backs on the
...t such societies can never be worthy of the name of God. All
...re free to ignore the prophets' invitations, but such societies bear
...blance to the realm that Christians call their first home. God
...ions responsible for those who must rely upon the grace, mercy,
...d hospitality of others. God judges nations based on how well

the stranger making their way in a foreign land, the Sinai tradition ensured people were cared and provided for at every level of the social structure. Moreover, when they were not, the prophets reminded those who govern to be mindful of the poor, the widow, the orphan, and the migrant.

The prophet Isaiah tells the rulers, leaders, and elders that for "grinding the face of the poor" judgment will befall them (Isa. 2:7; 3:13–15; 10:1–2). The God of Israel gives hope to the poor (Isa. 14:30; 25:4; 61:1). God will not spare those deserving of judgment but God will redeem Israel upon their repentance. There is a clear notion that people must be like the poor in order to understand their dependence upon God and how much God loves the least and lost. This is more than reconciliation; it is solidarity. When Israel becomes lost in the Babylonian captivity and remembers what it was like to be lost, poor, and a stranger, God can act. Isaiah's promise is that when God's restoration happens, the governors will remember and Israel will no longer have wicked rulers (Isa. 11:14; 45:14). When Jerusalem remembers the poor then they can be called the "City of the Lord" (Isa. 60:14).

The prophet Jeremiah gives word to his suffering spirit as he sees how the people are neglected (Jer. 4:19; 9:1; 10:19–20; 23:9). For it to be well, the people must remember the past and how their faith ancestors created a just and righteous society wherein the cause of the poor and needy was considered (Jer. 22:15–17). Jeremiah locates our responsibility within God's creative imaginary (Jer. 10:12–16; 51:15–19). He sees God not only as the God of Israel but of all nations. His is a universal call to serve the poor. Jeremiah understands that this national responsibility for the poor is met by the individual too. The problem is not something that exists at the monarchial level. The whole society from individual to the government is responsible for the poor.

The prophet Ezekiel argues that the people are a holy people because God is holy. They are to be a holy society—a holy land. They are, instead, a people of violence, murder, desire, *and* they oppress the poor and needy. They steal from one another and take advantage of the least all to benefit their own desires (Ezek. 18:10–13), which is a kind of idolatry because it rejects the social imagination of God. What are the highlights of this action? The people reject the Sinai covenant. They do not care for their parents, they oppress foreigners, they suffer the orphan and the widow, they loan money to the poor at high interest rates, and try to exploit their neighbors (Ezek. 22). Ezekiel prophesies that the work of the people is to do the work of God, caring for the poor. Moreover, only in this way will the people become an exemplar to the other nations. A nation cannot become great unless it serves the poor. We well remember Jesus's own invitation to become the least and to serve.

The prophet Amos takes the wealthy to task for their rich tables and furniture while people are hungry. Amos connects wealth and indulgence with the perversion of justice and the crushing of the poor. Some lose everything while others gain (Amos 3:15; 4:1; 5:11; 6:4; 6:6). God will bring about the lowering of the high and mighty. Amos prophesies, "Let justice roll down like waters, and righteousness like an ever flowing stream" (Amos 5:24). Micah condemns the leaders for not only rejecting the Sinai covenant, but also that, in so doing, they are oppressing the poor through dishonesty (Mic. 2:1–2; 3:1–3; 6:10–11).

Malachi prophesies after the Israelites return from Babylon, arguing— while they are rebuilding the temple—that there is more than worship. God's people are to serve others, especially the least and lost, which is true service to God. Worship and service to the poor are linked. What had they done specifically? They had stolen people's wages. The powerful defrauded the weak. They oppressed the widows and orphans and deprived foreigners of justice (Mal. 3:5). Malachi points out that God's social imaginary is not one where we honor God with our mouths and then ignore or oppress the poor and the foreigner.

Obadiah prophesies that nations will reap the rewards of their own actions. If they oppress they will be oppressed; if they take advantage, they will be taken advantage of; and if they create trouble and suffering, then trouble and suffering will befall them. This is not an eye-for-an-eye-type prophesy. It is more like what Jesus says about living by the sword. A nation's behavior has consequences. The way the nation treats others is how they will be treated. To deal harshly with others is, in the end, to receive harsh treatment.

There were women who prophesied Noadiah among them. During the time v occupied Judea under Artaxerxes I of Per is remembered for rebuilding Jerusalem many purity codes and social reforms (I him, along with others. Nehemiah asked (Neh. 6:1–14). She opposed his purity cod nic purity codes that required Jewish men had married and their children. We are t with them and cursed them and beat som hair; and made them take an oath in the not give your daughters to their sons, or ta or for yourselves'" (Neh. 13:25). Old Testa suggests that the reason for Noadiah's opp "breaking up families and leaving women out status or identity, neither shelter nor s forward because Nehemiah had forgotten ial faithfulness of the Sinai covenant requi foreigners and strangers who were helpless to a strange land, who could not speak Nehemiah's reforms, were becoming dehu place in the society, was being taken away f the leaders of Israel that God was interested

When we read the biblical accounts o with a kind of royal history that is well edited that embedded in this attempt to tell a unifi tive prophets. While the monarchy sought a defense of kingly legitimacy, the prophets k kings of Israel were plagued by mimetic vio and covetousness. The prophets refused to drew on their "prophetic imagination" and off attempt to make sinful practices normative. empire that God had a social imaginary whic rivalry as the *modus oporandi* of government a

of governm erning offi inserted th

These largely unl outside the necessary and widow ernance of sense of so

The w ities of nat our countr and scape dwells pri call the g works for advantage garden so the poor, we need criminal, meet. In tices of pa the disreg cies that l

The e is free to reject the needy, bu societies no resem holds nat justice, a the stranger making their way in a foreign land, the Sinai tradition ensured people were cared and provided for at every level of the social structure. Moreover, when they were not, the prophets reminded those who govern to be mindful of the poor, the widow, the orphan, and the migrant.

The prophet Isaiah tells the rulers, leaders, and elders that for "grinding the face of the poor" judgment will befall them (Isa. 2:7; 3:13–15; 10:1–2). The God of Israel gives hope to the poor (Isa. 14:30; 25:4; 61:1). God will not spare those deserving of judgment but God will redeem Israel upon their repentance. There is a clear notion that people must be like the poor in order to understand their dependence upon God and how much God loves the least and lost. This is more than reconciliation; it is solidarity. When Israel becomes lost in the Babylonian captivity and remembers what it was like to be lost, poor, and a stranger, God can act. Isaiah's promise is that when God's restoration happens, the governors will remember and Israel will no longer have wicked rulers (Isa. 11:14; 45:14). When Jerusalem remembers the poor then they can be called the "City of the Lord" (Isa. 60:14).

The prophet Jeremiah gives word to his suffering spirit as he sees how the people are neglected (Jer. 4:19; 9:1; 10:19–20; 23:9). For it to be well, the people must remember the past and how their faith ancestors created a just and righteous society wherein the cause of the poor and needy was considered (Jer. 22:15–17). Jeremiah locates our responsibility within God's creative imaginary (Jer. 10:12–16; 51:15–19). He sees God not only as the God of Israel but of all nations. His is a universal call to serve the poor. Jeremiah understands that this national responsibility for the poor is met by the individual too. The problem is not something that exists at the monarchial level. The whole society from individual to the government is responsible for the poor.

The prophet Ezekiel argues that the people are a holy people because God is holy. They are to be a holy society—a holy land. They are, instead, a people of violence, murder, desire, *and* they oppress the poor and needy. They steal from one another and take advantage of the least all to benefit their own desires (Ezek. 18:10–13), which is a kind of idolatry because it rejects the social imagination of God. What are the highlights of this action? The people reject the Sinai covenant. They do not care for their parents, they oppress foreigners, they suffer the orphan and the widow, they loan money to the poor at high interest rates, and try to exploit their neighbors (Ezek. 22). Ezekiel prophesies that the work of the people is to do the work of God, caring for the poor. Moreover, only in this way will the people become an exemplar to the other nations. A nation cannot become great unless it serves the poor. We well remember Jesus's own invitation to become the least and to serve.

The prophet Amos takes the wealthy to task for their rich tables and furniture while people are hungry. Amos connects wealth and indulgence with the perversion of justice and the crushing of the poor. Some lose everything while others gain (Amos 3:15; 4:1; 5:11; 6:4; 6:6). God will bring about the lowering of the high and mighty. Amos prophesies, "Let justice roll down like waters, and righteousness like an ever flowing stream" (Amos 5:24). Micah condemns the leaders for not only rejecting the Sinai covenant, but also that, in so doing, they are oppressing the poor through dishonesty (Mic. 2:1–2; 3:1–3; 6:10–11).

Malachi prophesies after the Israelites return from Babylon, arguing—while they are rebuilding the temple—that there is more than worship. God's people are to serve others, especially the least and lost, which is true service to God. Worship and service to the poor are linked. What had they done specifically? They had stolen people's wages. The powerful defrauded the weak. They oppressed the widows and orphans and deprived foreigners of justice (Mal. 3:5). Malachi points out that God's social imaginary is not one where we honor God with our mouths and then ignore or oppress the poor and the foreigner.

Obadiah prophesies that nations will reap the rewards of their own actions. If they oppress they will be oppressed; if they take advantage, they will be taken advantage of; and if they create trouble and suffering, then trouble and suffering will befall them. This is not an eye-for-an-eye-type prophesy. It is more like what Jesus says about living by the sword. A nation's behavior has consequences. The way the nation treats others is how they will be treated. To deal harshly with others is, in the end, to receive harsh treatment.

There were women who prophesied as well: Deborah, Huldah, and Noadiah among them. During the time when Nehemiah was governor of occupied Judea under Artaxerxes I of Persia, Noadiah rose up. Nehemiah is remembered for rebuilding Jerusalem and her walls. He also enacted many purity codes and social reforms (Neh. 2:1–20). Noadiah opposed him, along with others. Nehemiah asked God to protect him from her (Neh. 6:1–14). She opposed his purity codes because he was enacting ethnic purity codes that required Jewish men to reject the foreign women they had married and their children. We are told that Nehemiah "contended with them and cursed them and beat some of them and pulled out their hair; and made them take an oath in the name of God, saying, 'You shall not give your daughters to their sons, or take their daughters for your sons or for yourselves'" (Neh. 13:25). Old Testament theologian Wilda Gafney suggests that the reason for Noadiah's opposition is that the policies were "breaking up families and leaving women and children as persons without status or identity, neither shelter nor sustenance."[14] Noadiah stepped forward because Nehemiah had forgotten that compassion and the familial faithfulness of the Sinai covenant required that they be hospitable to foreigners and strangers who were helpless people who had been brought to a strange land, who could not speak the language, and who, under Nehemiah's reforms, were becoming dehumanized. Their humanity, their place in the society, was being taken away from them. Noadiah reminded the leaders of Israel that God was interested in such people.

When we read the biblical accounts of the kings, we are presented with a kind of royal history that is well edited. Walter Brueggemann argues that embedded in this attempt to tell a unified story we find these disruptive prophets. While the monarchy sought a kind of narrative "totalism" in defense of kingly legitimacy, the prophets kept disturbing the waters. The kings of Israel were plagued by mimetic violence, callous self indulgence, and covetousness. The prophets refused to legitimize these things. They drew on their "prophetic imagination" and offered a vision that opposed any attempt to make sinful practices normative. They constantly reminded the empire that God had a social imaginary which was the rejection of sibling rivalry as the *modus oporandi* of government and a refusal to lay the burden of government upon the backs of the poor. Whenever the leaders, governing officials, or society forgot their responsibility, the citizen prophets inserted themselves and disrupted the totalization of kingly storytelling.[15]

These prophets were regular citizens with big callings. They were largely unknown prior to their emergence on the scene. Most came from outside the ruling order—from the countryside. They rejected the myth of necessary violence and decried common disregard for the poor, orphans, and widows by the empire. "They have a very vigorous notion of the governance of God. But along with that sense of tradition, they have an acute sense of social reality."[16]

The work of prophetic citizenship is holding the powers and principalities of nations to the high standards of the garden social imaginary. When our country does not take responsibility for its own actions, or uses violence and scapegoating for the sake of dominion, then the Christian citizen who dwells primarily within God's garden social imaginary must engage and call the government to accountability. Furthermore, the Christian citizen works for a society that reverses the dominion principles when they take advantage of the poor for the benefit of the rich. The Bible is clear that the garden social imaginary foregrounds the needs of the widow, the orphan, the poor, and the foreigner—the stranger in a strange land. In our context, we need to add the homeless, the addicted, the generationally poor, the criminal, the prisoner, and those who work three jobs and can't make ends meet. In our own context, Christian citizens might fight to end the practices of payday lending, wage theft, the deprivation of justice for foreigners, the disregard for migrants and refugees, and regressive practices and policies that leave the poor in perpetual servitude to the wealthy.

The economy of empire does not have to do these things. The empire is free to act without compassion and familial faithfulness. It is free to reject the Sinai covenant. All societies are free to turn their backs on the needy, but such societies can never be worthy of the name of God. All societies are free to ignore the prophets' invitations, but such societies bear no resemblance to the realm that Christians call their first home. God holds nations responsible for those who must rely upon the grace, mercy, justice, and hospitality of others. God judges nations based on how well they treat the most vulnerable within their borders, and how they treat the nations who are their neighbors. Unfortunately, a rejection of God's social imaginary is becoming increasingly normative in our self-centered and individualist society. Many American Christians reject the scripture's prophetic witness in favor of a salvation-only narrative that is spiritual and individually focused.

Chapter Nine

A Step into God's Story

The basic fact is that Christianity as it was born in the mind of this Jewish thinker and teacher appears as a technique of survival for the oppressed. That it became, through the intervening years, a religion of the powerful and the dominant, used sometimes as an instrument of oppression, must not tempt us into believing that it was thus in the mind and life of Jesus. "In him was life; and the life was the light of men." Wherever his spirit appears, the oppressed gather fresh courage; for he announced the good news that fear, hypocrisy, and hatred, the three hounds of hell that track the trail of the disinherited, need have no dominion over them.

—Howard Thurman[1]

Jesus did not come to promote religion, morality, happiness, or the form of republican government we call American democracy. No, Jesus came to say God invites us into God's story. Christian citizens believe that America is invited into God's story and not the other way around. This story is perfectly encapsulated in the ministry, death, and resurrection of Jesus.

Reversing the origin story whereby God creates humanity from the man, the New Testament takes up the narrative with God recreating humanity from a woman: Mary. God spoke to Mary (Luke 1:28) and rehearsed the words used with Abraham. The messenger used words of peace (*shalom*) and said that she was to be a blessing. Sometimes we translate the words as "grace."[2] Mary accepted her role as a citizen prophet in this new kingdom-making. She agreed to serve God's mission. She would be responsible, accepting both the privilege of service and the accountability that goes with it. Not unlike the people at the foot of Mount Sinai, she accepted the invitation to be part of God's story and sealed the covenant with the words "Let it be done." In that moment she began her journey as an engaged citizen in both God's reign and in the reign of the religious and political powers of her day.

Mary's "yes" begins a slow-motion unraveling of the cult of imperial authority. Roman emperors were worshipped as gods. Their legitimacy to rule was grounded in the mythical stories of gods copulating with mortal women and birthing demigods. In these mythical narratives, one of the gods of the Greco-Roman pantheon forces himself upon a mortal woman. Modern retellings of these tales often omit or obscure the implications of rape, but such was not the case in the first century when Luke wrote his Gospel. René Girard calls these Greco-Roman narratives "monstrous births of mythology."[3] The mating of the gods with mortals was a violent oppression by a dominating power, undertaken by the gods and then repeated throughout the social orders of Hellenistic humanity. The story of Mary's invitation and acceptance to serve God's mission parallels these stories but also turns them on their heads. Mary's call narrative rejects violence by gods in favor of the peace of God. Girard writes:

> No relationship of violence exists between those who take part in the virgin birth: the Angel, the Virgin and the Almighty. . . . In fact, all the themes and terms associated with the virgin birth convey to us a perfect submission to the non-violent will of the God of the gospels, who in this way prefigures Christ himself."[4]

There was no violence done to Mary by God. She was the lost and least and was raised up. Mary did not resist her calling. There was no rape or sexual domination.[5] More recently, artists have portrayed the overshadowing of Mary as a kind of sexual ecstasy, but these interpretations say more about us than they do about Luke or Mary. The other modern trend, which is to "demythologize" Mary's experience by arguing that Luke has derived her calling narrative from those other more monstrous mythologies, misses the point. When we remove the mystery of God's invitation and Mary's acceptance and flatten Luke's narrative into an unremarkable recapitulation of Greek myth, we miss the message of shalom that is woven into the story of the Incarnation from the outset. When we deconstruct Luke's story in order to privilege our modern sensibilities about science, we rob Luke's Gospel of any chance of transforming us. Nonetheless, this was a predominant trend among many biblical exegetes writing when the gravitational pull of modern rationalism was at its peak. Episcopal bishop John Spong rejected Mary's call narrative as worthless mythology. Theologian Paul Tillich had no interest in the mythic birth of Jesus.

The story of God's invitation and Mary's willingness to serve is significant, not in the ways it mirrors the monstrous births of Hellenistic mythology, but in the ways it differs from those competing pagan narratives in order to undermine both the domination culture of antiquity and the domination culture of modernity. The total rejection of violence that was characteristic of New Testament Christianity is one of the reasons the early church struggled to achieve legitimacy within Greco-Roman society. God and the conception narrative of Jesus do not adhere to any of the mythic tropes known to paganism, and undermine all such tropes with a story of shalom. Our own sexually oriented culture, also consumed by violence, rejects the story, too. God soundly refuses to appease the violent expectations of either epoch.

If we had any remaining doubt about the radical message of peace that Mary entered into, her visit with Elizabeth dispels it. In the home of Elizabeth, who was to give birth to John the Baptist, we hear Mary speak about her ministry as God-bearer: *Theotokos*. Following in the footsteps of Moses and Esther, both of whom brought about dramatic social change; and Abraham, who was the first to be a blessing; and Isaiah and Jonah, who offered transformation to estranged people; Mary takes part in God's work of shalom by inaugurating cosmic change.

Mary told Elizabeth that she was humbled, and that God had invited her into the work of being blessed and being a blessing to the world. Perhaps reflecting upon the words of Hannah in 1 Samuel 2:1–11, Mary said that God's mighty acts throughout salvation history had benefited her personally and now she was part of the narrative. Remembering the words of Jonah, we hear her repeat that God was a God of mercy and quick to forgive. Mary said that God raised up the least, the lost, and the lowly. God laid low the powers and authorities of this world. God fed people good things. Those who wish for the ways of the world, the human ways of rivalry and greed, to prevail, would find the gospel of grace difficult and would be sent away empty. This was the reign of shalom. This was a new chapter in the promise God invited Abraham and Sarah into. From Luke's Gospel (1:46–55):

> My soul magnifies the Lord,
> and my spirit rejoices in God my Savior,
> for he has looked with favor on the lowliness of his servant.
> Surely, from now on all generations will call me blessed;
> for the Mighty One has done great things for me,
> and holy is his name.
> His mercy is for those who fear him
> from generation to generation.
> He has shown strength with his arm;
> he has scattered the proud in the thoughts of their hearts.
> He has brought down the powerful from their thrones,
> and lifted up the lowly;
> he has filled the hungry with good things,
> and sent the rich away empty.
> He has helped his servant Israel,
> in remembrance of his mercy,
> according to the promise he made to our ancestors,
> to Abraham and to his descendants for ever.

Many call Mary's song the most concise statement of the gospel. It is a statement of God's vision for a community of the least, the lost, and the lonely. It envisions a reign of peace and rejects any kingdom, nation, or state made from violence. It is such a radical statement of God's in-breaking peace that it has been feared by the powers and authorities of this world. Mary's song tells of a God who will overthrow the various states that humanity so violently brings into being. Mary's song has often been outlawed because it delegitimizes the violent structures of human power. Anglicans join the Roman Church in appreciation for Mary's song, called the *Magnificat* in Latin. The states supported by Anglican churches have not always been so appreciative, however. When India was ruled by the British, the recitation of the *Magnificat* in worship was outlawed. The same was true in Guatemala during the 1980s. Believing that the song of Mary was a rallying cry for the revolutionary and the poor, the government banned it. Guatemala was one of the first countries to practice forced disappearances—between forty and fifty thousand people were summarily murdered in this way. In South America, after the "disappearing" of many family members and children during the war in Argentina, the Mothers of the Plaza de Mayo (a square in the Monserrat barrio of central Buenos Aires) placed the words of the *Magnificat* on posters in the city. The military junta of Argentina responded by banning all public displays of the song for five years.[6] Protestant theologian and activist during Hitler's Germany, Dietrich Bonheoffer, wrote from prison in 1933:

> The song of Mary is the oldest Advent hymn. It is at once the most passionate, the wildest, one might even say the most revolutionary Advent hymn ever sung. This is not the gentle, tender, dreamy Mary whom we sometimes see in paintings. . . . This song has none of the sweet, nostalgic, or even playful tones of some of our Christmas carols. It is instead a hard, strong, inexorable song about the power of God and the powerlessness of humankind.[7]

Mary is an icon of faithful political engagement. She bears Christ into the world in a way that rejects the powers and principalities' mythic and real practices of violence. This story invites us to be God-bearers that witness to a different narrative than the one that legitimizes the ruling religious and imperial powers. Here we have a renewed origin story for the Christian citizen.

Mary's acceptance of the covenant with God was a declaration of responsibility for God's garden imaginary and a pledge to consider her role in relationship to others. Her "yes" undoes the warped desire, mundane violence, and constant scapegoating that arise out of sibling rivalry. Hers was categorically not an individual pietistic event or an internal private faith response to God. To view Mary that way is to read Enlightenment ideas back into Luke's text. Making the conception of Christ into a private event of Marian piety is to capitulate to the worldview that Christian and religious philosopher Charles Taylor calls the "immanent frame" where transcendence is discarded as useless and reality is explained self-referentially.[8]

Just as God invites Mary to take her place as a participatory citizen in both the reign of God and in relationship to governing powers, so, too, God invites John the Baptist. He takes the role of a prophet over and against the religious and political establishment and it costs him his head. John, like the prophets before him, invites people into a new way of being. He baptizes them and speaks about a reign of God citizenship. There was a new Lord coming who would bring about this renewal of all of creation. So powerful was this new reign, that all people would have clothes to wear, shelter over their heads, and food to eat. The rich would be good neighbors to those who had nothing, and share out of their abundance. A new economy would ensue and people would work and not take advantage of one another or enslave one another. The poor would no longer be consigned to a life without work and meaning. There would be an end to generational poverty. Vulnerability would not be something to take advantage of. The reign of God would reject the Pax Romana (the peace of Rome) that was built upon threats, false accusations, violence, and death (Luke 3:4–14). The realm of God would be a community with different kinds of members; uniformity would not be a value. People would pursue the vocation of shalom in the midst of everyday life. The reign of God would be a community that lived together differently, bringing judgment upon the practices of nation-states that used power and violence to promote a peace that was no peace.

John's vision and prophecy was not apocalyptic—unless you were part of the powers and principalities. If you were, things were going to change. His vision was an earthly one no less real than the prophets of old who warned those who would not take responsibility and who used violence to further the cause of the wealthy. John made way for Jesus. He opened our eyes. As a prophetic citizen in the Herodian kingdom subservient to Rome, he had very real-world intentions. John made way for the new reign of God to set foot on the earth again, to walk in the garden of God's own making again.

All of the gospel writers intend us to view John as the last in the long line of prophets. He prophesizes against the reigning lord and court, revealing how out of line they are with the origin story and the covenant at Sinai. John is both judge and jury of the house of Herod, all those who support him, and his alliance with Rome and Caesar. Like Elijah's prophecy against the house of Ahab with its foreign allegiances, John holds back nothing.[9] Even the first-century historian Josephus reveals that John was seen as a threat by the royal household. His call to repent and make a new way in the wilderness—a new way of governing, a new way of living in community, and a new economy—was a radical call to new life. John was serious, and Herod and the court knew it; John lost his head for it.[10] John was an engaged prophet citizen.

Christians believe in the eternal mystery of God who is Trinity. This means we believe in the eternal presence of the second person of the Trinity, the Incarnation of God. When we think of the work of God through creation, the calling of Abraham, the sending of Moses, the calling of prophets, kings, and the words of the prophets, we locate all of this in the work of the second person of the Trinity. God's living Word is a person through whom all things are made and come to have their being. The living Word was spoken to Abraham by the oaks of Mamre and was spoken to Pharaoh and the kings of Israel. This Word comes into flesh through Mary and is prophesied by John the Baptist. God in Christ Jesus is the perfect revelation of the living Word and eternal Incarnation, who comes as the Prince of Peace into the world to renew the face of creation. He is God and he is the living Shalom in our midst. God in Christ Jesus comes as a blessing of peace to the world. Jesus comes to do nothing less than renew the covenant of God with God's people and to fulfill the blessing for all people and not only those freed from Egypt. Jesus renews the garden social imagery and the virtue of covenant compassion and familial faithfulness.

The powers were concerned with the portents of Jesus's birth. In Matthew's Gospel, provoked by rivalrous envy and a Machiavellian desire to maintain the power of the empire, Herod the Great sent emissaries to find the child Jesus and his family (Matt. 2:13–15, 19–23). The king's desire was to kill Jesus. Out of compassion and familial faithfulness, the emissaries warned the family. The king then attempted to eliminate Jesus by killing all the children close in age. God sent word to the family to get up and go to Egypt, which connects Jesus and the holy family to God's narrative arc and the people of Israel. God's people arrived in Egypt because they were refugees from a drought. Jesus and his family were refugees from political violence. There are many who find it expedient to deny Jesus this experience as a refugee child, fleeing for his life from violent and oppressive political powers. Yet, this is exactly what Matthew tells us happened.

From the outset the Christ was a living icon of a humanity not subject to sibling rivalry, disoriented desire, scapegoating, or violence. He challenged the authorities, principalities, and powers of this world by his very presence, his healing, teaching, and engagement. His ministry revealed God's judgment upon the powers that be and he held up for every Christian a different way of living together. Over the years, many Christians have forsaken God's way in favor of the old ways of empire. But in doing so they have stepped out of continuity with the life of Jesus. His challenge to worldly power and authority began with his politically portentous baptism in the desert by John.

In Matthew, Mark, and Luke's gospels Jesus is led out into the desert where he makes his own personal wilderness journey. This recalls the Sinai wanderings of Israel, where Moses and Joshua taught the people dependence upon God. Jesus is in the desert for forty days and forty nights. He is hungry and we are told in Matthew's Gospel that the "tempter" comes to him. While our fascination with a Faustian devil causes our eye to be drawn to the evil one in this text, Jesus's temptation is intended to be a kind of simile. There is a Sinai reorientation of Jesus's ministry going on in this interchange (Matt. 4:1–11).

The tempter says to Jesus, "If you are the Son of God, command these stones to become loaves of bread." Jesus answers, "It is written, 'One does not live by bread alone, but by every word that comes from the mouth of God,'" drawing from the Sinai tradition for his response: Deuteronomy 8:3; Jesus reminds us that God's promise to provide will prevail. God's love and deliverance, whether it be with manna or any other sustaining gift, will endure. Jesus rejects the notion that earthly goods will indeed make heavenly stores. The desire for the fullness of God will not be quenched with earthly possessions—not even food.

Then the tempter takes Jesus to the holy city and places him on the pinnacle of the temple, saying, "If you are the Son of God, throw yourself down; for it is written, 'He will command his angels concerning you,' and 'On their hands they will bear you up, so that you will not dash your foot against a stone.'" Jesus responds, "Again it is written, 'Do not put the Lord your God to the test.'" Jesus recalls Deuteronomy 6:16 when the Israelites were frustrated and tested God by cursing that he had forsaken them in the desert. They cried out, "Is the LORD among us or not?" (Exod. 17:7). God told the Israelites to be faithful and trust that he will care for them. Here again Jesus is mindful that God is always present, God is to be trusted, and God is interested in us. Even in these temptations God will deliver Jesus.

Finally, Jesus is taken to a high mountain and shown all the kingdoms of the world and their splendor; and the tempter says, "All these I will give you, if you will fall down and worship me." Jesus said to him, "Away with you, Satan! for it is written, 'Worship the LORD your God, and serve only him.'" This passage recalls Deuteronomy 6:13, "The LORD your God you shall fear; him you shall serve, and by his name alone you shall swear."[11]

Jesus's responses to the temptations are clear: the God of the Sinai will deliver us, we will have no other God but God, and we will rest upon God's providence. Our covenant and community making starts at the foot of that mountain, and not in the courts of the powerful. We are witnessing Jesus making new the Sinai covenant.

Familial faithfulness includes a rejection of our mad scramble to accumulate more goods than our neighbor. We test God by acting and living as if God is not present and by dominating others. Power and dominion then enable us to become our own master and serve our own needs. This is the way of all governments at their worst. They shun responsibility and reenact the murder of Abel over and over again. Matthean scholar Daniel Harrington writes,

> Understanding this text against the background of Deuteronomy 6–8 allows one to go beyond the narrow themes of fasting and temptation to the level of Christology. As in the case of all the material in the opening chapters of Matthew, the focus of attention is the identity of Jesus. Understanding it as the testing of God's son allows one to see the nature of Jesus' divine sonship and its relation to Israel as God's Son.[12]

God in Christ Jesus rejects the powers of this world that seek to tempt and destroy the creatures of God. He rejects all forms of dominion and power that enrich individuals at the expense of the broader community. God rejects all religious, social, and political power that demand total allegiance. Such faith is summarized in Deuteronomy 31:6, "Be strong and bold; have no fear or dread of them, because it is the LORD your God who goes with you; he will not fail you or forsake you." Walter Wink, scholar and author of *The Powers*, captures this moment of temptation well: "Jesus is being nudged by God toward a new unprecedented thing, for which no models existed. No one else could have helped advise him. Scripture itself seemed loaded in the opposite direction—toward messianic models of power, might and empire. . . . Satan is offering him the kingdom of David, grown to the proportions of world empire. Scripture was rife with this hope."[13] This faith is no mere spiritual engagement. It is a political engagement that forces Christian citizens to see the powers of this world at work undermining accountability to God and to each other by hollowing out the virtues of compassion and familial faithfulness.

Imperialistic hope animated the political leaders of Jesus's day. The Herodian allegiance to Rome was a clear contradiction to God's social imaginary. The consolidated social, economic, and political power in Jerusalem was quite different from the vision God shared at Sinai. Again, Wink writes, "Israel seethed with longing for some form of its fulfillment. Jesus could not but have internalized that desire: freedom from Roman oppression, restoration of God's nation, the vindication of Yahweh's honor."[14] These are nothing less than the "highest goods known to the religion of the day."[15]

In fact, these temptations are the key motivating factors at work in some forms of Christianity today that make their own pragmatic allegiances with the empire. Some Christians desire a return to a Christendom that bought into the domination system that crowned kings, floated navies, colonized new lands, oppressed people, and burned those who disagreed. These groups seek a Christian nation and theocratic government. Wise Christian citizens must see this temptation clearly for what it is. The memory of Christendom in the age of Constantine is a mirage, another temptation that will spawn new systems of domination and power that legitimize death, oppression, slavery, and extermination. Wink reminds us it is always easier for us to be "pliant, docile, and obedient" Christians. He writes, "Is it not easier to let Jesus do it for all of us . . . rather than embark on the risky, vulnerable, hazardous journey of seeking to find God's will in all its mundane specificity for our own lives?"[16] This is the challenge for Christian citizens grappling with the powers and principalities.

If we have not yet understood God's handiwork in our previous chapters we see it clearly here. Jesus, God incarnate, is renewing the garden social imaginary, which includes familial faithfulness that challenges us to enter the lives of our neighbor and to be neighbor. We are to be compassionate to every stranger, tribe, and people, for they are our kin. We are to venture into the wilderness where God is present. Jesus invites our conversion at the foot of his cross, our own cross, and our neighbors'. None of this works if, like new wine in old wine skins (Luke 5:37ff), we try to fit it all into an American idea of Christian dominionism that works towards an idolatrous Christian nation. Jesus could have inaugurated a theocratic community, but he did not. He chose not to sit in the court of power and wear the earthly crown, but instead to engage the powers that dominate by rejecting earthly machinations. He offers a different way of being, of governing, of making community. Jesus lived prophetic citizenship.

Chapter Ten

A Different Destiny

Time and time again does the pride of man influence his very own fall. While denying it, one gradually starts to believe that he is the authority, or that he possesses great moral dominion over others, yet it is spiritually unwarranted. By that point he loses steam; in result, he falsely begins trying to prove that unwarranted dominion by seizing the role of a condemner.
—Criss Jami, poet[1]

God in Christ Jesus is born in non-violence and transcends the edifices of domination that rely upon the power of violence. René Girard argues that Jesus Christ is the only person able to "escape from these structures."[2] Our unity with him, through conversion, is freedom from their despotism. We are then not just any citizen, we are Christ's citizens. God gives a sign of God's presence to the creatures of this world by casting out the violence that is their inheritance. The gospels speak the truth that violence is not the way intended for creation. Their proclamation of Jesus rejects the myth that violence is a necessary part of the world. Girard writes, "Every [person] is the [sibling] of Cain, who was the first to bear the mark of this original violence."[3] Yet we pass from this mark of death into life precisely because of the abiding love that is made known in the Incarnation of Christ (1 John 3:11ff).

Christ took on the work of shalom during his first visit to the synagogue in Nazareth after a time of traveling (Luke 4:16–21). It was the

Sabbath, and Jesus unrolled the scroll to the prophet Isaiah and began to read. "The spirit of the LORD is upon me, because he has anointed me to bring good news to the poor. He has sent me to proclaim release to the captives and recovery of sight to the blind, to let the oppressed go free, to proclaim the year of the LORD's favor." He then rolled up the scroll and everyone in the synagogue watched as he sat back down. Then Jesus said, "Today this scripture has been fulfilled in your hearing" (see Isa. 61:1–9). Jesus's ministry would mirror what Isaiah foretold when he described God's garden imaginary over and against the societies of Uzziah (or Azariah), Jotham, Ahaz, and Hezekiah—the kings of Judah. Christ incarnates the community for the least and the lost. Jesus would inaugurate a community of release and freedom. He would bring God's blessing of peace into the world so all would know they were beloved of God, for he was the prince of shalom.

In Mark's Gospel this promise appears first in the prophet John's preaching, and then is made real when Jesus enters his home synagogue and heals a man with a withered hand (Mark 3). In that healing, Jesus makes manifest the promise from Isaiah that he and John the Baptist both proclaimed: the new reign of God would have real world consequences. Jesus diminishes the dominant powers of his day, and he is confronted immediately by those who are part of the empire.

The WEIRD (Western, Educated, Industrial, Rich, Democratic) citizen sees the world from the perspective of an individual. We are a series of communities of one. In non-WEIRD societies, identity comes from relationships with others. Self is always in relationship with kin. In Jesus's particular non-WEIRD society, there were kin and then there was the other—the stranger. In Nazareth, in both the sermon and the healing, Jesus introduces a broader understanding of the virtue of familial faithfulness so central to the Sinai covenant, where the individual, the kin, the outsider, and the stranger all congeal into community. He is breaking down the traditional dichotomy of kin versus stranger. With compassion as a lens he is saying all are family now—all are the body Christ.

He is then confronted by those who had previously defined his identity: his kin. (Mark 3:31) Today our networks of belonging are filled with individuals who do not understand Christian citizenship, many of whom are sold out to the gods of civil religion, nationalism, and patriotism. When we act as Christian citizens with the transcendent lens Jesus offers, we will receive pushback, just as Jesus did. Jesus challenges his kin to think for a moment about the boundaries of family. Who are our brothers and sisters (Mark 3:35)? He is not asking about positions of privilege in a hierarchy of domination. Jesus is pointing to a transcendent possibility of connectedness far beyond the carefully negotiated self-serving systems we construct.

The next to challenge Jesus are the legal authorities. Seeing his witness as a threat to the supremacy of empire, and realizing that Jesus is truncating traditional allegiances and recasting the narrative of God's people in a way that undermines the principalities of the status quo, the defenders of these traditional allegiances charge Jesus with being in league with the devil. He counters that only those who cannot tolerate the lifting of oppression and the healing of the sick are guilty of such accusations. Jesus, like the prophets before him, not only heals people, but makes it clear that healing people should be the concern of those who rule and make the laws. The lawyer's work is not to uphold unjust empires but to honor the original covenant with God at Sinai by ensuring the poor, the helpless, the least, lost, and sick are cared for. When the empire does not do this, it blasphemes against God's spirit of community (Mark 3:28).

To return to an earlier theme, the powers and principalities of the world are invested in a kind of totalism. *Totalism,* as defined by Walter Brueggemann, means a systematic aversion to any kind of narrative alternative to one's own. The story of the kings of Israel seeks total control over the story of God's people while the prophets in their midst offer a subversively different narrative arc.[4] Jesus is the icon of an alternative story that runs contrary to the totalizing ambitions of worldly institutions. It is the nature of the powers and principalities to erase any narrative that runs contrary to their own. They will cast fidelity as an unquestioned willingness to defend the dominant and dominating culture by painting all alternative narratives as dangerous insurrections. From the beginning of his ministry, Jesus was cast as a traitor.

Jesus expresses his alternative narrative not only in works of healing, but also through engagement with the community and its leaders. He creates a new community with different types of citizens. Jesus lives into what theologian Sam Wells calls "the Nazareth Manifesto." He casts a vision for this community. Jesus did not merely say nice things about the poor and feed them, he lived as a poor itinerant preacher dependent upon the hospitality of those who saw him as a homeless stranger.[5] The new community was imagined as one that was present in the lives of people. The Gospel was not an idea to be preached, but a life to be lived in and among people. The manifesto of Jesus offered a vision of life lived with the hungry, with the imprisoned, with the lost and least. Christ as the Incarnate One of God is living out this manifesto even as he offers it as a kind of new Sinai revelation. Jesus's Sermon on the Mount articulates such a vision (Luke 6; Matt. 5). Jesus's teaching from the mount is a retelling of God's visit with God's people in the wilderness.

It is rare that the Gospel writers recorded direct teaching by Jesus. Parables were the primary way he spoke about the kingdom of peace. This direct teaching recorded in Matthew and Luke begins with what we have come to call the Beatitudes, because Jesus's words distributed blessings, capturing the narrative of Abraham and Sarah and bringing it forward. People who lived in this new community built around Jesus were a blessing and would be a blessing to the world because they lived *with* the poor. The poor in spirit, those who mourn, the meek, those who deeply long for goodness and faith, those who make mercy happen, the humble, and those in whom there is no guile—all of these people were beloved of God, blessed by God, and were a blessing to the world (Matt. 5:2–8). These are the people God welcomed into the bosom of blessed Abraham—as in the parable of Lazarus and the rich man (Luke 16:19–31). The least were the first citizens in the reign of peace—a new family oppressed by the systems of domination. Jesus used blessings instead of violence to create citizens.

The second citizens were the peacemakers (Matt. 5:9). The community of shalom was to be filled with peacemakers, and Jesus was committed to growing the number of peacemakers and equipping them for their work. People would know who was a member of the community of shalom because they would live outside the system of powers, domination, authorities, and violence, waging peace instead. The peacemakers would join the ranks of God's beloved, and they would be known by the way they lived their lives as children of God. Living as peacemakers, though, would not be peaceful, as Jesus taught later on. Those who were afraid of the authorities and principalities or who gained from the systems of domination would not be happy with the peacemakers and would punish, persecute, and martyr them because of the discomfort they felt about the evil that peacemakers revealed in the various edifices of society. For this reason, their witness to peace would bring about division between those who were peacemakers and those committed to the status quo of violence and greed.

A sharp edge quickly emerged between those who made peace and those who would not join Jesus's community of shalom. This division was not brought about by the peacemakers, but by those for whom peace only came through violence (Matt. 10:34–39). The keepers of the Pax Romana persecuted the peacemakers, who suffered for righteousness sake. Despite their trials, those who lived in peace, who constituted the community of shalom, participated in God's reign in this world and the next. Those who were reviled and persecuted, who had all kinds of evil muttered against them because of their witness to God's peace, and their participation in the great narrative arc of God, joined the ranks of Abraham, Sarah, Moses, and the prophets (Matt. 5:10–11).

This alternative narrative undermines the narrative of empire. Jesus declares God's rejection of the illegitimate powers of the rulers in this world. God alone is sovereign. Jesus breaks out of the lens that frames the world within the reign of the princes, and in favor of the topography of power that emerges from the origin stories in Genesis. Jesus's manner of life, his inauguration of a new community, his prophetic witness, teaching, and healing constitutes an enacted judgment upon the dominant narratives of the world, regardless of all its many variants.[6] You can only have one primary narrative. Whatever your primary narrative is, it will bend other competing narratives to its principles. God's invitation into the garden social imaginary bends all other narratives by judging them corrupt.

Jesus also offers a manner of life for his new community. He gives Christian citizens of the reign of God a new way of living together. They are to forgive those who offend them. They are to embrace the inevitability of suffering for their rejection of violence. They are to create an economy founded on sharing money. When there are problems in the community, each citizen uses their own humble gifts for the purpose of leading. And, when confronted with a corrupt society, they are to create new structures and systems to overcome the old.[7]

The Nazareth Manifesto and the Beatitudes are a call to dual citizenship. Christians are members *first* of a different community founded upon a social imaginary rooted in the origin stories of scripture; then, they are citizens.

Jesus's voice echoed over the hillside, declaring that those who took his name would work within their own societies to bless the world like the patriarchs, matriarchs, judges, and prophets before them. They were to be salt. They were to be light. Jesus appropriated these images from the religious elite and offered them afresh to members of his new community. He did not envision a new religion or the renewal of an old religion. His vision was no religion at all. It was a cosmic citizenship above and beyond any one nationality. Jesus's vision was a universal invitation. Jesus spoke out against the powers and principalities of the day who sought a conformist totalism. He called into existence a community of mutuality that did not use hierarchy to oppress, or create an economy that enriched the privileged. Jesus offered a higher way of living together (Matt. 5:11–21). Such a citizenship does not deny national citizenship or state laws but calls its denizens to function as prophets in a strange land, forever caught between two competing cultures.

WEIRD American Christianity is and has been about forcing people into becoming something they are not. It has been just another way for citizens to live out a life of domination and manifest destiny. Colonialism of the New World easily transitioned into theological colonialism. When Jesus names the poor in spirit, those who mourn, the meek, those who hunger and thirst for righteousness, the merciful, the pure in heart, and the peacemakers, he is naming us for who we are and who we are created to be. His Nazareth Manifesto enables us to become something we already are: members of the body of Christ, a community that knows and extends God's shalom to the world. This new community creates relationships of peace beyond kin. The natural human way of practicing religion and government generates oppressive violence. Jesus's community has a higher rule of peacemaking. It is concerned with restoring broken relationships and making peace among neighbors, which means all people (Matt. 5:21–26). Women, for instance, are not objects to be coveted or property with no self-determination. Women and men live together in healthy relationships (Matt. 5:26–32).

We are invited as Christian citizens to engage the powers and principalities with compassion and faithfulness that can be transformative. We are invited to speak truthfully and not engage in sophistry—to use words to gain power (Matt. 5:33–37). We are invited to be salt and light, to be peacemakers who joyfully sacrifice themselves for each other. Moreover, we are called to give our lives for our enemies as well as our friends (Matt. 5:38–48; John 15:9–17).

The Word of God, Jesus upon that holy hill, spoke God's mission of shalom into existence as creation itself was re-birthed. It was nothing less than a new Genesis—another new beginning. Jesus, the Word made flesh, articulates the blessings from Sinai with extreme clarity in the Beatitudes. He declared God's intention to steward a community of shalom that witnessed against systems of domination by reversing their downward flow.[8]

Walter Wink calls this peacemaking community a "domination free order."[9] It was an alternative to communities based upon sibling rivalry, the repeated (mimetic) desire for improvement of one's own state over and against one's siblings, as in the story of Cain and Abel. The peacemaking community was an alternative to communities that lived by the law of vengeance, where women were property, violence against other tribes was sanctioned, and religion was linked with the powers of the nation-state. The peacemaking community rejected wealth as a driver of connection and source of power, setting aside practices of economic oppression, so that all were fed and had what they needed for shelter, clothing, care, and sustenance. The Jesus Movement, if it was to be a movement at all, had to unbind the community of shalom from the myth of legitimate or transformative violence. In Matthew 6:19–34, Jesus replaced a dark, violent vision of community with trust in God and pursuit of life in God's new order.[10] Socially, politically, religiously, economically, Jesus subverted the domination system and the spirit that drove it.

The peaceable kingdom envisioned in Isaiah's scroll and Jesus's sermon is deeply connected to the call stories and vocation of Israel we discussed in the prior chapters. The reign of peace is less concerned with order and control and more concerned with enabling all of us to play our part in the narrative arc of God's garden imaginary. Seeing the world through the lens of shalom cannot be undone, though it can be rejected in favor of a personal or national Pax Romana that perpetuates economic and social violence for the sake of individual or tribal peace. There are plenty of authority figures who pretend that "peace" in the world can be purchased by violence, but that is a complete rejection of Christ's reign and our citizenship in it, which is purchased by loving enemies and laying down swords. The peace of God is procured by Christ's victimhood and not by God's own violence.[11] God's story of peace is rooted in the world like a cedar of Lebanon by the suffering Incarnate One, and not by a faithful war led by disciples. When Peter dared to raise a sword to protect the Savior, Jesus healed the man wounded by his blade, and told Peter that the kingdom of peace would not be seized by violence (John 18:10–12).

For the Christian citizen, the work of creating this new social imaginary in our country is very real. Our country has been involved in military action of one kind or another since its inception.[12] Good Christian men and women have served in these wars out of duty to their country. Administering these wars does not make them bad people. They have given their life for their country. We should pray for them and care for them as they deal with the posttraumatic results of doing horrible things to other human beings. We should provide healthcare, and psychological and spiritual counseling for them. We should ensure they have a living wage and that they can take care of their families. We do all of this so that the sickness of war does as little damage as possible. War, though, is a cancer.

We could easily debate the just participation of a nation in these wars, but that is not my point here. When we support and pray for our troops it easily morphs into God supports our nation in particular, or worse, God supports our war against others. My point is that Jesus Christ, the Prince of Peace, offers a different social imaginary for the Christian citizen. Regardless of our participation in our nation's military efforts or the justice questions that proceed from such participation, war and violence that support systems of domination are not part of God's reign. This does not change the Gospel or our story. God in Christ Jesus does not sanction war.

Christian citizens have to negotiate the tensions that arise from this clear conflict of interest. Changing the story of Jesus into one of domination only supports the powers and principalities of this world. We have to live with the difficult questions that God's narrative asks of our cities, our nations, and of us when we are so fixated on a violent means of keeping the peace. Violence has become our nation's first response. The story of Jesus rewrites citizenship by relocating it in the garden. His invitation to live as citizens of a different realm is not about how to be a better American (or insert your own nationality). The invitation is to be released from our attachment to dominating our brothers, sisters, and neighbors. Our culture has desensitized us to violence. Jesus is inviting us to be sensitized to peace. To be a Christian citizen means that our relationship with others is now part of a different order by virtue of our own new relationship with God.

In this new citizenry, our relationships of love are the foundation of shalom, rejecting sibling rivalries and misdirected desires. We are invited to be citizens of a new reign through the security of God's redeeming act of love and the establishment of a kingdom in this world and the next that flows from the Cross of Jesus. The inauguration of the new reign of God makes present in this world a citizenship that is removed from the urgency of dominion.[13] Jesus's engagement with the powers reveals the virtue of a life lived as a prophetic citizen.

Chapter Eleven

A Decolonized Citizenship

*The colonized mind is a telltale sign that the urban disciple has been indoc-
trinated with a false theology that derives from the Empire instead of from
the Kingdom of God. Empire theology is focused on the temporal without
regard for eternal things, which are unseen. It only serves the interest of the
powerful, maintains the status quo, and perpetuates the demonic narrative
of white superiority over against those in the margins. Empire theology
prances around like an angel of light; it cloaks itself with a domesticated
gospel void of self-sacrifice, but inwardly it is a ravenous wolf. It requires
nothing of its propagators and everything of those on the margins to whom
the theology is given. It ensures that the first remains the first and that the
last remains the least.*

—Ekemini Uwan[1]

Jesus undertook his prophetic citizenship by means of miracles, mass feedings, teaching, and engaging in dialogue with institutional representatives of Second Temple Judaism. Jesus's home turf was the countryside around the "ten cities," or Decapolis, an area occupied by the Roman army. It was a pocket of Hellenistic urbanism plopped down in the Judean countryside where reminders of Roman authority were everywhere.[2] For example, the land Luke refers to as the land of the Gerasenes was given to Roman military veterans as payment for their service (Luke 8:26).

Jesus got off the boat in the land of the Gerasenes and conflict immediately commenced (Luke 8:27; Mark 5:7). The land was unclean because it
was dotted with graves and tombs. Luke tells us that Jesus was approached
by "a man from the city who had demons, who for a long time had worn
no clothes and lived not in a house but among the tombs" (Luke 8:27). We
are reminded of Isaiah 65:4, "They live in tombs and spend nights in dark
corners, eating the meat of pigs and using unclean food." The demoniac
addressed Jesus using a Hellenistic name, one used by the Gentiles, calling
him the "son of the Most High God" (Mark 5:7).

To reduce this encounter to a run-of-the-mill exorcism is to miss the
dramatic implications of the event. Medical doctor Frantz Fanon wrote
about incidences of possession during the Algerian rebellion against
French colonialism in the 1950s. Fanon argued that demon possessions in
Algeria were consequences of the economic assault on the people and were
a form of protest and escape from the reality of occupation.[3] In Mark 5:5,
we are told that the demoniac inflicted wounds upon his own body. He
expressed the oppression that was an inevitable part of Roman occupation;
he was turned against himself and his own body. The projected violence
was internalized to the point that he was no longer the person God meant
him to be. His possession was rooted to the occupied land and rooted
in Roman oppression. Jesus's encounter with this demoniac is a spiritual,
physical, and political confrontation with larger implications.

Ched Myers points out the difference between the ways that Luke and
Mark tell the story. In Luke, the possessed man was under watchful eye of
the authorities of the region, and kept breaking free to flee into the wilderness, which foreshadowed Luke's use of the same imagery in reference to
the disciple's imprisonment by the Roman authorities (see Mark 5:5 and
Luke 8:33).[4]

Jesus took control and asked the man to name the demon who possessed him. His name was "Legion" (Luke 8:30; Mark 5:9). Roman legions
were the detachments of soldiers infamous for keeping the Pax Romana
through violence. A legion was a unit composed of some five thousand
men, plus their support and crowds of hangers-on who made money
from them. During the first century, there were a total of four Roman

legions deployed to Judea and Galilee, and they maintained the dubiously legitimate Herodian monarchy and kept order in the outlying areas. Ched Myers writes,

> A third century CE dedication plaque for a Legion found in northern England reveals Mars, the Roman war god, brandishing a spear, and Hercules holding his club. At bottom is a running boar, symbol of the 20th Legion. This is truly the propaganda of world domination: "Do not cross us, or we will beat you down."[5]

The Tenth Legion that conquered Judea at the time of the writing of Mark's gospel also took a boar for its mascot.[6] The meaning is all too clear. Legionnaires were holy warriors of the Roman Empire, and they offered themselves as living sacrifices for the sake of the nation. They were vassals of dominion. In the case of this demoniac, "Legion" dominated the man, the land, and its people.

The demon called Legion called out to Jesus and "begs Jesus eagerly not to order them [legion] into the abyss" (Luke 8:31; Mark 5:10). Then the demon asked Jesus to send them instead into the "band" (ἀγέλη, *agelē*) of pigs that was by the seaside. The word is used in both Mark 5:11 and Luke 8:32; its military meaning is a group of new recruits. The political military narrative continues. It is a double entendre of course. On the one hand, the swine cult within the Roman army was favored among legionnaires and on the other hand, pigs were unclean for the Jews.[7]

Jesus then "dismissed" (ἐπέτρεψεν, *epetrepsen*) the legion. Again, the same word is used in both tellings. We normally translate it as Jesus "allowed" them, but to do so misses his continued prophetic and political action. He commanded them. He had the power, not the military who seemingly possess the land. The word used is a military term. Jesus barked an order to the herd and they went into the sea; they, like a legion of soldiers, charge.[8] The fact that the story ends with an army being overwhelmed by the sea is perhaps more than a mere allusion to the Exodus story. This occupied land is God's and God takes interest in the people there.

Immediately, the Gerasenes requested that Jesus and his people leave the area. Why? If this were a healing with no political implication, people would have gathered rather than run away, as they do in other narratives in the gospels. This Jesus that confronts the powers will invite reprisals; he cannot be allowed stay. The people want no part. Sometimes it is easier to peacefully go along with oppressive norms than to stand against foreign powers. After all, you can end up possessed.

Jesus offered an alternative narrative to the political occupation of the Pax Romana, which was no peace at all. His prophesy inserted itself in the body politic, freeing people from what oppressed them so that they become who God created them to be. No longer was the demoniac cast out of community. Instead, reclaimed by God's recreative act, he was restored to community with others and God. No longer a citizen in a city of the dead making his home in tombs, he was free to make a life among the living.

Jesus's engaging of the political powers in no way lessens the spiritual element of demon possession in the story. Powers and principalities of this world that use violence as a means of keeping the peace are demonic; they destroy the creatures of God. This man was freed from his spiritual shackles.

Jesus's political exorcism triggers fear for some, just as deep readings of scripture that don't agree with our nation's accepted values raise anxiety in churches afraid of lost parishioners and dwindling pledges. Again, we turn to Frantz Fanon. The impact of a settled foreign power is that violence seems the only possible response.[9] Fanon's experience in Algeria taught him that people living through occupation feel more and more powerless. They become like zombies. Like the demon-possessed man at Gerasene, their powerlessness is more terrifying than their colonizers.[10] People in pews will resist the change that Jesus offers in the beginning, until revolution breaks out. People revolt, Fanon writes, because they can no longer breathe. He believes there is a cognitive dissonance in the beginning from which people have to break free. This is what the people of Gerasene experienced.[11] This is what people in our pews experience if they read scripture as only a spiritual sustenance and not as political engagement. Remember this exorcism took place only thirty or so years prior to the Jewish revolt that ended with the destruction of Jerusalem! Violence to keep the Pax

Romana—or the Pax Americana—always begets more violence. It took a lot of money, people, and acts of violence to bring about a "peace" whose purpose is to maintain dominance.

We as Americans and as Christians have been silent too often as the overarching political zeitgeist of America's civil religion has taken hold. Our silence has buoyed nationalistic fears of scarcity. We did not push for or contribute to important conversations that have been needed for decades. In the end a strong sense of disenfranchisement built up and in 2016 we had a social and political explosion. Instead of engaging intentionally in conversation with the political world around us, we raised our fists, got angry, didn't listen, painted extreme pictures of the world, gobbled up lies about one another, then spit them out as truths and called for seemingly justified extreme responses. We estranged ourselves from our neighbors and did violence (real and virtual) to the people around us. The Gerasene demoniac, Legion, was the first evangelist in the Gospel account of Mark who was freed and went on to tell a different story of political engagement. But we have merely became evangelists for our opposing political parties. In our context we have not freed people from their zombified and colonized experience. We have demanded greater occupation of religious space by political parties with the hope that people would join our side. Instead of restoring people to each other to live together in harmonious relationship, as Jesus did, we shackled ourselves and each other, and condemned ourselves to dwell among a politics of tombs and gravestones. Christian citizens must rise above political narratives of estrangement. Those stories are legion and they want only one thing: power. They serve only one master: the demonic powers and principalities that use us. We are challenged to honor Jesus's exorcizing work, to take our place in the political world without doing violence to our relationships and our communities. This kind of exorcism demands the virtues of compassion and familial faithfulness.

I am not advocating passivity in regards to the world around us. As Christian citizens, we cannot be silent in the face of dominating violence no matter what flag it drapes itself in. Jesus casts out Legion through nonviolent engagement. It is all too easy to become the monsters we fight and to legitimize violent reprisal. Nietzsche once warned, "Whoever fights monsters should see to it that in the process he does not become a monster. And if you gaze long enough into an abyss, the abyss will gaze back into you."[12] We cannot become violent Christian monsters in the political arena, in our congregations, or otherwise. There is no "onward Christian soldiers" and no "either you are for us or against us" in the story of Jesus.[13]

The demonic forces of colonization are present throughout the Gospels. The freedom of the people from these forces is only one of the narrative threads we find in Jesus's ministry. A similarly crucial political metanarrative has to do with the responsibility of political leaders to care for the hungry. There are numerous feeding stories. What I want to point out is that the feeding stories have largely been spiritualized or sacramentalized. However, ensuring that people have food was the responsibility of the government. Hunger was directly tied to the responsibility of those in power, as we discussed in the chapter on kings and prophets.

We know that the scriptures interpret the responsibility of feeding the poor as a governor's work because of the story of Joseph. He went to Egypt and helped the Pharaoh ensure the people were fed during a famine (Gen. 41). The people expected Moses to feed them in the wilderness, which is clear by the fact that they turned on him when they teetered on starvation's brink (Exod. 16). There are numerous feeding stories in the ministry of Elisha the prophet, occasioned by a widespread famine (2 Kings 4:38). He laid the fact that the poor and hungry were not being cared for at the feet of the king, and saw the king's negligence as a sign that the covenant with God was broken.

The political motif that captures this expectation is the recurrent metaphor of the shepherd. Recently, the shepherding business has become a spiritual metaphor, but for Jesus and his disciples, and in the arc of God's narrative, it was synonymous with leadership.[14] The prophet Ezekiel said clearly that shepherds (kings/governing politicians) should care for God's people. They were to feed and protect them. He also lamented that the shepherd-king cared for the wealthy but provided nothing for the poor. There were fat sheep and lean sheep (Ezek. 34). Ezekiel understood that those who ruled were to be shepherds and share their wealth for the good of the whole herd. The ruler who did not feed and care for the sheep was a bad ruler.

I find it interesting that the prophets don't deny asymmetries of wealth. They accept the inevitability of social stratas within society. What the prophets are clear about is that the garden social imaginary of God is one of plenty. There is actually enough to go around. It isn't that the rich should give everything away to the poor. It is that there is enough in the whole society for people to receive what is needed and to be cared for. There is proportionality within the understanding of the society as a group. Good shepherds take good care of their responsibilities, one of which is to make sure that people are fed.

Let us look at how Jesus prophetically engaged the economics of hunger. There were crowds of people everywhere. In both Matthew and Mark the word is *ochlos*, Ὄχλος. In the stories of the feeding of the five thousand, Jesus saw that the crowd was hungry. He was connected to them, had a sense of mutuality with them. He was in a reoriented garden social relationship with the crowds. Jesus saw hungry people and was moved in his gut (Mark 6:34; Matt. 9:36). He saw them as sheep without a shepherd. They were in a lonely place. It was on the shoulders of those who govern to feed them, and because of power and perverted desire they had shirked their responsibility. When Jesus saw these people he made clear that hunger was a sign that the leaders of society had failed. They were bad shepherds because their sheep were hungry.

Jesus miraculously did a king's work instead. Many people were fed in the stories of Matthew and Mark. Many people who were hungry found food at a table with Jesus throughout God's narrative. They were not spiritually hungry; they were simply hungry. Hungry people can't do anything else unless they are fed. Jesus fed them. Jesus also taught about how a society with its different social strata was supposed to work. When we look at how Jesus handled the situation in Mark 6 we see something interesting.

The disciples, in Mark's version of the gospel, came to Jesus and told him the people were hungry. They tried to make it Jesus's problem (6:36). He explained that the work of prophecy and good citizenship meant engaging with the basic needs of the crowd, not shirking them. Jesus told the disciples to give the people something to eat.

The responsibility of feeding people belongs to the society under the direction of its leaders. It is the citizen's responsibility in the reign of God to prophetically reveal the hungry people who are present and ignored. It is also their responsibility to do something about it in concert with others and the government. The Gospel does not support a privatized *noblesse oblige* theology of the wealthy.

The disciples heard Jesus's words and thought they were to spend their own money. Their comments to Jesus about having to spend two hundred dinarii is a reproof.[15] They were shocked, astonished, and incredulous.[16] Jesus was unflappable and sent them to discover how much food was out there: how much food did they actually have? The disciples came back and still wanted to buy food. In Mark's version, there is enough food; it is the reordering of resources that is important. Jesus determined what they had, organized the people into groups (Mark 6:39), blessed the food, redistributed it (Mark 6:41), and the people ate (Mark 6:42). Again, the responsibility of the government in concert with the people is to see that there is plenty and to create systems by which everyone can eat.

Now don't dismiss this as Marxism. That is a failed political system of power manipulation. That is not what Jesus is doing. While Marxist critiques can help us reread traditional narratives, Marxism is just another way in which politics have been used to give the few power and wealth over and against the many. Marx was offering an alternative political narrative to the dominant political narrative of the day, which was monarchy and oligarchy. But sin and human frailty corrupt every such alternative, which is the problem that plagues Marxism and every political narrative when they are unmoored from the garden social imaginary.

When we read the story of the feeding of the five thousand, our ears should be pricked to the idea that the political leadership is responsible for making sure people have what they need to live proportionally within society. That is a non-WEIRD response. However, as WEIRD Christians, we hear the story through our chosen political party's filter. We are either to "redistribute wealth so everyone is equal" or we dismiss the story because "nobody should get anything for free." Both of these reinforce the mythical inevitability of scarcity. The first is about the redistribution of scarcity. The second is about protecting what we have because of scarcity. In his book *Righteous Minds,* Jonathan Haidt argues that humans hate cheating and have a gut reaction when people get things they don't deserve. We are fearful of scarcity or people taking things that are ours. Politicians are constantly manipulating these gut reactions so we will vote for them. They don't solve the issues they promise to solve.[17] This is decidedly not what is happening in Jesus's feeding miracles. If anything, Jesus was suggesting that God's social imaginary had a "responsible proportionality" to it that was essential, one that undermined the economics of empire. Jesus's narrative is based upon a faithful expectation of plenty and abundance instead of scarcity.

Jesus, like the prophets before him, expected that a society affected by God's narrative would be led by people who ensured everyone had food enough to live. Jesus was suggesting not a blanket redistribution of wealth, or a social program where rich people bought things for poor people and the power dynamics stayed the same. Jesus was also not suggesting that caring for the poor was the sole responsibility of a church that was disconnected from the state. This reading of his actions denies the scriptural demand that nations care for their marginalized and poor.

When "charities" are solely responsible for the care of the poor, then the corrupt power and economic differential stays the same. God's desires are clear. God intends a garden social imaginary where all are cared for within the political life of the society. The same prophetic words to the kings of Israel can be leveled at any government that evades its responsibility for the least who live within its borders. God's narrative reminds us that society has enough and that systems can exist that enable hard working people at the top and bottom of the society's class structure to eat and live well. There is always the possibility of a reasonable proportionality of resources.

We can talk about this story spiritually. We can speak of the miracles. But as Christian citizens we need to read the story in relationship to our dual citizenship. When governments are unjust, they do not enable systems that ensure people have what they need to live. In nations of bounty, where there are enough resources and plenty to eat, it is a matter of distributive systems working to share that bounty. The Christian citizen's work is to take a role in using the power of government to make sure people can eat and live well. Notice that the disciples kept wanting to buy food, which kept the system of feeding the hungry within the existing economic system of the day, allowing the shepherd leaders to maintain their lack of responsibility.

Jesus's miracle is not just feeding the people for the day. That alone does not change the system. Instead, Jesus models a different way of doing things and reveals that the shepherds were not shepherding. Is it any wonder that the people wanted to make Jesus king? They were awe-struck because Jesus was actually allowing God's garden social imaginary to take root in the world around him, including the economic systems in which he lived.

Cornel West criticizes theologians and clergy for inadequately addressing this reality. He writes that black theologians do "not emphasize sufficiently the way in which the racist interpretations of the gospel they reject encourage and support the capitalist system of production, its grossly unequal distribution of wealth, and its closely connected political arrangements."[18] We have a responsibility as Christian citizens to read our narrative closely. We have a responsibility to honor our role as dual citizens. I am not suggesting a theocracy or a kind of socialist government. I am suggesting that Jesus as a prophet had a critical eye, and challenged his society to make real God's social imaginary. This is the work of Christian citizenship.

Jesus rejected the powers of dominion and their colonizing influences. Jesus also rejected the principalities' shirking of responsibility. Jesus then recast a narrative of God's social imaginary and bid the Christian citizen to see the world through that lens.

Chapter Twelve

The Story of the Disinherited

Reformation theology . . . pretends to prefer Pharasaic ostentation to a modest invisibility, which in practice means conformity to the world. When that happens, the hallmark of the Church becomes justitia civilis instead of extraordinary visibility. The very failure of the light to shine becomes the touchstone of our Christianity.

—Dietrich Bonhoeffer[1]

God's intention that we live in community together is clear. Our deepest cherished freedom is rooted in our responsibility to live together. We are community and connected. Our individual narratives are located in the midst of God's narrative, and so is everyone else's. We are a web of story and connection. God's social imaginary and its arc from Abraham to Moses to the prophets to Jesus reminds us we are all connected.

So, let us consider for a moment the crowd—the *ochlos,* ὄχλος— that Jesus saw before him. The *ochlos* was a particular kind of crowd: the unwelcomed members of society. This group of people is mentioned some thirty times in Mark—they are ever-present in the ministry of Jesus. Most people (preachers and teachers) assume that this is a generalized term for people—in Greek, *laos.* But Mark is trying to break down our lens of the insider/outsider. *Ochlos* oftentimes refers to a "confused" group of people. It can also refer to those who travel with soldiers and clean up after them.

Ochlos is a mass of people who follow along, a motley crew, stragglers, and the disorganized.

As Ched Myers puts it, since "the time of Ezra [the term *ochlos*] came to mean specifically the lower class, poor, uneducated, and ignorant of the law." The religious leaders of Israel made it clear that the faithful were not to "share meals nor travel together" with this group. Jesus travelled with them openly. They were constantly with him. He went even further: he called them family. In Mark 3:32 we read: "A crowd (the *ochlos*, the 'am ha'aretz, the people of the land) was sitting around him; and they said to him, 'Your mother and your brothers and sisters are outside, asking for you.'" (Remember his family thought his behavior was crazy and they wanted Jesus to stop embarrassing them and breaking the law.) Jesus replied, "Who are my mother and my brothers?" And looking at those who sat around him (the crowd), he said, "Here are my mother and my brothers!" Jesus called them family, reorienting the social structure itself.

Jesus has brought people into relationship across the social divisions of society across the ages. His action clarifies not only who is family, but also how responsibilities between these classes work. He has demonstrated who we are to be compassionate to. He has made clear who we are to be faithful to. Again, Jesus sees the new family as including the rich and the poor: the hard workers at the top of the food chain and the hard workers at the bottom.

The poor do not become poor of their own volition. They bear the brunt of political systems made up of socially prescribed relationships. Jesus explored the nature of such prescribed relationships of power in his own day and culture. In his ministry, he confronted the suffering that resulted from a social caste who was dependent on the symbolic structures of honor and shame. "Honor cultures," as they are called, are built so that honor and shame parallel privilege and poverty. People from privileged casts receive honor while the impoverished are shamed.

Sociologist Bruce Malina remarks that, in honor societies, social standing is evidenced by sexual status, marital status, rank, and power. These things prescribe how people interact: who can talk to whom, who can eat with whom, who are peers and who are subordinates; all of these relationships are carefully marked by custom and "cultural cues."[2] Molina also notes that there are prescribed roles for people within these cultures who police the boundaries and ensure that they are honored. Men control the honor system through the use of power and violence, while women in these societies use the power of shame. Molina calls this the "moral division of labor."[3]

As Jesus claimed the crowd as his family; as he ate with political and religious leaders, as well as the poor; and as he healed and touched the unclean; he was undoing those boundaries and recreating God's garden social imaginary. Some will say he was challenging the social order. Some will say that it was all about spirituality. Still others will not reference these parts of scripture too often because they are uncomfortable. Jesus reconnected the fractured social classes into a community. Jesus's work was not new, though. He was purposefully enlarging the community beyond its honor/shame boundaries to reorient people back into God's narrative.

Let us consider Jesus's healing of two women in Mark 5:21–43. This passage comes after the exorcism of the Gerasene demoniac. In God's narrative, Jesus was on his way—the way of prophetic imagination. Jairus, a man who led the local synagogue, met him. Jairus was a man of honor in the society, of high station, and of power. He was not a typical member of the crowd in the story, so he stood out. His daughter was ill and Jairus felt powerless. He told Jesus that his daughter was in urgent need of saving so that she might live again.

Urgency, resurrection, and living again are all particular words used in the passage. We cannot but hear, perhaps as Mark's first readers did, the parallel with the urgency by which Jesus made his way to the cross, the death and resurrection which were to take place, and the opportunity we receive to live again on Calvary. The Greek is clear: Jairus's daughter was not sick but dead![4]

As Jesus made his way to Jairus's home, a hemorrhaging woman touched him. She occupied the bottom of the honor/shame society caste system. She was outside of community. People may not have even spoken to her, and they certainly would not have touched her. She may have even had to live outside of village. The narrative tells us that the woman was terrified. Scholars differ in their understanding of her emotion. She may well have been afraid of being seen in the crowd, infecting others, or being found out. She may have been afraid of contaminating Jesus himself.[5] Certainly all of these fears indicate a woman oppressed under a cultural weight of shame.

When she touched Jesus's clothes she became aware of being made well. He was aware of the healing, and he told her that it was her faith that made her well. Jesus looked at her. We are reminded of his looking upon his followers and calling them his new family. He looked upon her and he called her "daughter"—Θυγάτηρ, *Thygatēr* (Mark 5:34). She became family, a follower, a believer. She was able to live life in a new way. Perhaps she was afraid because her own life within the prescribed social order was not only restored, but changed and reoriented. Her healing is paralleled in the new family with Jairus's daughter, who was healed and made to live again as well. She was at the upper end of the honor/shame system.

There was no fear in Jairus coming to Jesus. There was no fear of contamination or uncleanliness. Jairus was a man of power and came as if to direct and to take charge. Unlike the pouring out of his spirit that took place with the hemorrhaging woman, Jesus's intervention with the girl is more like the stilling of the storm or the Gerasene demoniac. The words here are powerful (Mark 5:41). We see in the midst of the room: mourners cast out, death in power, and then a God of creation at work remaking the world. Death was vanquished with powerful words and she rose.[6] She was restored into her family, and given food to eat. The healing of Jairus's daughter was another act of power. For those of us who know the rest of the story, the words and images the narrative conjures up are the resurrection of Jesus.

Here we have two women. The first woman was old, contaminated, and at the bottom of the system. The second woman was young, wealthy, powerful, and at the top. Jesus united them both to himself and to each other. The narrative plays itself out as one unified story. Two separate narratives become part of God's narrative. If they were merely two separate and unrelated healings, then Jairus's bringing him to the house would be superfluous to the story's timing. These two strands are connected in the narrative. One cannot be healed without the other. One daughter of Israel

(Jairus's daughter) is in relationship to the unnamed daughter of Israel (the hemorrhaging woman). You and I exist together. We are always in relationship with the unnamed other. Jesus heals all. Jesus's healing action rewove the seamless woven fabric of God's narrative wherein all the stories are God's. Jesus restored what had been estranged by the honor/shame dynamics of Second Temple culture.

This may seem odd to our WEIRD ears that are so adept at seeing individuals instead of crowds. We see ourselves alone and disconnected, rather than in relationship to others as of part of a wider web. Our WEIRD eyes are used to seeing two women, and two separate healing stories. We probably even find the idea of the honor/shame social system to be unAmerican. We might be offended by it and easily persuaded that Jesus's healings are meant for other societies that clearly have such systems.

Not so fast. Jonathan Haidt, in his book *Righteous Minds*, reveals that all humans are motivated by their gut reaction to what he calls the sanctity/degradation foundation—even Americans. It is one of the key foundations that motivates us politically, and is played upon by politicians. Yet, we deny it. He points to the fact that actually learning to eat things that don't kill you, or do things that won't get you killed, is part of our ancestral heritage. The principle actually works to protect human communities. The "triggers are smells, sights, or other sensory patterns."[7] Malina reminds us how honor and shame work. Haidt reminds us that such a social system is rooted in our prehistoric survival and ensured tribal survival. Insiders and outsiders are placed in their spots within the social group whether through the action of an honor/shame dynamic or the sacred/degraded dichotomy, because to do otherwise jeopardizes the society.

The principles of sacredness and degradation have found their way into every society around the world. They impact internal policies as well as politics around foreigners, immigrants, and strangers. On the one hand, the foundation binds us into moral communities and protects us.[8] It also creates and influences systems that degrade and shame human beings, creating untouchable castes and enabling abuse of power and scapegoating.

Americans may wish to pretend that we do not operate such systems. Haidt and scientists like him reveal nonetheless that this dichotomy is one of the socio-psychological motivations that undergird all human systems. Rather than reason, it is instincts like the sanctity/degradation dichotomy that create culture. We have a very real emotional "ick" factor built into our psyche that derives from the sanctity/degradation impulse. We have a system of honor and shame that is triggered by and sorts out our own class systems and it is not run by reason.[9]

Jesus reinvented social norms again in Mark 10:13, Matthew 19:13, and Luke 18:15. People brought children to Jesus, even babies. The inner circle around Jesus said, "Not so fast." This scene is sentimentally memorialized in church windows all over as part of a sweet let-the-little-children-come-to-me spirituality. Now, I am quite sure that Jesus did want the children to come to him regardless of their parents' place in the wider social system, but Jesus was suggesting a community where all strata were connected and in relationship. So, his invitation runs parallel with the previous conversation. Meanwhile, it is evident in this story that the social imaginary of the teacher/disciple remained hierarchical. Jesus disrupted all of it by putting the children at the center of the community (Mark 9:36). He explained that he was in relationship with them. In a culture where one's value to the family was based on what one did, to consider a child a person, to put one of the least of the members of community at the center, to recognize an unproductive (indeed, vulnerable) person there, reorderd the social structures to be garden-like.

Given that they played such a crucial role in Jesus's ministry, centering children is a key part of the Christian citizen's responsibility: the structures of state should be oriented towards the well-being of children. Children are often the most vulnerable in power systems characterized by the interplay of honor and shame, or sanctity and degradation. They are the first to go hungry. Without proper nutrition, their brains don't form properly in the first three years of life, perpetuating the cycle of poverty into the next generation. They are seen as the property of the parents or the ward of the state. They are seen as assets for our future: future church members, future workers, future soldiers, and future consumers. Jesus changed this orientation. Children are no longer appendages to the social imaginary of a tribe, city, state, or nation until they are productive members. In this act, Jesus turned the tables upside down. Literally making the least the first, Jesus reoriented every member of society as part of God's narrative.

In his relationship with the crowd, and in his relationship with the two women and children, Jesus revealed how God's narrative offers a different social imaginary that keeps our natural ways of shaming/honoring under check. It isn't enough that a transcendent God far away is in relationship with us. Jesus revealed that our relationships are intertwined with God, as are our stories. Our futures are tied together with God; therefore our politics, economics, and health are also tied together with God.

One of the values of American civil religion is individualism. It is a value that is strong, and is tied to our collective passion for freedom and self-determination. It is reinforced by our national birth story, our mythic characters, speeches by our leaders, and our civil liturgies. Think of those mythic tall tales of George Washington, Molly Pitcher, Daniel Boone, "Davy" Crockett, John Henry, the unsinkable Molly Brown, Buffalo Bill Cody, Annie Oakley, and Calamity Jane. Add to the list Paul Bunyan and Pecos Bill. Individualism has become our dominant language as well as our philosophical frame.[10] However, "individualism" is not a strong enough shared value to help this country manage the challenges that face us in our next age. In fact, it may undermine our future if it remains the sole arbiter of truth.

In God's social imaginary, we have described community in terms of relationship and responsibility. The stories of Jesus point us towards the virtue of interconnectedness. This is not a new term in social systems and politics. Some fifty years ago, author Dan Beauchamp argued that interconnectedness as a kind of "group principle . . . has tended to be subordinated to the language of individual rights." Nonetheless we remain a body politic with shared commitments and responsibilities.[11] In the last fifty years, people working on the nature and philosophy of community as lived out in our American context have wrestled with the idea of our interconnectedness. Ann Robertson, a professor working in the field of theoretical considerations for health, calls this a "moral economy of interdependence."[12] People like political theorist Mary Ann Glendon are beginning to have conversations that challenge the notion of individualism, defined as the "self-determining, unencumbered individual, a being connected to others only by choice."[13] Unencumbered self-determination is not a reality in society, and it is certainly not a value in God's garden social imaginary. There is a real balance being worked out in this discourse. George Lackoff, who is a linguist, suggests the language of "cultivated interdependence," in which those who have been nurtured accept a corresponding responsibility to nurture others.[14] This is where we want to land: cultivated interdependence.

God invites us into God's narrative as partners. We are connected to both God and others. As MacIntyre suggested, we are intertwined in one another's stories and in God's story. God has also created us free. Our freedom is how mimetic desire and sibling rivalry enter our relationships. Desire and rivalry perpetuate scapegoating and violence, thereby fraying the fabric of our interconnectedness. Jesus told the story again, as if for the first time, and invited us back into relationship with one another. What we see in God's narrative arc with the crowd, women, and the children is a cultivated interdependence.

This is not a new idea in my tradition. In 1988, then Archbishop of Canterbury Robert Runcie faced a trying time of great division for the Anglican Communion. Social change, the lack of response by governments (including his own), ecumenical challenges (including the relationship with Roman Catholicism), the ordination of women, and global church struggles with theological colonialism all made for a toxic soup of division within the church. At the 1988 global gathering of bishops, called the Lambeth Conference, he suggested cultivating the idea of interdependence. He questioned the group directly, "Are we being called through events and their theological interpretation to move from independence to interdependence?" He grounded the notion of shared values and unity in the word "interdependence." He suggested that it was the only way for a diverse group to be unified, and he called for the envisioning of new structures. Continuing as a community with the high value of independence, he prophesied, would inevitably end in a religious society of decay.[15]

In that creative and challenging moment, I believe Runcie, steeped in scripture, was calling upon the deep social imaginary of God's garden.

Christian citizens must in some manner, some way, say no to the endless division of humanity that privileges ego over the needs of community. The struggle is always framed between the extremes of independence versus connection. It was not individuals who withstood tyranny at America's founding, but a new community who worked together and saw that their futures were intertwined. They each had to give a little to work together. In the end, their shared responsibility for each other—their cultivated interdependence—gave life to a new and unique republic.

The word interdependence captures well the essence of God's given freedom in our origin story of Christian citizenship. Coupled with a life of compassion and familial faithfulness lived within community, interdependence is a word for our time. It pulls on the strands of God's social narrative in a way that is helpful. We must labor on and discover real ways to engage on the ground with one another as responsible citizens who are interdependent.

Chapter Thirteen

The Hive Lens

Political compromise is difficult in American democracy even though no one doubts it is necessary. It is difficult for many reasons, including the recent increase in political polarization that has been widely criticized. We argue that the resistance to compromise cannot be fully appreciated without understanding its source in the democratic process itself, especially as conducted in the U.S. The incursion of campaigning into governing in American democracy—the so called "permanent campaign"—encourages political attitudes and arguments that make compromise more difficult. These constitute what we call the uncompromising mindset, character- ized by politicians' standing on principle and mistrusting opponents. This mindset is conducive to campaigning, but not to governing, because it stands in the way of necessary change and thereby biases the democratic process in favor of the status quo.

—Amy Gutmann and Dennis Thompson[1]

The fact that our founding fathers were able to craft a federal politics that has lasted this long is amazing. Jonathan Haidt believes that large-scale human societies are miraculous. His research has led him to believe that it is the combination of social inventions (complicated moral psychology, religion, tribes, agriculture, and systems of social hier- archies with "parochial altruism") that have enabled them to survive.[2] Haidt's work indicates that large societies have to be made up of smaller groups. These smaller micro-societies enable the stronger macro-culture to evolve, change, and grow. Economist and philosopher Adam Smith believed that our system's wider civil religious values allow plenty of room for people to find small niches that could be improved. People exerting their own creative impulses within the framework of smaller groups and local problems is a good thing.[3] This was certainly our founders' thought, too, as they left most of the governing up to the local states and communities.

Nassim Taleb, a philosopher and author of *Antifragile: Things That Gain From Disorder*, says there are two kinds of organizations: fragile or antifragile. A glass mixing-bowl is strong until it is dropped on the tile floor; it is fragile. Organizations that only do one thing or have one focus are extremely fragile. A muscle is strong but elastic and takes a great deal of tension to break. It resists fragility because it is built up by stresses and strains upon it. Systems and institutions that have a diversity of resources and aims resist fragility in the same way. Systems that disperse creativity and failure throughout the wider organization are stronger and build strength for the stresses and strains of the organization's existence. Such systems have an ability to allow "fear to be transformed into prudence, our pain into information, our mistakes into initiation, our desire into undertaking."[4] The antifragile systems allow a large organization like a nation to grow stronger by the dispersal of risk through these smaller more local communities.

Sociologist and researcher Émile Durkheim believed that people had an "inter-social" quality. This interdependence leaves individual autonomy and personality almost intact. While particular passions drive us, we are part of a corporate life as well. The act of coming together in these smaller groups stimulates a common life, and tugs against the individual passion to stay separate.[5] Jonathan Haidt, Patrick Seder, and Selin Kesebir argue that this "hivishness" is a basic part of our human nature. Small hives that are "egalitarian, and communally oriented," are helpful to the wider organization or community. However, they also can be used and manipulated.[6]

Robert Putnam and David Campbell, in their book *American Grace*, tell us that people who come together in tightly knit groups for common work (in the case of Putnam's research—religion in America) are bound together in a relationship of mutual trust and responsibility that inclines them to be less selfish.[7] They also found that when these groups accentuate difference versus unity, they are pulled apart. As socially meaningful differences such as race, religion, and language are emphasized, division and distrust appear inevitable; group cooperation internally and externally is reduced.[8] In this way hives can be manipulated to work against other hives. Much of politics seeks to do this. Political narratives build large groupings of smaller hives on the basis of *difference*. An emphasis on various ideological purity codes has left the political field divided without much hope for coming together. In fact, these purity codes demand an aversion to compromise with the other.

James Baker, secretary of state for George H.W. Bush, is a parishioner of one of the churches in my diocese, and he has coached me on many issues. He is adept at rising above divisions that threaten the success of necessary endeavors by building coalitions. He has been in politics a long time, even though his father told him to stay out. He says that the more recent political environment is much uglier than it used to be, and that compromise has become a dirty word. When division across the various small groups that make up our larger whole is normative, such that there is a hopeless sense of bridging differences, we "turtle"—we pull ourselves back into our hives and defend our positions. We hunker down.[9]

Christian citizens often hive up and hunker down across our own ecumenical and interfaith divisions, but Christians also steward a deep story that counteracts this natural way of behaving in the face of division. Jesus's parable often called the "Good Samaritan" underlines his message of interdependence, but before we look at the parable, there are two lenses we need to deconstruct that are typically used to read this text: the hive lens and the morality lens.

Let's look first at the hive lens. It used to be that religious communities were composed of people with diverse backgrounds and narratives. Even with the presence of denominational sects, church communities were made up of a wide variety of people. This diversity was amplified in the wider culture, as people would bump into one another at the only high school, the only butcher shop, the only coffee shop, and the bus ride across town that threw all kinds of people together in tight quarters. There were many "melting pot" opportunities, Marc Dunkelman says in *The Vanishing Neighbor: The Transformation of American Community*; this is no longer true. People now live, work, and play in ever more segregated neighborhoods. We are hiving off in more ways than ever before. We move into parts of town that isolate us across ethnic groups or based upon our political ideology.[10]

The garden social imaginary is one of a community of all people. It raises our eyes above the local, to the wider social groupings and communities. It raises our eyes above the individual hives we create. "The Good Samaritan" reorients our vision.

The second lens we need to deconstruct is the morality lens. We often think of the story in individual moral terms. We assume that Jesus is exhorting us to try harder to be better people. In fact, we may even be tempted to read this book as a new form of moralism. It is an understandable error and one that stems from our failure to make a distinction between moralism and virtue. The former offers us an external standard of ethical behavior and then exhorts us to use effort and make sacrifice to achieve that standard. Moralism is always up to *us*. Virtue, however, is different. In the Christian life, virtue is the fruit of grace and encounter with God. Virtue results in changed external behavior, but that change is born out of a renewed internal state of being. When virtue takes hold of our lives, we are led to a different way of imagining ourselves, our relationship with God, and our relationships with other people. God's garden imaginary is not a human project, but a reality that we can taste when our lives are aligned with the life of God and we are committed to the cultivation of virtue. Thus, I invite you to read my words as descriptive, and not prescriptive. I am *describing* what citizenship looks like when, out of a deep encounter with God, we commit ourselves to the cultivation of virtue. *This* is the lens I invite you to put on as we explore Jesus's parable of the Good Samaritan.

The message of the parable of the Good Samaritan is well known. The story redefines who is like us—who is our kin. Other parts of the New Testament provide a few clues to what Jesus was doing in this radically subversive story about neighbors. Jesus continuously expanded the Sinai law to include all people, Gentiles and Jews alike. He equated hate of the enemy with murder, and even said that if we are going to worship, we should make amends first. Jesus encouraged passive resistance and is clear that violence is not part of how we are to follow him. In Matthew 5:43–47, Jesus said:

> "You have heard that it was said, 'You shall love your neighbor and hate your enemy.' But I say to you, Love your enemies and pray for those who persecute you, so that you may be children of your Father in heaven; for he makes his sun rise on the evil and on the good, and sends rain on the righteous and on the unrighteous. For if you love those who love you, what reward do you have? Do not even the tax-collectors do the same? And if you greet only your brothers and sisters, what more are you doing than others?"

Jesus expanded the law, beyond the bounds of Second Temple Judaism, but in a way that was faithful to the priorities of Sinai. Jesus said that living and loving goes beyond our hive or tribe. He taught that the Nazareth Manifesto had implications for neighborliness of all sorts. With this in mind, we must retell the story of the Good Samaritan to see it again for the first time. We need to see who we are in God's eyes and how God invites us to be curious about the way we do politics together.

The parable of the Good Samaritan is found in Luke 10:25–37. The question that invited the parable from Jesus was asked by a lawyer. Before we go any further, it is important to highlight that lawyers of Second Temple Judea and Galilee were not the lawyers of today. They were experts in the law—the code of law that governed Jerusalem's religious, economic, and political systems. Jesus's interlocutor knew the commandments and was highly invested in their keeping. He was part of the wider circle of religious leaders. It is highly likely that this lawyer represented the institutions that made the culture of politics run. He was certainly part of the establishment. The question he posed to Jesus was about eternal life; he wanted to know what one had to do to inherit it. Jesus answered the question with a question, "What is written in the law? What do you read there?" The religious leader answered, "You shall love the Lord your God with all your heart, and with all your soul, and with all your strength, and with all your mind; and your neighbor as yourself." Jesus replied, "You have given the right answer; do this, and you will live." It is unclear if the leader was trying to trick Jesus or simply engage him. Jesus seems a little coy. The leader continued to press Jesus, though, and asked the big question, "Who is my neighbor?" Jesus, warming up to the conversation, told a story.

There was a man going down to Jerusalem from Jericho. The trip from Jericho to Jerusalem is a downward trek, a descent from a high place to a low place. Having made this trek recently on a trip to Israel, I can personally testify that the journey is a radical decline across a significant distance. The topographical drop is the first clue to our parable, according to theologian Robert Farrar Capon. Jesus was indicating the descent of God in Christ Jesus through the Incarnation.[11] Paul invoked the same thing through an ancient Christian hymn in Philippians 2:6–7, "Though he was in the form of God, did not regard equality with God as something to be exploited, but emptied himself, taking the form of a slave, being born in human likeness." The man destined to be robbed is the incarnate God. Furthermore, the man in the story was going down to Jerusalem. Jesus was on his way to Jerusalem as he told the story. Jesus was going to Jerusalem to be tried and found guilty so that the whole world would fall upon him and kill him. The downward walk into the heart of darkness is a foreshadowing of what was coming in the wider gospel narrative. The traveler fell among thieves. For Capon, the man in this parable is the Christ.[12]

The man—the Christ figure—fell into the hands of robbers "who stripped him, beat him, and went away, leaving him half dead." Then, two religious officials passed by. They are us, the church and the religious. Both of them crossed to the other side of the road. Preachers often make a lot of this detail. In exegeting this parable for a WEIRD culture, we often make the story into a cautionary tale about being moral, pointing out that "we" mustn't be like "them;" we want to be like the Samaritan instead. We even name him the "Good Samaritan." We want to be like him and not like those other religious people. The church unconsciously draws attention away from the man, God in Christ Jesus, and focuses on the transactional act of mercy by the Samaritan. When the church does so, it misses Jesus's criticism of hives and moves our attention from the person lying in the ditch to the individual who serves him. In other words, this interpretation changes the story from a story about interdependence to a WEIRD story.

The religious leaders believed, because of their transactional faith, that they had done all that was required. They kept the law. They made their religious offerings. They said their prayers. In fact, nothing else could possibly have been asked of them. Therefore, the religious passed by the man. They had no need of him.[13] He was half-dead already.

Jesus then introduced the Samaritan. Samaritans were not of the same tribe as the man or the religious leaders. They were a Yahwist sect that followed the ancient Sinai tradition, and rejected the trappings of Davidic empire and temple religion. They did not recognize the religious supremacy of Jerusalem, so they were ostracized from the family of Israel. They were definitely not of the same hive. Samaritans were seen as outcast in the Gospels; whenever one shows in a story or a conversation, Jesus is usually redeeming them. This sinner in the eyes of the religious establishment, this outsider, the Samaritan, stopped to help. He drew near to the beaten man, and was moved in his gut by what he saw. This is important. The Samaritan was going down the road. He did not wait for the man to find him; instead, he found the wounded one in the ditch. He was outside the comfort and protection of his hive. He was not afraid, but came close enough to find him and to see him—to see his wounds and the damage done by the robbers.

The Samaritan entered into the passion of Christ by stopping to help the beaten, robbed man on his way to Jerusalem. The Christ figure was in the midst of his passion and the Samaritan comes and kneels with him. He was present in his passion. The Samaritan saw this "other" man as kin and acted out of familial faithfulness. He joined in the Christ figure's passion through his compassion. The meaning of compassion is to "suffer with," which is what he did. The Samaritan then took up his own cross and continued down into the passion with the Christ figure—the one who imaged God for him. He stopped his journey. He "bandaged his wounds, having

poured oil and wine on them," an act that was expensive and precious. He
put "him on his own animal." Capon points out that such an act of charity
sacrificed convenience and time, because the Samaritan must walk.[14] He
spent money on the beaten man, and asked the people at a nearby inn to
take care of him. It was not enough to simply drop him off; he sacrificially
offered money to care and feed the Christ and he left it to the innkeeper
to do what was needed. He would pay the bill.

Jesus then asked the lawyer, "Which of these three, do you think, was a
neighbor to the man who fell into the hands of the robbers?" He said, "The
one who showed him mercy." Jesus said to him, "Go and do likewise." Jesus
flipped the original question. The lawyer asked, "Who is my neighbor?"
Jesus invited the lawyer to ponder who was neighbor to the Christ. Who
was he, the lawyer, to be neighbor to?

This is a different way of seeing, rather than thinking that to be a loving neighbor means some kind of legal requirement to be overly nice to
others. A neighbor is the person who becomes an outcast like Jesus and
enters into the passion of other outcasts. Becoming a neighbor is picking
up our cross. Being a neighbor is costly. This parable is not about good
behavior. We are to live in the world in relation to the Christ and his passion. Capon writes that Jesus is telling us to "stop trying to live and to be
willing to die, to be willing to be lost rather than to be found—to be, in
short, a neighbor to the One who, in the least of his brethren, is already
neighbor to the whole world of losers."[15]

You may say that I've slipped back into a morality play, but the imitation of Christ is not about simple morality. To imitate Christ is to
prioritize relationship and sacrifice instead of doing nice things out of
obligation.[16] Humans want to codify this behavior and make it into a
mandate—do nice things for others—and then to let it gradually slip into
an economy—do nice things for others so you can get into heaven, or be
loved by God. This codification is always dependent upon the individual
and motivation, and frequently rooted in the immanent frame or tribal
systems of rewards and honors.

Austrian philosopher and Roman Catholic priest Ivan Illich believes
that the Gospel offers a different way of engaging the world around us.

It breaks open these naturally formed codes.[17] The Samaritan's actions were not generated by a code outside of himself. Instead the Samaritan responded to a shared humanness. Charles Taylor digests Illich's thoughts on the Samaritan this way:

> He feels called to respond, however, not by some principle of "ought," but by this wounded person himself. And in so responding, he frees himself from the bounds of the "we." He also acts outside of the carefully constructed sense of the sacred, of the demons of darkness, and various modes of prophylaxis against them which have been erected in "our" culture, society, religion often evident in views of the outsider as "unclean."[18]

The Samaritan's actions show a new way of being in relationship outside of the boundaries of religious morality. Jesus calls us to see what we have by our shared humanity and our common creation. We are all members of God's community—God's garden's social imaginary.

The Samaritan is an extension of love and agape in the same way that Christ is an extension of these things. Both the Samaritan and Christ create a new "kin" out of relationship and "enfleshment." In the Samaritan's actions we see a new fitting together of people outside of their hives with their own codes, moralities, and formed way of being.[19] The Samaritan is surrounded by religious codes and breaks them by involving himself in the beaten man's passion. He moves across tribalistic boundaries in his act of compassion and familial faithfulness. The Christian citizen has many opportunities to do the same—to reject the religious and political codes of society or the self-focused codes of niceness and kindness. Jesus invites us to dispose ourselves, especially to the strangest and "least deserving" folks we know.

Capon writes, "If you want to read his selfless actions as so many ways in which he took the outcastness and lostness of the Christ-figure on the ground into his own outcast and losing life—then I will let you have imitation as one of the main themes of the parable." Where do we find the passion? The passion of Jesus is always to be found in the "least of his brethren, namely, in the hungry, the thirsty, the outcast, the naked, the sick and the imprisoned in whom Jesus dwells and through whom he invites us to become his neighbors in death and resurrection."[20] The passion of Christ invites the Christian citizen to put aside comfort and enter the Way of the Cross. We may be motivated by our passions and emotions, but the story invites us to an expanded understanding of hivishness. We are invited to enter the lives of others by entering into their passion and daily crucifixion. We are invited to see not only our interdependence, but also that our interdependence requires sacrifice. Theologian Fleming Rutledge says, "This is not a parable meant to inspire us to go out and do good and then feel good about ourselves because we have been good neighbors. This is about entering the way of Christ."[21]

If the world could be fixed by nice people doing kind acts, then everything would be fixed by now, but this is not the reality of Christ's sacrifice, nor is it the reality of the world in which we live. Paul wrote in Galatians 3:21, "If a law had been given that could make alive, then righteousness would indeed be by the law." Rutledge says, "Handing down a new law does not create new people. Something more is required than an exhortation to good works."[22] The social imaginary of God is not merely a way of practicing good citizenship. The deep theology of the Cross and its grace is part of a narrative intended to enliven the whole world.

Luke offers another story in Acts 9 that echoes the parable. It is the story of how the Lord sent Ananias to find Paul and restore his sight after Paul's conversion experience at the hands of God. We know Paul had a huge influence on Luke and Acts. We also know that Luke is keen to show the continuation of the tradition of Israel in the new Christian community. Who better as an illustration than brother Paul? Just like with the story of the man who fell among thieves, we have an interpretation bias that perverts how we read Luke's story about Paul and Ananias: we often make this story about the persecution of the early church, and thereby a persecution of Christ, which allows us to be on the hive side of things. Bulwarking ourselves in this manner places us on the inside and those who are different on the outside. Paul's story is the same as the good Samaritan. Here though, the Christian Ananias is invited to enter the passion of Paul and vice versa.

The early church was not immune to thinking that they should bulwark themselves against the evil world. Even today, there are many Christians who believe we should become a diaspora community and isolate ourselves in the midst of an evil world. Yet, Christ's understanding of the garden social imaginary undermines such thinking. For early Christians, Christ's expansive vision of the garden caused them to oppose the Manichaeans. Mani was the name of the Christian who started a religious sect in Mesopotamia in the middle of the third century. It was popular; even Augustine spent time in a Manichaean community.

There was a complicated cosmology and theology that went with Manichaeism. I will be brief: in this heresy there was good and evil in the world and they were of equal power. God was good and had the same power as Satan/the Devil, who was bad. People were caught in between. There was a whole exchange of light and dark that balanced or created an imbalance in the world; it gets super complicated from there. Manichaeism was a convoluted hybrid of regional religions. It was Christianity with a touch of secret knowledge borrowed from another heresy called Gnosticism. It also included a bit of astrology and Zoroastrianism. The Eastern and Western powers, along with Christianity, opposed it and worked against its spread across the Roman Empire. It took strongest root in Egypt. The church ultimately rejected it because it undermined the sovereignty of God. It argued the devil and evil had the same power as God. It undid our origin stories for one much more akin to the mythos of classical Greek gods connecting God's power, influence, and livelihood to humanity. It perpetuated mimetic violence and scapegoating.

A Manichaean view of our parable would take the side of the political and religious leaders who have nothing to do with the half-dead man and leave the Christ figure to die by the side of the road. Manichaeism rejected interdependence. Their worldview was dualistic; there were good and evil forces and you don't mix the two. A number of years ago Glenn Greenwald, a journalist and author, coined the term "Manichean politics," which, he said, pervades our political discourse.[23] Greenwald argued that this dualism took root some time ago in American politics as it made the case for the defeat of foreign powers: they are evil; we are good. Many people do not remember that President Dwight D. Eisenhower defined the Cold War as a battle between good and evil. In the years that followed, church attendance rose gradually. We often talk about this as baby boomer attendance growth; certainly, there were many reasons. I would argue that the Cold War Manichaean frame was the first time that churchgoing was a fundamental part of being American. You were doing your part to win the Cold War if you went to church.[24]

Manichaean politics have now taken root internally as part of our civil religion in the midst of our own internal political debate. We are in a political season of extreme hivishness, where political powers and principalities use Manichaean philosophy to cast the world in threatening terms of good and evil. One political party is good, the other evil. Both parties and everyone in between now operate out of a hivish Manichaean political framework. Regardless of the party, the hive approach will be Manichaean: there can be no compromise; only defeat or victory. This is how the two opposing political parties have captured the imagination of the people.

Faced with inadequate health care, a weakening birth rate, the dying off of the boomer generation, the increased need for skilled and unskilled labor, and failing systems of infrastructure and education, we will not be able to adapt if we cannot concede that we are intimately connected to each other, and are a part of each other's narrative. The narrative of Christian citizenship turns on sacrifice for the other. It is rooted in the idea that we are at our best when we are willing to enter into another person's loss and suffering and become sacrificially responsible. Putnam and Campbell find that religious people are better friends, neighbors, and members of society. We give more and do more for the good of the whole community.[25] The Christian community is an important part of forming Christian citizens who are neighbors to the Christ figures in their contexts.

The Christian citizen's understanding of cultivated interdependence is intimately tied to our understanding of the Cross and sacrifice for others, regardless of ethnicity, language, nationality, or narrative. The Christian citizen rests upon the power of cultivated interdependence for the sake of relieving the suffering of people within the system, by changing the system politically. Yes, we resist withdrawing into our hives by being a good neighbor. The Good Samaritan invites us to resist division when confronted with diversity. It invites us to resist our hives' desire to support political theories, policies, and practices that demonize the other. It also challenges us to confront the powers and principalities of the world that gain power out of this division.

Chapter Fourteen

Vineyard, Sword, and Cross

And we too might have to die in faith, as did all the saints of old. None of them received the reality of a new age in their lifetime that they worked so hard to produce . . . Even though we do not see that full sun rising, we work with the promise of God knowing that morning always comes. That is the way that all saints and revolutionaries must work—with the assuring promise of God that morning always comes, with or without us. And that is why we work in faith, not seeing the promise of God, but believing in God that if I plant my life, if I plant a seed in your soil, something is going to happen. God is going to see that it happens, because morning always comes after the night. And it tells me something about God. Just as that sun never fails, God never fails. Morning always comes.

—Katie G. Cannon[1]

There is an old story within God's narrative often called the "Song of the Vineyard." The prophet Isaiah talked to the political leaders and took them to task for "grinding the face of the poor" and prophesied that judgment would befall them (Isa. 2:7; 3:13–15; 10:1–2). It was a failure of justice by those who governed. Isaiah used the image of the vineyard to make his point (Isa. 5:1–7). The image hearkened back to God's garden social imaginary. The song goes,

> My beloved had a vineyard on a very fertile hill. He dug it and cleared it of stones, and planted it with choice vines; he built a watch-tower

149

in the midst of it, and hewed out a wine vat in it; he expected it to yield grapes, but it yielded wild grapes.

The sower of seeds sowed a vineyard—God planted a garden. Isaiah prophesied that God would not hold back the enemies of the state; the song continues,

> I will remove its hedge, and it shall be devoured; I will break down its wall, and it shall be trampled down. I will make it a waste; it shall not be pruned or hoed, and it shall be overgrown with briers and thorns; I will also command the clouds that they rain no rain upon it.

Jesus turned to these words as he engaged the dominant narrative of violence by the ruling class in his day.[2] He compared the political leadership of Israel and Rome to an absentee landlord and tenants (Mark 12:1–12). Moreover, by doing so he not only critiqued the present political system of domination he equated with previous scriptural examples of the same. In the parable of the vineyard, Jesus placed the political leaders of the day as the tenants of the garden vineyard. God planted a vineyard, built a wine press, tower, and a wall (Isa. 5:1–2 ≈ Mark 12:2a). God allowed the rulers to take charge as tenants (1 Sam. 8:6; 8:22 ≈ Mark 12:2b). God sent prophets who were beaten or killed by the political leaders (Matt. 23:31 ≈ Mark 12:3–5). Jesus continued with his story, sowing the idea that God sent God's son and the tenants did the same to him that they had done to the prophets. Why were they so violent? There was an old tradition that the tenants got to keep the land if no one claimed it.[3] They rejected God's social imaginary out of greed. Like the prophets before him, Jesus reminded the political leaders that God required mercy, justice, and the care of the poor. God required responsibility. If we hearken back to Isaiah's vineyard song we see, "For the vineyard of the Lord of hosts . . . expected justice, but saw bloodshed; righteousness, but heard a cry!" (Isa. 5:7) The political leaders wanted to arrest Jesus and kill him, but the crowd was too big.[4]

Jesus, having confronted the leaders of Israel in the "wicked tenant" parable, turned his attention to the Roman Empire. The political leaders conspired with religious leaders to try to trap Jesus by bringing him a Roman coin (Mark 12:13–17; Matt. 22:16–22; Luke 20:20–26). The trap is still deployed today against Jesus's own intentions to suggest that there is a separation between church and state. People quote this passage *ad nauseam* without any sense of what they are doing to Christianity, or what the passage actually means. Before we clarify what Jesus intended, we need to clarify how we do damage to our faith when we use this passage about Caesar's coin to defend the separation of church and state.

First, let us be clear: "the separation of church and state" is not in the Constitution. The Constitution *does* say that there shall be no state sanctioned establishment of religion. This means there will be no state religion or church. The First Amendment to the Constitution says that the state cannot interfere in religious practice. This means that the state has to leave the church alone except in very particular situations. The Lyndon B. Johnson Amendment in the tax law prevents preachers from supporting candidates. But there is nothing in the Constitution or the laws of the country that says that the church must unquestionably go along with the state. There is nothing that says that churchgoers and churches cannot deal with political issues. The laws of the country do not silence the church.

There are many who reject this view and suggest that faith is a private matter and that churches have no business talking about politics. Such a view sidelines Christians and Christian citizenship. What is worse, this is taught by and argued by Christians. In his book *Civil Religion: A Dialogue in the History of Political Philosophy*, Ronald Beiner argues that what we do when we make this case is support civil religion or modernity's secular frame. On the one hand, making such a case that churches and Christians should not talk about politics means that the state and politicians get to form citizens based singularly upon civil religion. Secondly, when we do this we completely gut the idea of Christianity and Christian citizenship all together by relativizing the Christian spiritual life to a private individual experience, which supports the secular frame and rejects the God narrative we are actually participating in.

To make the argument that there is no place in our nation's political discourse for the expression of Christian citizenship is to relegate

Christians to a "voluntary association of like-minded individuals" that should support the nation or be quiet.[5] Any religious conviction that runs contrary to the civil religion and politics of the state will, in the end, be silenced if this opinion prevails, which will be bad for Christians, Jews, and Muslims along with any other religious communities. Remember, a state unmoored from God's social imaginary will sink beyond subjectivism to nihilism and eventually collapse under the weight of its own despotism. Moreover, to read the passage about Jesus and Caesar's coin as revelation about the separation of church and state is poor scholarship. It isn't even a good surface reading of the text. In the beloved words of Admiral Ackbar at the Battle of Endor in the movie *Return of the Jedi*, "It's a trap!" This showdown about the coin is a confrontation with the empire.

The goal of the politically motivated leaders was to get Jesus into trouble publicly—to trap him in his own words. They came to him solicitously: "Is it lawful to pay taxes to the emperor, or not? Should we pay them, or should we not?" (Mark 12:15; Matt. 22:17; Luke 20:22) There were seven levels of taxation in the region where they were standing. Most likely the tax they were referring to was the poll tax, which supported the occupying army; it was levied on every person. They knew that if Jesus answered, "No," then he was liable for rebelling against the empire. If he answered, "Yes," he would be liable for heresy by suggesting the emperor was God. It was such a big issue that Jews would not handle Roman coins because of the heresy and idolatry involved.[6]

Jesus was pretty crafty in his response. He knew they were putting him to the test (Mark 12:15b; Matt. 22:18; Luke 20:24). It was their question and their coin, so he made it about them. First, he asked them to present the coin, which meant they had to handle it, and they were liable for heresy and idolatry. The accusers became entangled in a trap of their own making. Jesus then asked whose likeness was on it and what the inscription said (Mark 12:16; Matt. 22:19; Luke 20:24). They answered, "the emperor's," and, "August and Divine Son"—which was Jesus's title. The next time the phrase would be used was on his cross.

Jesus said, "Give to the emperor the things that are the emperor's, and to God the things that arc God's" (Mark 12:17; Matt. 22:21; Luke 20:25).

Jesus's answer invited the political leaders to act according to their own allegiances. Jesus knew they were in league with Caesar. He called their bluff.

We might ask, "What is God's?" The point of course is that everything is God's. The creation is God's; it is God's vineyard. Jesus's reply further challenged the rule of both the local political authorities and Rome's taxation, which was burdensome to the poor. Non-payment of the tax resulted in a person losing their land and property. In essence Jesus confronted the ruling powers with the truth of their allegiances and critiqued their treatment of the poor. The word used in the Markan account is of note: ἀπόδοτε (*apodote*) means to "repay" not merely to "render." Jesus's answer may better be framed: repay to Caesar what is owed and repay to God what is owed. In this way we see that Caesar was placed back into the role of the wicked tenant from the parable above.[7] Moreover, Caesar was to repay what was owed to God as well. Caesar was not left out of the parable of the coin and was accountable to God.

This is not a story about the separation of church and state. This is a story about how Jesus reasserted God's garden social imaginary as the dominant narrative. He did it by linking the narrative of both the local authorities and Rome into God's narrative and not the other way around.

There are some in the wider Christian community who want no separation of church and state, and instead work towards a Christian theocracy in America. American theologian and pastor Roger Williams (1603–1683), founder of the first Baptist congregation in America, was the first person to use the phrase "separation of church and state," not Thomas Jefferson, as many believe. In Williams's mind it was the distance that was needed in order to protect the church from its misuse and corruption by political leaders:

> The church of the Jews under the Old Testament in the type and the church of the Christians under the New Testament in the antitype were both separate from the world; and when they have opened a gap in the hedge or wall of separation between the garden of the church and the wilderness of the world, God hath ever broke down the wall itself, removed the candlestick, and made his garden a wilderness.[8]

Williams understood the importance of keeping the politicians from using the church or from the church misusing politics. Politicians would like nothing more than to manipulate and motivate voting blocks of church members. The more we sideline our Christian citizenship, the better the politicians are at defining Christianity for themselves and using Christians as a means to their own ends.

Jesus was not interested in a theocracy. All too aware of the abuse of the tenants in God's garden, he warned his followers to be wary of those who would use them for political gain. Jesus, in one of his last teachings, warned his followers to avoid those who used their ministry as a means to power. He told them to watch out because those seeking political power (rebelling against the state in order to rule themselves) wanted to deceive them. Jesus told his followers that rebels and politicians just wanted power for themselves. Our historical critical eye suggests that Mark, the author of this passage, was saying a similar thing to his community. We know the text was written in the middle of a rebellion that sought to vanquish Rome from Israel and regain power of the state. Either way, the passage is clear: those who seek political power are merely another set of tenants of whom we need to be suspicious.

Jesus continued by warning his followers that these would-be rulers looked like they were on their side. They would feign unity and act as though they were the good ones. When people promised messianic delivery through war or politics they were not to be believed. Jesus told them to remember, and he repeated himself. He told them there would be people who tried to manipulate them into joining in the fight, but not to do so. His teaching was filled with end-time imagery, but it was as much about the present as it was the end time. It is, in fact, about our time. Jesus warned his followers not to be deceived or drawn into sibling rivalry. He talked about the local political powers as deceitful, and out to gain dominion: nation would constantly rise against nation because they were in a political battle of violence for the sake of themselves (Mark 13). Jesus told them, "Do not get involved," in part because Christians themselves would end up as scapegoats. Their work was the nonviolent work of making real God's social imaginary.

It is all too easy to be distracted, pulled in, and manipulated by the political powers and principalities. Christian citizenship has an agenda and it is not the same as the agenda of the state, even though our dual citizenship requires that we be a part of the wider community. Jesus reminded his disciples that their loyalty should not be to the empire or to the rebels. They were to be loyal to God's garden social imaginary of compassion and expansive familial faithfulness.

The loyalty to God was no more sharply represented than in the street theater that was Jesus's triumphal entry into Jerusalem. Many believe that Jesus entered into Jerusalem during the festival of Sukkot. People would have been wandering through the streets reciting Psalm 118: "Save us, we beseech you, O LORD . . . Save us . . . Hosanna . . . Blessed is the one who comes in the name of the LORD." As we read the passage from the Gospels, we recall that Jesus's entry mimics Zechariah 9:9, "Rejoice greatly, O daughter of Zion! Shout aloud, O daughter of Jerusalem! Lo, your King comes to you; triumphant and victorious is he humble and riding on a donkey, on a colt, the foal of a donkey" (Matt. 21:1–9; Mark 11:1–10; Luke 19:28–38; John 12:12–19).

Jesus has been very clear from the beginning of his ministry (in Mark's Gospel) that to walk the *Way* (the reoccurring theme of this Gospel) is to walk towards the Cross. This was true for Jesus's own ministry, and in the life and ministry of all those who have followed him. The principalities of the world will do whatever violence is needed to protect their power. Here in this passage the *pilgrim way* leads directly to Jerusalem and to the temple. The *Way* is tied inextricably to the faithful traditions of our Abrahamic ancestors and will unleash God's presence in the world, God's embrace of the world. Jesus's triumphal entry was the point at which walking the way *to* the Cross, arriving at the backdoor into Jerusalem, became the way *of* the Cross.

In Jerusalem the social imaginary of God's narrative took an important turn as it came into the starkest contrast with the ruling powers. Jesus's entrance rite was royal (Gen. 49:10–11 and Zech. 9:9). His was an eschatological (end time) and messianic reign that was being unfurled in real time. The stage was set and the plan was underway; the unfurling of creation and opposing order of living was at hand. Jesus stood in contradiction to the power of kings and the supporters of empire.

Jesus's entry was juxtaposed with a victory parade of Pilate who was entering the city at the front gate, on a stallion, with the might of an army behind him. Whenever there was a Jewish festival in Jerusalem, the legion occupied key points to keep the Pax Romana—with violence, if necessary. Pilate entered as an icon of the empire. His procession was about dominion and domination. It invoked a social imaginary with human demigods at the top of the hierarchy. Along with imperial power, Pilate also made a show of imperial theology. The emperor was not just viewed as the ruler of Rome, but also declared to be the son of god. It began with Augustus, who ruled from 31 BCE to 14 CE. His father was said to be the god Apollo. Inscriptions refer to him as son of god, lord, savior, and one who had "brought peace on earth." His successors continued to take on the divine titles. Pilate normally lived in Caesarea Maritima (Caesarea on the Sea), but he brought his soldiers in to reinforce the Fortress Antonia. The Roman son of god took possession of the city by means of his legion and representative.

Theologian William Stringfellow writes, "[E]xile, imprisonment, slavery, conscription; impeachment, regulation of production or sales or prices or wages or competition or credit; confiscation, surveillance, execution, war" are the hallmarks of the state. Every political leader is sullied with the countless histories of their involvement.[9] What is true today in our culture of violence was true in the age of Jesus. Military parades do not only tap into deep American emotions of patriotism and nationalism, they remind us of the power to subdue and dominate.

Jesus's followers often had a hard time with this fact; just as his followers today struggle. Think of the story from Luke 9, where Jesus and his disciples entered a Samaritan city. Things didn't go well for him there and he was rejected. Jesus continued to make his way towards Jerusalem. His disciples, though, asked, "Lord, do you want us to command fire to come down from heaven and consume them?" Jesus rebuked them. His entry is emblematic of a ministry that flatly rejected domination and violence. It also ended with a rejection of such violence.

The religious and political leaders came for Jesus in the garden—our metaphor for God's social imaginary. They found him where he and a few disciples were praying together (John 18). Recalling Genesis 2, Jesus was speaking with God in the cool of the evening, returning to the eternal beginning of the origin story. In that moment, even Jesus's own prayer ran right up to the edge of discarding his responsibility for engaging the powers. He asked that the cup might pass. In the end, he resigned himself to the prophetic engagement ahead. A few of his followers were there, asleep, waiting to be remade into a new community through the cross and resurrection. Prayer was all around, as the garden social imaginary was interrupted once more by the powers of the world.

Simon Peter drew his sword and struck the high priest's slave, cutting off his right ear; the slave's name was Malchus. Jesus said to Peter, "Put the sword into the sheath; the cup which the Father has given Me, shall I not drink it?" (John 18:11) Jesus made clear that violence was to be met with peace and nonviolence. He refused to raise an army, to defend himself, or to save himself. In his crucifixion he truly rejected any idea that there is a "redemptive" power of violence.[10]

As one who lives in Texas, I acknowledge the ambivalence some may feel towards a no-gun policy in a pro-gun world and state. However, it would be inauthentic to say that we desire to walk Jesus's narrow road of death with all of our being, for there exists in each of us a readiness to defend ourselves when threatened. It is our natural instinct, and it is our instinct to want to protect our loved ones. Like Jesus's first disciples, we may boldly proclaim, "Even though I must die with you, I will not disown you" (Matt. 26:35). But we, too, are ready to deny Him to save ourselves: "All of them deserted him and fled" (Mark 14:50). We are all willing to deny God's narrative in favor of the narrative of our rights. We will deny God's narrative in order to protect our things. We will deny the narrative to take up arms against other people. We are human and humanity uses violence in the vain hope of protection, retribution, vengeance, and as a misplaced tool to maintain freedom and peace. We are all too ready to lift our sword and defend ourselves under the guise of serving our Lord or legitimizing our right to bear arms.[11] We are just like Peter—we are human and we reject Gods' social imaginary for narratives that run contrary to it. Jesus's own words and actions remind us that God's garden social imaginary has a higher and more costly way. Jesus quite literally says that human weapons have no place in God's garden. Christian citizens are challenged by this story and we should not change it for the sake of convenience. Instead we must engage one another in order to figure out how such a narrative informs the wider discourse.

The trial of Jesus proceeded quickly the next day. The trial was not, in the end, the trial of Jesus. It was the trial of the political authorities. It is true that what happened to Jesus was exactly what Jesus had foretold about the powers and principalities. The people had to be silenced and sidelined, so the religious powers worked with the political powers to bring about Jesus's death. The Romans were as uninterested in a revolution as the Sanhedrin. They saw Jesus's death as a way to appease the people.

Jesus became a scapegoat. He heard the hailing voices worthy of an emperor. He wore a robe and a crown intended to mock him.[12] He took on all of the might of the empire in vestige, abuse, and political torture. The people and the powers condemned him to death because of his subversive teaching and actions; his healing the sick and eating with the unclean and unholy; his engagement of powers calling them to accountability; his rejection of violence for both Rome and the rebels. Stanley Hauerwas, in his exposition of Matthew's telling of the crucifixion, says:

> Jesus must be killed because Jesus is the Son of God. Jesus must be killed because Jesus has called into existence a new people who constitute a challenge to the world order based on lies and deceit. Jesus must be killed because he is a threat to all who rule in the name of safety and comfort. Jesus must be killed because we do not desire to have our deepest desires exposed. Jesus must be killed because we do not believe in a God who creates us and who would come among us after our likeness. So we have learned from Matthew.[13]

Jesus was sacrificed on the altar of violence and power. He was killed by humanity as a reenactment of ancient religious and political sacrifice. Jesus's death was the world's rejection of God's narrative that no sons and daughters shall be sacrificed. Instead of sparing him like Issac, the powers demanded his death. Jesus participated totally in the mimetic sacrifice that God wanted no part of. If that were the end of it, then we would be invested in just another community with a scapegoat theology that repeated the violence of mythic gods.

Instead, God took our violence and broke it open. Jesus was raised from the dead by God and in so doing, Girard says, God "refutes the whole principle of violence and sacrifice. God is revealed as the 'arch-scapegoat,' the completely innocent one who dies in order to give life. And his way of giving life is to overthrow the religion of scapegoating and sacrifice—which is the essence of myth."[14] God does not let the world's demand of sacrifice have the last word.

God's social imaginary reveals God to be the maker of shalom, whose action of nonviolence undoes the endless sibling rivalries and repeated sacrifices that bend humankind toward vengeance. The story of Jesus lines up with the stories of Cain and Abel, Abraham and Sarah, Moses and the Israelites in Egypt, and the prophets.

The story of Jesus as the Prince of Peace is a story that reverses all scapegoat typologies. It redeems all the unnecessary deaths of sons and daughters who have been sacrificed for the sake of violence and desire. Christ is innocent and reveals the violence and scapegoating of the world. Only in the shalom community's innocence can the Christian citizen strive for peace and reveal the violence that dominates every age.

God in Christ Jesus, the Incarnation in history, enables the Christian citizen to read the scripture and understand that inside our shared monstrosity there is a fragment of humanity in perfect communion with God. Walter Wink says we are "fleetingly human, brokenly human." We are created in the very image of the Incarnation: "Only God is human, and we are made in God's image and likeness—which is to say, we are capable of becoming human."[15] Jesus the Prince of Peace helps us glimpse our true humanity by revealing a capacity for peace-building that has been deep within us since our creation. Jesus helps us to see we have been in the garden all along. It is our brokenness and inability to accept responsibility that creates a competing narrative.

Jesus turns our inherited notions about God upside down. We were taught that God required Jesus's death, making God a mythic monster instead of seeing God's work to free us from the powers that bind us. But the theory of substitutionary atonement does not line up with the story of the sacrifice of Isaac, where God made clear that no human sacrifices were required. It does not line up with the idea that humans are modeled on the eternal Incarnation. By contrast, the gospel of peace reveals God as a victim of violence, and as a human worth saving.

The Gospel reveals that we are connected to the Incarnation itself, in our innermost parts. Though we can see that we have taken part in many systems of domination, we stand in the middle of God's narrative. Following Jesus is an embrace of the Incarnation and a rejection of the old mimetic tendencies that inevitably find their way back into religion—even Christianity. By the grace of God, the Incarnation is our hope and our potential. The world is truly turned upside down by the resurrection of God in Christ Jesus.

God is interested in a continuing narrative of peacemaking and community-building. Mary says yes to this work and makes the uniqueness of God in Christ Jesus manifest. Jesus himself, being found in human form, does not inaugurate an institutional church but rather a community of shalom that has been part of the story since the foundations of creation were set. Christ and his body are the actual icon of our realized humanness. His body is also the image of the community at work. Where he goes, what he does, who he meets, and what he says are ways the community of shalom works in the world around us. They are models for Christian citizenship that is prophetically engaged in the world and nation around us. It is the work of the Christian citizen to own up to our part in this system and to resist powers, authorities, and the violence they beget in this world.

Christ chose to honor his place in this narrative of peace. Christ, whose equality with God was already established, bridged the gap between heaven and earth, between God and humanity (Phil. 2:5–11). Christ's invitation, preaching, and his sacrificial death inaugurated a peace that passes all understanding, giving us the possibility for peace in our own lives (Phil. 4:7). Through our own participation in God's great gift of death and then resurrection, we find peace. We find peace with ourselves, with others, our enemies, and with the God who remains so different from us.[16] Jesus puts flesh on this vision of the divine community. Jesus calls us to go. We are God's messengers of this kingdom of peace. Isaiah prophesizes:

> The wolf shall live with the lamb, the leopard shall lie down with the kid, the calf and the lion and the fatling together, and a little child shall lead them. The cow and the bear shall graze, their young shall lie down together; and the lion shall eat straw like the ox. The nursing child shall play over the hole of the asp, and the weaned child shall put its hand on the adder's den. They will not hurt or destroy on all my holy mountain; for the earth will be full of the knowledge of the LORD as the waters cover the sea.
>
> Isaiah 11:6–9

This kind of shalom is possible because God in Christ Jesus becomes a victim. It is true that Jesus gave himself over to the authorities. He willingly, and with full knowledge of what humans do to prophets, carried the cross to his end. Upon a dung heap he would be despised and crucified. All the powers of humanity and all the evil in the world met him there on Golgatha. He died on behalf of and in place of all humanity. He became a victim of the systems of power and dominion in this world. We must be clear: Jesus's willingness as "the heir of all things" (Heb. 1:2) was a willingness to allow a murderous and unjust court of powers, principalities, and religious authorities to have complete power over him. In this way even his willingness to sacrifice himself does not undo the story of Abraham and Isaac or the parable of the vineyard in Luke 20:9–19 wherein the tenants kill the landowner's son. The idea that Jesus willingly goes to the slaughter, takes our place, and that God raises him from the dead in no way diminishes his victimhood.[17] In so doing Christ joins in solidarity with all victims. There is no victory without victimization by the powers that be. Jesus's willingness to participate cannot lessen his full sacrifice and his complete death. Jesus's final laying of the foundation stone of the peaceable kingdom was in his willingness to die for the righteous and the unrighteous alike, and to be raised for the righteous and unrighteous alike

(Matt. 5:45). This is much more than the notion that life is sacred. What separates Christianity from religion is that Christ gives himself over for the sake of the criminals, enemies, hatemongers, violence-makers, and victimizers, too.

As Christians who follow this Christ, we not only give ourselves over to the other, but we are also responsible for the sacredness of life that belongs to our neighbor and enemy alike. To divide the world into groups of people whose lives are expendable and those whose lives are sacred is to advocate for communal action contrary to the will and actions of God in Christ Jesus. God imagines a different kind of faith community altogether. In the great tradition of the Sinai prophets over and against a temple-centric faith engaged in nation-building, Jesus initiated a community grounded in the historic community of Abraham and Sarah, and in the Creation narrative itself. While creation was brought forth out of nothing (*ex nihilo*), the shalom community arouses the memory of Edenic fellowship among its members. The memory of Eden is the icon of the Incarnation—a longing for such harmony is found in each human being by their very nature as a creature of God.

Chapter Fifteen

The State's Accountability to God

The Christian gospel is more than a transcendent reality, more than "going to heaven when I die, to shout salvation as I fly." It is also an immanent reality—a powerful liberating presence among the poor right now in their midst, "building them up where they are torn down and propping them up on every leaning side." The gospel is found wherever poor people struggle for justice, fighting for their right to life, liberty, and the pursuit of happiness.
—James Cone[1]

Mark's Gospel ends with the disciples gathering together and then going out. God's resurrection of Jesus is the great exclamation point in God's narrative. The undoing of the powers, the resetting of the garden social imaginary, and the establishment of this narrative as *the* narrative is done. The Cross has had the last word. Death met Jesus in the tomb and lost the battle. A renewed narrative is carried forward in the lives of those who follow Jesus. Christian citizenship is an expression of this victory, enveloped by the imagery of the Cross. A Christian citizen rejects the story of empire in order to honor the prophetic legacy of Christ's victory against the colonizing powers.

We are to engage and work towards God's social imaginary by being blessings of shalom and creating communities of shalom. There is depth and complexity to this work. The church's vocation is found in honoring this overarching call; the same is true for our Christian citizenship.

Christian citizens are invited to disrupt the notion that the only stories about us that matter are the ones we write ourselves. To explain this further: a fishing metaphor.

The first disciples Jesus encountered beside the Sea of Galilee were invited to be "fishers of people." This was not a general invitation to follow. It was not a mere pun. The church's unconscious habit of reading scripture as legitimation for a vast institution has used these call stories about bringing people to Jesus for the sake of church growth. In this way, we shoehorn the fractured narratives of modernism into the Gospel by focusing on how church members should bring other people to church where they can meet Jesus. Within the context of God's social imaginary, a different meaning is revealed in these stories.

"Fishers of people" create the shalom community. By calling his disciples to become fishers of men, Jesus harkened back to the Old Testament, and the patriarchs and matriarchs of God who made a community for all people.[2] The first mention of fishing is in the prophecy of Jeremiah:

> I am now sending for many fishermen, says the Lord, and they shall catch them; and afterward I will send for many hunters, and they shall hunt them from every mountain and every hill, and out of the clefts of the rocks.
>
> Jeremiah 16:16

Jeremiah reminded the people of Israel to be citizens who bless their community with shalom. He called them to care of the poor and the least and the lost. He asserted that the blood of the innocent poor was on Israel's hands (Jer. 2:35). Through Jeremiah, God declared the leaders of God's people to be poor shepherds, scattering the people rather than gathering them (Jer. 23:1–6). God pledged to overturn Israel because it had forgotten itself, its work, and its God (Jer. 18:15; 30:14). As a consequence, God would gather God's people anew and frustrate those who preyed on the poor. For Jeremiah, fishing was about justice for the poor. The image of "fishing for people" also harkened back to the prophesies of Amos (4:2). Through Amos, God declared that those who forget the needy and live upon their backs would be taken away by fishhooks. Again, in Habakkuk

(1:13–16), God caught the people up in God's dragnet. Ezekiel prophesied that the people were the fish and would be gathered in (29:3b–4).

Jesus's ministry was linked to the prophets who lived in communities that rejected their responsibility for the least and lost. Jesus's fishing metaphor connected discipleship, apostleship, and Christian citizenship to the work of prophecy in a foreign land. Using the Hebrew scripture and the language of prophets, Jesus declared that all were citizens in God's unfolding reign of peace (Matt. 23:37–39). This gathering included the rich and the poor, the found and the lost. All people would be gathered into a community of peace; exploitation, injustice, and violence of any sort were anathema. In this community, neither the poor nor the rich would be scapegoats. God's people would be gathered in like fish caught in a dragnet. Jesus's message was consistent with the scriptural narrative from Abraham and Sarah to Mary. Jesus called these fishermen from the Sea of Galilee to be part of a different community doing a different kind of work. Their way of their life was to be different from the world of violence that surrounded them. They were invited to join Jesus in his work of prophesizing shalom. In the face of oppressive domination by both the local authorities and Rome, Jesus imagined a society where captives were free, the blind could see, and the oppressed were unbound. God's blessing was proclaimed, all were to be gathered in, and a new order of living was to be established (Luke 4:16–19).

This story locates our participation in God's story outside of social and governmental engagement. Our faith ancestors' story of calling into vocation links the prophetic work of citizenship with the whole narrative arc of God's communal engagement in the world. There are plenty of people out there who suggest this narrative only pertains to Christians, or American Christians. This is another way the nation's story about citizenship privatizes gospel work, restraining the church to the sanctuary and limiting religious obligation to Sunday morning.

In Matthew 13, Jesus returned to fishing images when he said, "The kingdom of heaven is like a net that was thrown into the sea and caught fish of every kind" (13:47). This parable was the last in a long series about the kingdom of peace. Robert Farrar Capon uses this parable to speak eschatologically about the kingdom at the end of the age. [3] While I concur with Capon's interpretation, I want to broaden it to fit a wider discussion of our work as Christian citizens. I think Jesus was also speaking of the reign that is at hand in this world. We are peace builders, because followers of Jesus are doing work in this world that will remain at the end of the age. Jesus used the dragnet as a metaphor for this peace-making enterprise. The community the apostles built was to be universal and catholic—everyone was included.

Dragnets gather in everything because they dredge the sea floor. They capture wood and plants as well as fish. They capture inedible fish as well as edible ones. The community of peace that Jesus invites in this world is identically indiscriminate. God makes a community that connects—or networks—all kinds of people. The narrative is not only about Christians. It includes ecumenical and interfaith partners. There is no isolation in a dragnet.

We normally turn the dragnet imagery into a parable about heaven and its other-worldly implications, but that spiritualizes and privatizes the story. God's dragnet is bigger than heaven. It is also bigger than a story about peaceful relationships with other human beings, though that is included. God is calling us to a bigger vision of the Christian citizen's work.

Many people deny our responsibility to engage in the care of creation. They say that our scripture does not say anything about such work. Such a reading of scripture denies and limits God's garden social imaginary. We can strive to keep this work a private spiritual affair, but that is like trying to fit a square peg in a round hole. God creates a garden where people are placed. It is God's garden and we are placed there to partner with God in creating community. The garden provides food and shelter. Certainly, God's creation has social implications regarding the poor, which means the garden imaginary is about economics, and economics is not simply about money, but has to do with the wider creation in which we live.

The net that Jesus used when talking about the work of the people is a kingdom-net that not only contained fish, good and bad; it also contained everything: the weeds, the detritus of dysfunctional relationships and human brokenness, the debris of daily life lived in service to the masters of economies and political power mongers. The community of shalom, our dragnet, "touches everything in the world: not just souls, but bodies, and not just people, but all things, animal, vegetable, and mineral."[4] God in Christ Jesus is in this world gathering into the community of shalom the whole of creation, not just human beings. As the Book of Revelation indicates, all of creation is drawn to God in Christ—not just people. As God in Christ was lifted up on the Cross, the great crossroads of community was bridged—heaven with earth, humanity with God. All was drawn to God's self (John 12:32). This means that Christian citizenship that avoids responsibility for all of the elements of creation is not fully participating in the great vision God has for the garden.

Christian citizens advocate radical change for the institutions that enforce order. Jesus's own experience demonstrates that building the kingdom of shalom requires direct confrontation with the powers of this world. Jesus, like his faith ancestors Abraham, Moses, the prophets, and others, took on the powers that preyed on humanity. Christian citizens must take on edifices of religion when they abuse their power. Christian citizens must take on the powers of state when it does the same. Jesus illustrated in his own life and action that citizenship is not only an internal ministry that takes place behind the walls of religious separation. All who followed him suffered for their own messianic vocation. Across all the ages, when those who follow Jesus engage in the prophetic work of Christ, the powers will react. Christian theologians have long understood that a person in the middle of God's narrative experiences more suffering than triumph. "Take up your cross and follow" is no mere campaign slogan. It means that Christian citizenship, when done well, may indeed be about enduring losses worthy of Christ's.

We must admit that a Christianity protected by the boundaries of congregational life and ministry is comfortable. We can sing sweet songs of our faith and our salvation. But when we settle for this, we deceive ourselves. We are called to leave places of comfort that are under the watchful eye of the religious authorities. We are to practice our life, work, and our citizenship in the middle of God's narrative. There will be political consequences of this work. There were very real political consequences for the

work of Abraham, Moses, and the prophets. There were political consequences for Jesus, his first disciples, and the first generations of followers.
So radical was their prophecy against the state, that the first generation of
theologians would have found the theology of a state theocracy that was
proclaimed by later generations heretical. The first Christian theologians
looked upon the empire with "indifference and its rulers with contempt,"
writes historian Arthur Herman in *The Cave and the Light*.[5] It was Lucius
Caecilius Lactantius (b. 240 CE) and Eusebius (b. 216 CE) from Caesarea
in Syria who assimilated Christianity into the philosophy of the empire.

The state had been the most despotic persecutor of Christ and his
followers for hundreds of years. Rome's worship of gods and demigods,
and the use of these cults to legitimize imperial rule, were heresy to the
first Christians. Herman writes, "To Origen [one of the first Christian
theologians (b. 184 CE)] and his generation, the idea that Christians had
anything to gain, spiritual or materially, by supporting Rome's governing
institutions would have seemed absurd."[6] Another first-generation theologian, Tertullian (b. 155 CE), wrote, "I owe no allegiance to any forum,
army or Senate. . . . All secular powers and dignities are not merely alien
from, but hostile to God."[7] This is the earliest testimony of the church
about how Christian citizenship was to view the governing powers and
principalities of the world. Many look upon the victory at the Milvian
Bridge by Constantine as a victory for the church. Eusebius and others
certainly did. The Roman emperors Constantine I and Maxentius met
for battle at the Milvian Bridge on October 28, 312, a central cross-
ing point over the Tiber. Maxentius drowned and Constantine was
victorious, setting him on a path to the throne as the sole ruler of the
empire. Eusebius of Caesarea used the moment to interpret a vision that
Constantine had prior to the battle that caused him to have the soldiers
paint a Chi-Rho on their shields. The two theologians used the vision
to craft a story about how God delivered the battle into Constantine's
hands. But was it a victory? Or was it the moment when the state consumed the Christian movement and disempowered it forever, uniting it
with state violence? God's shalom does not look much like the heroic
and oppressive Pax Romana of Constantine, or any other power for that

matter. This is something that the persecuted Christians like Tertullian and Origen knew and left as a legacy in their writings. It took only one hundred years for Christianity to be enveloped by the same empire that crucified Christ. While the Christians were spared in the following years, many others were not. In this way Christianity, as it made its way into the hierarchy of the empire, became complicit with violence for the sake of the Pax Romana.

Jesus's very first act of calling was an invitation to "leave" places of comfort amidst the prevailing social and economic orders in order to follow. Following included fishing for people and using a dragnet to do so. Jesus imagined his disciples reinterpreting the prophetic work of jubilee for their time. Jubilee was when the poor were released from debt and the fields rested. It was the festival that Jesus referenced in the synagogue at Nazareth as a time for the healing of the sick (Lev. 25 and Luke 4). Jesus imagined an enacted Jubilee festival that had a real impact on people, society, and the earth. His second invitation reimagined death. Jesus's second call articulated the political consequences of prophetic engagement practice (Mark 8:34). The politics of the strange land, corrupted by powers that no longer resemble the garden, would bring about cruciform consequences for anyone who followed.[8]

Christian citizens take up their crosses and follow. We do this by declaring peace in a world of violence; members of Christ's community of peace lose their lives. The community of shalom is a community that is willing to lose. This is most clearly articulated in the three sayings of Jesus about "the way." Jesus said, "For those who want to save their life will lose it" (Mark 8:35); "Whoever wants to be first must be last of all and servant of all" (Mark 9:35); and, "Whoever wishes to become great among you must be your servant" (Mark 10:43). The victory of the Cross is no worldly victory; it is complete loss. The Christian citizen accepts this loss as "our way." It may look like the powers and authorities have won, but Christians proclaim that "Jesus's nonviolent power has actually begun to unravel their rule of domination."[9] As Paul wrote to the Colossians, "He disarmed the rulers and authorities and made a public example of them, triumphing over them in it" (Col. 2:15). The community of shalom continues as new

Christian citizens take up their own understanding of this mission, and walk out into Easter morning.

The first apostles ventured out declaring that God had undone the religion of vengeance, just as God did between Ananias and Paul. They went from Jerusalem and Galilee to Samaria, Caesarea, Antioch, Laodicea Cyprus, Perga, and Pisidian Antioch, Tiberias, Caesarea Philippi, Damascus, Tarsus, Troas, Thessalonica, Beroea, Pireaus, Athens, Corinth, Ephesus, Miletus, Cnidus, and Rodhos. They went to Crete and Sicily and Rome. In each place we see footprints of the movement of peace, and the creation of multiple types of Christian communities. These diverse communities engaged with the powers and principalities of every nation as Christian citizens made their case for a different world in people's homes and in the courts of emperors.

Paul certainly did. We see the first generation of Christian citizenship captured in Romans 13. Paul writes that the Christian citizen is a dual citizen. We are subject to governing authorities. Paul says that the authorities are given power by the way God has given freedom to the world. Similar to Jesus's reminder to Pilate that he has no power but what is given, Paul says the powers are part of the creation. They can be used for good or ill (Rom. 13:1). In his 1939 essay *The Church and State,* Karl Barth argues that Paul is advocating an approach to common government that respects Jesus Christ in order to make the state better.[10] We breathe life into the image of the garden through our work of shared governance. We often use elections as proxies for God's will—at least when our chosen candidate has proven victorious. But Paul did not think of the emperor as God's hand-picked appointee. Paul is merely pointing out what the scripture said: power is part of a free creation.

In the next verse Paul suggests that our work is not to resist authority. When we do, we incur judgment. Paul then says that if the authorities act justly, then we should act within the good; but if we act against injustice, we will ensure the state's wrath. Ultimately, we hope that the state will do more good than bad. But, whatever the state does, it uses the sword. "Be afraid, very afraid," Paul warns (Rom. 13:2–5).

Repeating Jesus's sayings about taxes, Paul places our duty within the state to do what the state asks. If revenue is due, then we are to honor our social agreement and pay it. We are not to build up debt with the state or others (Rom. 13:6–7). Then Paul reminds his readers that they are part of God's social imaginary. He tells them they are to love and follow the commandment to love. They are to live out the Ten Commandments from Sinai. They may live in Rome, but as Christians they are a dual citizen. Their Christian citizenship is first because they are part of God's reign (Rom. 13:6–10).

As Christian citizens, we are to be awake because we have accepted our place in God's story. We must see things differently. We have to put away the works of darkness, powers, and principalities and take on the work of light. We are to live honorably and live virtuously (Rom. 13:11–13). We are to live our citizenship by creating a just society within our smaller communities, and we are to make society just through our prophetic engagement with the authorities.

Many Christians have read this passage and come up with a completely different understanding of Romans 13. For them, Romans 13 mandates that we follow the law and obey the God-chosen powers of this world. Across history, people have used Romans 13 to support their political bias.[11] In 1933, on the eve of the rise of Nazi Germany, Joachim Hossenfelder preached a sermon at Berlin's Kaiser Wilhelm Memorial Church. He used the words of Romans 13 to suggest that the German citizen should obey the authority of the state. This text was used repeatedly to create support among Christians for the Third Reich. The church's authority to read scripture was morphed into using the church to support politics, law, and the domination of humanity by a governing power.[12] We must remember that it wasn't that the government itself used the passage to justify their power; it was the church that used Romans 13 to justify its support of the government and its rule of law. It is all too easy to suggest that the use of the passage was a Nazi ploy. That is far from true. Good German Protestants used Romans to justify their support for the unjust rule of the Nazis.[13]

There are two important ways in which Christians have used Romans 13 in American history. During the American Revolution, loyalists in the new colonies (including Samuel Seabury of my own tradition) used Romans 13 to suggest that the rule of England should prevail and that the revolutionary fervor of the patriots was immoral. Romans 13 was trotted out again to counter the arguments of the abolitionists. American Christians used Romans 13 to justify the ownership of people.

Romans 13 has justified all manner of human domination and violence by the empire and state all in the name of God. This text shows up so reliably as a defense for bad government that demeans humanity and supports dominion and violence, that it can almost be seen as a canary in a coal mine. If it is being used—and especially when Christians are doing so—it is likely being deployed to excuse a nation's vices.

Karl Barth opposed any reading of Romans 13 that gave a blank slate to the state. For him, such a reading was unmoored from Christian theology. It favored natural theology to such an extent that its proponents had lost the mind of Christ. If Romans 13 is disconnected from the garden social imaginary and the Cross of Christ, it has no purpose in the great narrative arc of God's community. Barth believed the church had a responsibility to hold the state accountable to the rule of love, and that this responsibility became more urgent as the state moved away from the mind of Christ.[14] Barth did not advocate indiscriminate support of the state. The state was subject to the same narrative framework held within the Christian narrative.[15] Contemporary theologian Stanley Hauerwas likes to remind us that we need to read Romans 13 only after reading Romans 12, where Paul says that if we are to be Christian citizens, we are to be siblings first. We are to place our whole selves into this work as beings in relationship to God and to each other. If we choose to worship God, then our work of citizenship in the world is to be formed as worship itself (Rom. 12:1–2). We are not to be "conformed" to the world and its powers and principalities. In other words, the narrative of these institutions neither dictates nor takes precedence over the urgency of God's garden narrative. Our minds and our wills are to be conformed to God's garden social imaginary. In the garden we find the grace that makes us one in relationship to God and neighbor. We live in a new garden that is birthed from the dung heap of Golgotha. God in Christ Jesus is buried in the ground as the first seed of the new garden, replanted in the world. This is what Paul means when he is given grace by God (Rom. 12:3a).

Paul calls us to see that we are one body made up of many members. We are different and we have different work. God in Christ makes us one through the work of the Cross, just as God the creator formed us as one in the garden. God raised Christ after raising Israel, and will raise us on the last day. Yes, we are different, but all our gifts work together for one garden society. These gifts are given to everyone regardless of their knowledge of God. Everyone is a member of the garden society by virtue of their creation. Christ's mission is to redeem the whole world. In this way, the body is proportional. The more we live within the narrative of God, the more our gifts are used for the garden social imaginary. Paul writes, "We have gifts that differ according to the grace given to us: prophecy, in proportion to faith; ministry, in ministering; the teacher, in teaching; the exhorter, in exhortation; the giver, in generosity; the leader, in diligence; the compassionate, in cheerfulness" (Rom. 12:6).

Paul says, "Let love be genuine; hate what is evil, hold fast to what is good; love one another with mutual affection; outdo one another in showing honor. Do not lag in zeal, be ardent in spirit, serve the Lord" (Rom. 12:7–12). He continues by saying that we are to support those close to us, the poor, those who are strangers. We are to be patient when our actions bring about suffering or when we are suffering with others. We are to, "Bless those who persecute you; bless and do not curse them" (Rom. 12:12–14).

We express our Christian citizenship by living in harmony. We are to live the life of Christian virtue: temperance, prudence, courage, and justice. Moreover, we are to not repay evil for evil. We are to live a life of shalom—of peace. We are to live within creation and with our neighbors in a peaceable kingdom. This is the garden social imagery brought into the frame of Christ's gospel.

There are times when it is difficult to live peaceably. Paul reminds us that we are not to avenge ourselves but we are to be like Christ and the prophets. If we have enemies who are hungry, then we are to feed them.

If our enemies are thirsty, we are to give them something to drink. This is a reminder that violence is always rooted in mimetic desire. To fill the hungry with good things is to deal with the desire that so often leads to violence. Paul also says that to repay violence with peaceful acts is judgment itself. We are to overcome evil with good (Rom. 12:19–21).

Hauerwas challenges us, and calls Americans out on their blatant misuse of Romans 12 and 13. He says we read Romans 13 as an unchallenged support of the government while we read Romans 12 as a private rule of life. Americans forget that they are Christians before they are American citizens. Recovering our own place in God's narrative means that we can no longer sacralize our own American democratic presuppositions about government. Romans 12 does not only apply to the Christian citizen, it is the measure by which we understand the kind of just government we can support. We cannot read Romans 13 without first applying the criteria we find in Romans 12 to the empire.[16]

In this way, we see what a just empire that deserves our support looks like. Our governments must also read, mark, and digest Romans 12. Paul says that our governments must remember the whole of the citizenry. They are to reject the mimetic desire that leads to violence and scapegoating, rather than conforming to the distorted and fractured world (Rom. 12:1–3a). We are called to see the importance of all people and their gifts for the good of the whole. Governments are called to see all citizens as having a role in the society. Everyone is a member of the garden society by virtue of their creation. As the state embodies the garden social imaginary, it can see that (Rom. 12:3–6). The state is to build its government on love and to reject evil. The country is to focus and work towards the good, honoring all people inside and outside of its boundaries. Though it is hard work, the just state will not flag at difficult challenges (Rom. 12:7–12). Governments are to bring all people close, work on behalf of and with the poor, and be hospitable to the stranger. We are to care for the suffering as a nation, and reject persecution in all forms. The state is to bless instead of curse, seek peace within and beyond its borders, and reject violence and consumption as the first course of action (Rom. 12:13–18). This will not always be possible, but the challenge for the state is to look first for hunger and thirst and offer help, rather than to retaliate with violence. What is true for the high road of Christian blessing is to be true for the road of the nation itself. The nation is to repay violence with peaceful acts, for this will be judgment itself. We are to overcome evil with good (Rom. 12:19–21). These are the characteristics of the just empire. As the disciples said to Jesus, "This teaching is difficult; who can accept it?" (John 6:60).

When the empire is unjust and rejects the image of God's garden, there is work to do. As Christian citizens we undertake that work with Romans 12 and 13 in mind. God's narrative of the garden social imaginary does not change in the midst of difficult times or even war. The belief that God's call to a just community can be suspended or marginalized has plagued American Christianity for far too long. In our humanness we forget the proper order of things. We are too easily persuaded to believe the maxim of our particular political age that Christianity is a private affair. All too often Christians are forced to work within the landscape of politics instead of the other way around. We are convinced that we have to shoehorn our Christianity into the world of American politics; this kind of compromise is not necessary or fruitful.

Martin Luther King Jr. imagined what Paul would say to Americans in his sermon "Paul's Letter to American Christians":

> Ye are a colony of heaven. This means that although you live in the colony of time, your ultimate allegiance is to the empire of eternity. You have a dual citizenry. You live both in time and eternity; both in heaven and earth. Therefore, your ultimate allegiance is not to the government, not to the state, not to nation, not to any man-made institution. The Christian owes his ultimate allegiance to God, and if any earthly institution conflicts with God's will, it is your Christian duty to take a stand against it. You must never allow the transitory evanescent demands of man-made institutions to take precedence over the eternal demands of the Almighty God.[17]

Chapter Sixteen

A Tabling Christian Citizenship

From Moses to Jesus, the Bible tells us that those who fought for justice—those who spoke truth to power, those who refused to accept that injustice and inequality had to exist and that there was no better way—always found themselves hated, hounded, and heaped upon with false accusations simply because they believed in the necessity of speaking and working for the cause of righteousness and building a more just community. This lack of majority support is why the just must live by faith and must know exactly who we are.

—William J. Barber II[1]

Episcopalians are proud of our Anglican legacy in supporting the creation of the first English Bible translated by John Wycliffe in the fifteenth century and then William Tyndale in the sixteenth century. People love the King James Bible. It has had a long shelf life. As they were translating it, the scholars dealt with numerous issues. One was that King James was adamant that no matter how the rest was translated he didn't want his people to get the idea that there was a godly admonition towards kings or an empowerment of the people to take corrective action when monarchs misbehaved. In James's eyes, previous versions were fraught with "seditious . . . dangerous, and trayterous" translation. I imagine you were not even allowed to bring up the Geneva Bible in his presence because it was so radical. It included the suggestion that it was okay to overthrow a despotic ruler if they were unjust. King James wanted to make sure that the people knew they were to "resist not" their king and ruler.

The King James translation of the Bible, and others like it, support "monarchical absolutism" and "submission,"[2] as though Jesus invites us to submit based upon terms set by the government. Walter Wink argues that such a revisionist gloss on Jesus's words does not capture the whole picture.

Jesus is inviting his followers to define their secular politics by their citizenship in the reign of God. The powers of this world cannot tell us what the Christian story is and we needn't accept the secularist maxim that we have no story until we choose theirs. Jesus invites us to transcend the narrative of this world with a different narrative. We are to engage the world by rising above passive submission or violence. We are invited to find a third way. Wink reveals that the correct translation (without the king's fingerprints all over it) reads: "Do not repay evil for evil" and "Don't react violently against the one who is evil" (Rom. 12:17; 1 Thess. 5:15; 1 Pet. 3:9 and Matt. 5:39a). We are to take a stand against ἀντιστῆναι, *antistēnai,* evil and injustice (Eph. 6:13).[3]

Wink suggests that a good translation of the scriptures helps us see Jesus inviting the citizen of God's reign to engage the powers and principalities of this world just as he did. If we act out the instructions in the passage we often describe as "turn the other cheek," we see that we are to step into the swing of the abuser (Matt 5:39; Luke 6:29). This stops the master from giving a backhand that asserts dominance and requires a punch with a fist that implies equal human status. The next verse says if we are in debt, we should give our clothes away, which rejects the dominance of those who lend at high rates. For a debtor to be left naked brought shame on the creditor (Matt. 5:40; Luke 6:30). Walking the extra mile had a direct connection between the *ochlos* and the military. The military could require the occupied to carry their pack, but only for a certain distance. To go an extra mile was to flip the burden to the soldier because the person was breaking the law. Walking the extra mile was an engagement of the colonial powers (Matt. 5:41).[4]

We are used to reading the Bible by ourselves. We believe that our common-sense reason, our pragmatism, enables us to read the Bible alone. The Bible does not stand alone in a corrupt society that worships the god of civil religion with a biblical literacy gleaned from the dim memory of Sunday school class. It is the church's responsibility as a whole to engage in biblical interpretation. Despite people believing they have a right to do this and that, individuals do not interpret scripture for themselves. The Reformation doctrine of *sola scriptura*, combined with the powers and principalities' ability to affect translation and the Western secular frame, and our insistent deferral to the common person's common sense is challenged by God's narrative as understood by the church. Following Stanley Hauerwas, I believe in a community that is under authority; such authorities within the ecclesiastical tradition must be listened to, if we are to mine the depths of scripture and invoke God's social imaginary and engage the powers and principalities of this world.[5]

It may appear that I am rejecting the individual's right to tell me what they think scripture is saying. I am in some way, but I am so suspicious of the interpretation formed by powers of this world that I no longer trust it. For me, God's call to Christian citizenship has priority over the demands of order. The more God's call challenges my preconceived notions about my place in God's narrative and the narratives given to me by the secular society the better. Far too many Christians, possessed by the political powers, parties, and their own preferences, rush off to fight the good fight as pawns of the culture rather than reading scripture in the context of the church to be challenged by the diversity of voices from that history, alternative perspectives within the church community, and even from those that hail from different traditions. Before we engage with our culture, we must re-engage our own sacred texts and rely upon the wealth of witnesses surrounding us.

We also must rethink our context. While it is true that many people in our present day feel powerless, the idea that ours is a unique time in the history of the world robs God's narrative of the persistent, quotidian way it has grappled with the powers of the world from the beginning.

Our present political context is no more or no less dangerous than all the moments that have come before it in both scripture and in our history.[6]

While there is a certain "natural theology" to the discourse of politics, believing that politics has a self-sufficient integrity that can stand without the intervention of the Gospel is a subtle and dangerous idea. Deprived of conversation with the Christ, political systems begin to act as though they themselves are revelatory of the Gospel and the reflection of God's character. This manifests in the political utopianism that buoys the hopes of many a liberal or conservative who trust that our political systems can "make progress" and save us, and that such saving can come without faith, the community of faith, and the garden social imaginary. We should be troubled that political systems seek such salvation without any interest in the revelation of Jesus Christ.[7]

The truth is that our laws, natural and political, along with our civil religion, do not reveal God as the creator of the garden social imaginary. Neither do these natural laws express the deep theology of the Trinity or God in Christ Jesus and the work of solidarity and reconciliation. They do not speak of humanity's inability to break free of sibling rivalry, mimetic desire, or the violence that accompanies our brokenness.[8] There is no revelation to be found in the founder's common-sense reason, just as there is none in Ralph Waldo Emerson's culture of creative democracy based upon American philosopher John Dewey's pragmatism, the chief intellectual inheritors and political philosophers of America's "coming to age" story.[9] This bankruptcy of revelation caused Cornel West to say, "Revolutionary Christian perspective and praxis must remain anchored in the prophetic Christian tradition."[10] He is quick to add that such an anchoring requires attentiveness to the experience of African Americans and other minorities within the Christian culture of America.

Karl Barth reminds us that

> . . . the so-called exact sciences built on empirical observation and investigation on the one side and mathematical logic on the other, are constituted in virtue of the knowability and in the knowledge of laws . . . these formulae which have partial and formal validity within the

world as descriptions of relative necessities, and which really count, and may be counted upon, when they are defined in this way.[11]

We must remind ourselves that such laws and natural revelations can undergird important breakthroughs of knowledge and technology, but these breakthroughs remain bound up with human fallenness, and are often seconded to the powers of dominion. The insights of natural theology are too easily co-opted by the ruling political party to buttress their power.

Before we look at the political context we must be steeped in God's narrative and garden social imaginary so that we have clarity about the higher narrative in which we participate. Then we must treat the world as if God is active within it—as if God genuinely cares for it. Such a vision helps us to see those who (Christian or not) may be working to furthering God's interest in the least and the lost in our world. Armed with our unique knowledge of God's character, we can begin to look for partners in the political sphere that are using a multiple of ideological approaches to the problems of our context. Beginning with our tribalisms rather than what we know about God through Jesus is a rejection of God's continuing work in creation and a flat refusal to God's co-creative invitation into the garden narrative.[12]

We must also reject the enticing message of political candidates that suggest utilitarian reasons for voting for this or that candidate/law when there are voices from our own tradition prophetically calling out from God's narrative saying not to do so. The various and embarrassingly compromised Christian theologies of modernity have made apathetic, non-participatory Christian citizens, or Christian citizens who have abandoned God's garden imaginary for the sake of political expediency. In both cases such "Christian realism" precludes a Christian politics rooted in Sinai's compassion and familial faithfulness. Stanley Hauerwas says, "Christians in America have played this game for so long now and with so many half-baked strategies that they can no longer differentiate between America and God, something scripture calls *idolatry*."[13]

Jesus invites the Christian citizen to reject politics as usual. Our deepened understanding of scripture enables us to see the difference between

America's version of God and the God we receive through the narrative of the garden. Acknowledging that our political systems of so-called natural laws and pragmatic philosophies contain no divine revelation and that we have been duped into believing they do through the shuffles and slights of hand of modern theologies like "Christian realism," gives us the necessary distance to engage the public square afresh. We have interrogated our understanding of scripture and carefully considered the source of our ideas about Christian participation in politics. We have screwed up enough courage to reject the lens forced on us by America's civil religion with its common-sense reason. What comes next?

The first thing I am going to say is that partisan pontificating from the pulpit is not the way to engage the public square afresh. While better engagement with God's social imaginary as it comes to us in scripture will assuredly reinvigorate Christian homiletics, partisan preaching—taking sides—is not our business. First, it doesn't do any good. In their book *American Grace* Putnam and Campbell reveal that fifteen minutes of preaching on Christian behavior and neighborliness once a week doesn't change very much about people's behavior. They argue that sermons don't impact social and political engagement or neighborliness. Relationships do.[14]

Before we move on to the relationship part of our work, let me pause for one more word about preaching. It is against the law for a preacher to promote particular candidates. Many preachers make their preferences clear anyway. When a preacher declares that one or the other political party, or the political system itself, is to be trusted and that our Christian duty extends no further than pulling the right lever or punching the right button in the voting booth, they forget that, from the vantage point of God's garden social imaginary, the entire edifice of modern democracy legitimizes the violence of the powers and principalities. When we make partisan politics the subject of our preaching, in subtle or not so subtle ways, and give the message that one party or the other is right, we inadvertently promote the fiction that rightly-ordered politics can redeem us. Politics does not save us. It is always a golden calf.

Preaching aside, politics is always making its influence felt in local congregations. Religious communities are often sorted politically. Because of this it is easy for church to become a kind of "echo chamber" for one-sided political half-truths.[15] Christian citizens need to view their conversations with each other as conversation with peers, rather than an exercise in clumsy solidarity, or an overworked talking past each other. If local churches can engage the Bible with the church's witness at hand, and have conversations in smaller groups about our political participation, the result will be a more coherent articulation of Christian citizenship and a better engagement by Christian citizens in the public square.

Friendships, and the bonds within small communities and groups, have a tremendous impact for good when it comes to ministry. The perspectives of fellow members in our community are so effectual that atheists attached to a congregation and its social life through marriage who participate with their spouse are more likely to serve the poor and needy. Not only that, but that atheist is more likely to do good works on behalf of others than the most earnest believer who prays alone.[16] Community life is essential when it comes to caring and neighborliness, and it is essential if we are to engage as Christian citizens in the work of politics. A person who feels like they belong will be a better and more engaged Christian citizen by virtue of their connections with others.

It is also interesting that theological and denominational differences do not affect neighborliness or caring for others as much as the priorities of the people we are in relationship with. Interaction, study, and service are all interconnected. In fact, you don't have to preach at all on the topic for these to have the same positive affect upon the congregation and the wider community.[17] What this all means is that the formation of Christian citizens through relationship building matters more than leadership from the pulpit. Having open dialogue and small groups that engage strong biblical and thoughtful theology on citizenship will have a greater impact than all the preaching on politics in the world. This requires leaders in congregations to think carefully about the leaders of these groups, the Bible texts used in the study, and the kinds of extra-biblical sources. Such intra-congregational work is enough. What we know from neighborliness studies is that engagement outside the congregation with fellow members, friends, and relations has the greatest impact. If we want to influence Christian engagement in the public square, it is enough to gather together in a church with like-minded people and talk about politics. Just as we seek to get people out of the building to do the ministry of neighborliness, we need to think of political engagement by Christians in the same way. We have to break out of our echo chamber.

Jon Meacham's book *Soul of America* is a great place to start thinking about this future for the church. He suggests that we need to take the duty of American citizenship seriously. Those of us who intend to be good citizens, Christian or other, need to "enter the arena" with those who are already there. Brené Brown talks about this a lot. It is easy to be in the cheap seats and stay out of the fray. Citizenship is nothing if it is not active. We must "resist tribalism," Meacham says. With our working understanding of Christian citizenship, enough room for partners across ecumenical and interfaith boundaries, and a strong center, we can easily and non-anxiously join the conversation in the public square. Remember, we seek convivial relationships and conversation-building on unity for the common good.

Meacham argues that we need to work to "respect facts and deploy reason." We must support a free press, difficult answers, and difficult questions. We must think well together and do so publicly. Finally, we must "keep history in mind." One of the things we must remember is that those who think they know the future are dangerous. The future of our nation is dependent upon us and our cooperative and imaginative engagement. Meacham says that history tells us our government is responsible to the people and to a higher authority. "A demagogue can only thrive when a substantial portion of the demos—the people—want him to."[18] I must add, if we are to engage in this way we must do so not only out of a sense of deep understanding of our own American civil religion, but also by engaging as those who claim a dual citizenship in the reign of God—our fellow Christian citizens.

In *Formations of the Secular*, Talal Asad thinks through political engagement from a Christian tradition. How do we live a Christian life that dovetails the other six days and twenty-three hours we are not in church with what we say and do on Sunday? How do we live a continuous life as a Christian that includes the work of politics? How do we do so in cooperation with other faiths and denominations and the non-religious fellow citizens? We are not trying to live out of some kind of nostalgic American civil religion, or even a nostalgic faith that believes the present is a uniquely different time than all the history that precedes our witness. We are trying to trace the shape of a non-defensive engagement with the public square that does not create a privatized faith subservient to the wider secular frame. We seek instead to overcome the fracturing of society through the creation of a "conflictive cooperative" that seeks ways of "discerning, protecting, and creating commons of every kind of citizen where there is a searching out of common good." Our engagement with others must disrupt the conflictual tribalism that gives powers to the parties rather than the people.[19]

What we seek is the fullness of community and the fullness of humanity as it appears to us in God's narrative of the garden. Compassion and familial faithfulness towards the whole human family are not undertaken out of a sense of wanting simply to be a partner in the secular work. We have rejected the idea that any work can be secular to begin with. We are suggesting that secularism itself is a kind of idolatry. Modern politics promotes a merely human flourishing; whereas Christian citizens are seeking to replant the garden.

As Malcolm Guite said, we must move out of the realm of syllogisms and into the world of human interaction and art. The nature of being human and living in human community is a story of lived experience. This "cultural repertory," as ethicist Willis Jenkins calls it, will inevitably lead us to new understandings.[20] Convivial communities, or even conflictive cooperatives, must resist prophetic work in its normal political forms. The church has fallen prey to prophecy rooted in the practices of our modern politics: name-calling and lampooning foes. We harbor a false belief that such prophetic work (better described as fomented righteous indignation) will lead to social action. The truth is that these forms of appropriated political snark extend the inhumanity of the political process that oppresses us. I prefer Walter Brueggemann's kind of prophecy: "The task of prophetic ministry is to nurture, nourish, and evoke a consciousness and perception alternative to the consciousness and perception of the dominant culture."[21]

As John Milbank has seen, if the political structures of the nation hold within them revelation because of their root in natural law, then there can be no requirement that such structures be answerable to theology. In contrast, we propose an engagement that assumes God's grace as the underpinning and support for the whole of God's garden social imaginary. All forms of common life (public education, social systems that support first responders—police, fire, and healthcare professionals—our public transportation, creation care, defense, and all the rest of the national infrastructure) are to be elevated by grace. Christian citizens must be grace-filled political players. We have said that God's social imaginary has the key virtues of compassion and familial faithfulness. Grace is not an added extra something, a change in our sinful status. When we are engaging well, grace will abound. There is no politics for politics sake. There is no "self-referential grace," for that is also a "mask for mere worldly ecclesiastical dominion." Compassion and faithfulness must instead be lived out.[22]

Grace must break us out of what political philosopher Romand Coles calls our "gated political communities."[23] This means venturing out of our diaspora churches. If we have programs on Christian citizenship in our congregations, they need to have diverse voices. If we meet in people's homes to discuss Christian citizenship and political engagement, we need to have diverse voices present. We must build conflictive and cooperative groups and mix in a full dose of cultural reparatory. Only through such reconciliation will our praxis mimic God's garden imaginary and reject the political powers' view of totals. It will protect us from becoming tools of parties and break the chain of fools, as Aretha Franklin once sang.[24] These engagements, if they are to embody God's grace, will need to be praxis built upon listening, relationship-building, and community flourishing with a full measure of vulnerability. This approach has to be moved into by the individual and community (if a church is hosting) from the position of vulnerability.[25]

Such manifest vulnerability by the individual is rooted in what we might call Hauerwas's Christian citizen rule of life. We first must understand our commitments. I believe this book has helped to elucidate those with some measure of clarity. The rule of life rejects the notion that somehow the church has it right and all we have to do is coerce or force the other worldly institutions to follow suit. We, as the church, are not a social justice institution. Jesus is not "coercive, selfish, nondialogical, or invulnerable."[26] Let me put it this way: we are only the church when we gather with people of the community around us. We are a church when we work with people who are not of the church. Social justice organizations promote ham-fisted prophecy by championing causes without doing much for our neighbors.

Jeremy Neill, in his essay "Political Involvement and Religious Compromises," reminds us that voting, circulating petitions, and helping to pass legislative bills are all good political forms of traditional engagement by citizens. But as Christian citizens, we must undertake this work without supporting the legitimizing narratives of institutions themselves or by surrendering our own identity as a Christian organization or citizen.[27]

Finally, Hauerwas's rule includes gentleness. After working with Jean Vanier and the L'Arche communities, Hauerwas understood that it was not enough to be vulnerable with neighbors; if political citizenship was going to work it had to be gentle. If we do our work well, our diverse conversations of conflicted cooperation will include a variety of people. Our groups must include the vulnerable.[28]

I think this last piece is so important as we move outward into engagement. What we are doing is much more than applying some political philosophy or a theological principle of reconciliation. If grace is the intended consequence of our Christian citizenship then we must not only enter into relationships with a diverse group of people, including the marginalized, we must also live as engaged members of our communities, like Jesus did. We must be in solidarity with them for the good of the community and the good of all human flourishing with our community. Apathy grabs hold when we vote but believe that is all that is required of us. Political parties gain power when we vote (win or lose) and then get ready for the midterm elections so we can regain our footing or keep our power. Christian citizenship is about a completely different narrative that promotes working together to build a society that looks more like God's garden narrative. That means we live and work with each other. We know each other's names. We work for the betterment of life for all those in our community. I find that Hauerwas's rule of life helps us to flesh out a bit the Sinai covenant's virtues of compassion and familial faithfulness.

There is plenty of opportunity for Christians to engage in the work of national politics. We can be informed by finding media that are reporting from the middle, support the freedom of the press, get off the internet. Or, if we are going to stay on, share only fact-checked news. We can figure out issues we care about and follow them. We can sign petitions and write letters, attend civic, city, school board, and town hall meetings. If we have kids in school, we can join the local PTA and volunteer. We can serve as a juror, or run for office. We can go to rallies and march. We can vote in elections and arrive prepared. We can volunteer to work at a polling place or register voters. We can study American history and be an informed citizen. We can share what we learn.[29] There are many ways that citizens can be involved. Christian citizens can do all of these things, but we must do them from the perspective of God's narrative and our place in it.

In Romand Coles's book *Beyond Gated Politics*, he describes our work as listening, traveling, and tabling. I think we have covered the ideas of listening and the work of engaging our communities pretty well—the work of traveling. It is the idea of tabling that is so important for the Christian citizen and is a good way to end our discussion on engagement. "Tabling" is a term often used in meetings to take an issue out of debate and set it aside for further discussion before a decision is made. That is not what it means here. Coles talks about tabling as the art of a re-conceptualized engagement about governing that constantly draws others into the conversation from different walks of life in order to increase who is at the table. It is to have a table with a different collective around it. This idea does not replace public space, but instead breaks public space up into smaller more interactive tables, creating spaces where a different imaginary can take hold.[30]

For the Christian citizen tabling is rooted deeply in the table ministry of Jesus. Jesus sat at people's tables: all kinds of tables with all kinds of people. Christians are a people of the table where Jesus breaks bread and shares wine and is both giver and guest. We know how to set a table. Nobody starves at our tables set in our parish halls, or in our dinner groups. It is time for the Christian citizen to go traveling, to go listening, and to go and set up a table in the wilderness and engage those we find there.

Conclusion: No Pleasant Valley Sunday

Then let the dream linger on. Let it be the test of nations. Let it be the quest of all our days. The fevered pounding of our blood, the measure of our souls, that none shall rest in any land and none return to dreamless sleep, no harp be quieted, no tongue be stilled, until the final man may stand in any place and thrust his shoulders to the sky, friend and brother to every other man.

—Pauli Murray[1]

We recognize the failure of politics, its vulnerability to the dehumanizing forces of sibling rivalry, mimetic desire, violence, and scapegoating. Politics is not a sacramental vessel that reveals God, nor is the god of America's civil religion the God of the Bible. The various systems of modern political philosophy have saved no one, but made a lot of people's lives worse, including women and people who are part of various minority populations. Modern politics is fundamentally intolerant, and reliably produces all kinds of indefensible discriminations and biases. Modern politics demands total acquiescence to the empire's grand narrative, lived out as ideological lockstep with the micro narrative of one political party or the other.[2]

The empire's values are shaped by a capitalism unmoored from civil and moral virtue, an estrangement made more acute by the fact that religious participation has become apathetic and absent. The market is strong, but society suffers under the burden of its demands. Moreover, an epistemological infatuation with common-sense reason has undermined any account of personal value beyond our roles as consumers and workers. The politics of our age is a civil capitalism, a society with no uncommodified thing that relies upon the dark force of sibling rivalry for its livelihood. This new civil capitalism depends upon the idea that humans are selfish and unsympathetic to the idea of a shared public good.[3] The citizens of the nation have become lonely individuals whose estrangement from each other makes corporate America run. Any alternative narrative is seen as unpatriotic. Nationalism reigns and sports have become the opiate of the masses. If cries for political justice transgress our sacred pastimes, they are immediately sidelined. Our convictions about the public good, and any religious perspective that might undergird such convictions, are to remain private. The public square exists solely to support the reigning powers.

We are a WEIRD society whose relationships are defined by an individual rather than a corporate bias. Western, educated, industrialized, rich, and democratic, we see everything as separate and individualized. We see fractured narratives. We do not see our interdependence, our desire for solidarity, and our hope for meaning. Yet we pour ourselves into a future where the mechanical, synthetic, and electronic both feed our hunger for transformation and tame our hunger for objects. We long for a biotech fix for all that ails us. Our world, with its narrative of an ever-progressing capitalist empire, is devoid of spirit. Our current reality reminds me of humanity's naïve optimism before both world wars, when we thought our minds and mechanical tools would save us.[4]

Meanwhile the values of lived communal compassion and faithfulness are disregarded as unneeded virtues. The law itself and politics are revelatory and require no additional correction. We are deaf to any narrative besides what desires pass across the screen of our television. Those things that are not against the law are acceptable; in fact, we have a right to do them, have them, and use them without judgment. Corporations have the same legal rights as individuals, and are therefore granted the same carte blanche. Freedoms abound without reflection. At the same time there is mass incarceration, where whole generations of Americans are incarcerated for minor offenses.[5] As Charles Taylor has warned, a society with no transcendent narrative is locked into subjectivism or nihilism.

What we have is a society of opposites: enemies and compatriots. One side defends our self-described freedoms. The other side defends the regulation of assets—administrative oversight of the goods held in common. They are both "self-described protagonists." There is harmony on but one thing and one thing only: that there are two ways of living as community. Philosopher Alasdair MacIntyre says, "There are only two alternative modes of social life open to us, one in which the free and arbitrary choices of individuals are sovereign and one in which the bureaucracy is sovereign, precisely so it may limit the free and arbitrary choices of individuals."[6] There is no shared common good. The only common ground is that there is none. Our common-sense civil religion offers no answer to these problems. Instead, it requires patriotic allegiance to a government hostile to the sorts of relationships that bring about the common good and the best life for the individual.[7] Our fractured fairy tale suggests that patriotism/nationalism will unite us and to the victor will go the spoils. It is a vain hope that individuals can flourish without societal/communal flourishing. Contemporary conservatism is just as committed to this functional impossibility as liberal progressivism. There is no common narrative and no common value. [8]

The Gospel offers a different vision of human community. Using a hermeneutic of imagination and a different narrative frame, we have described God's invitation to participate and find our place in a garden social imaginary. Rooted in our origin stories we have rejected the idea that God intends a world of fractured narratives. We have seen that sibling rivalry, mimetic desire, violence, and scapegoating are perennial companions along humanity's journey. We have suggested the characters of Abraham and Sarah; Moses; the prophets; Mary, John, and Jesus; and Paul as particularly evocative of God's social imaginary. Loving God and neighbor have been expanded into a wider Sinai covenant, where healthy relationships can be differentiated from desire and envy. Together with compassion and an expansive view of familial faithfulness, I have sketched a different way to engage in politics as Christian citizens. Christian citizens are the disruptors to *dominionism* and *totalism*. They cultivate the Nazareth Manifesto through works of peace, relationship, and stewardship. They balance interdependence and responsibility. As Christian citizens, we are prophets cursed to live as dual citizens in a strange land.

I will tell you that I see people who come from every kind of political background engaging across my diocese in the work of compassionate and faithful Christian citizenship. I see people in small towns pulling apart the racisms of the past. I know people in the city saving youth from going to prison and creating peer mentoring and sports organizations to keep them out of gangs. I see people coming together to intervene in state-sponsored education and to hold vigils on death row. Some of my flock even saved a man who killed his father, who was a priest of the diocese. Women have provided a home for other women trapped in the sex trade. Still others in a different city work to get women off the streets and out of enslavement. I can tell you the story of small-town politics and violence interrupted by a common meal shared by a little church who decided to do something. Talk about setting up a table in the midst of the community. Today they are convening a conversation about their community that has brought hope to a troubled place.

I know of a church that, when Hurricane Harvey hit, opened its doors and took in another church, convened the city to deal with the crisis, and provided space for the largest outreach center in the area that flooded. I know of an ecumenical, interfaith, multiethnic group who come together to share poetry, art, and talk about issues of race. These folks now go on field trips to experience other people living in their context in order to bridge the great social and cultural divide, which is as big as the Grand Canyon. We have congregations that are involved at the state house and others involved in the streets and within neighborhoods. There are some that march, that is true. But the best stories are those where Christian citizens are transforming their local community through engaged prophetic imagination.

I could tell you hundreds more of these stories and not tell the half of it. This is the benefit of being a bishop: I get to see that God's garden social imaginary is not some theological idea on paper, but the reflection of God's hand at work in the world through Christian citizenship. Here is what I have learned. In each of these instances what has happened is that congregations have gotten politically involved because of personal connections with people in the wider community. Urgency has been created where people feel the need of the other, where there is connection, the importance of involvement. The challenge for the engaged Christian citizen is to create relational capital so that they feel connected, involved, and a part of the wider political life that surrounds them. Real change happens because we are involved in another person's life. This is the incarnational model of Christian citizenship that we have been talking about. The work of Christian citizenship is not mere theology. It is, always and everywhere, theology and politics practiced together through the vessel of human relationship rooted in the relationship with God and God's narrative.

Maybe you have read this book in the midst of what the classic rock band the Monkees called a "Pleasant Valley Sunday here in status symbol land." Maybe you live in a world where your ears have been numbed into passivity because of the cynicism and pessimism that is all around. Maybe you are apathetic or can't imagine how to engage. Either way, I fear we have lost our sense of urgency. It feels like there is not much movement left in this movement.

God in Christ Jesus comes to us in the midst of our citizenship in this and every land. Jesus invites us to wake up and see that God is on the move. The seeds of this kingdom have been sown and the harvest is plentiful. The garden needs tending. Like a weed, God's realm will not be stopped; even now spreading. The light will not be hidden. Those that have no place to call a home, or lay their head, or dwell among loved ones are the ones who, like birds of the air, will find a home and nest in the arms of Christian citizens who follow the way of Abraham and Sarah, Moses, the prophets, Mary, John, and Jesus.

There is no doubt in my mind that Jesus never imagined he was securing a private spiritual faith for the individual through his death and resurrection. I do not believe he had any interest in starting a church with no voice in the public square or at tables in people's homes. He was not an American citizen, but instead he was a part of God's reign. He had no WEIRD sensibility. His was a global vision of a new garden. A garden that was more like the social imaginary of the Garden of Eden and less like the gardens of this world.

The time is now. There is work to do in God's garden social imaginary as Christian citizens. There is compassion and faithfulness to be enacted. Hear, see, go, do, follow the way, and like a weed it will grow.

Acknowledgments

I had several conversation partners for this project: Miroslav Volf, Walter Brueggemann, and Stanley Hauerwas. Each of them had a profound effect on my thinking. Each challenged me to be courageous and to not shrink from the work. I read a ton of Alasdair MacIntyre and am grateful for his reminder not to trust the empire.

I am grateful to the Episcopal Diocese of Texas and its people, who continue to press me into conversations about the future mission of the church and why it matters. In particular, they have questioned if the church's mission has a voice within the wider community and nation. Some have argued "no," others with a "yes." All have desired to seek the wisdom of God about our present time. It is their seeking and questions about what the church's mission is and has to say about our political time that has inspired this book.

I am grateful for the support of my staff that enables me to have time to write. The Rev. John Newton especially has been supportive of the work and an encourager along the way, as has the Rt. Rev. Kai Ryan. I am also grateful to Canon Christine Faulstich who helped ask important questions as I was drafting the document. My first reader and conversation partner for this book was the Rev. Patrick Hall, who has my gratitude for the work and time he put into the book, and the gratitude of my wife, JoAnne, who served as the first reader for the last five books.

Of course, there is Milton Brasher-Cunningham, my editor, and the team at Church Publishing who are always wonderful to work with and supportive of my projects. Without them I would not be able to bring the text to life.

Finally, I am grateful to JoAnne and the kids. JoAnne, because she knows I sneak off to the desk in the early morning hours and late at night to work on my writing, and who is always caring, encouraging, and excited to hear what is next. She gives me courage and faith at times when I am lacking. She shows me the importance of caring and speaking honestly about what Jesus and Christianity have to say about the present time. There are of course my two daughters. They are making their own way in the world. They are bold, concerned, and eager to believe in a God who wants a better world. I am very fortunate.

Notes

Epigraph

1. This is attributed to Montesquieu from his book *The Spirit of the Laws* (1748). However, a reading of the text reveals that Montesquieu would have agreed with the sentiment but it is not found in the text. There may be a unique translation of the text somewhere; however, while there are a lot of attributions, there is no document with this quote in it. Research reveals that the earliest attribution is from a 1954 book entitled *The World In Crisis in Maps* by Dimitrije J. Tosević.

Introduction: Engaging an Apathetic Christian Citizen

1. Thurgood Marshall, "Who Is Qualified to Be a Judge?" (speech, American College of Trial Lawyers, California, Coronado, March 14, 1977). It also may be found in a collection of his manuscripts entitled *Supreme Justice: Speeches and Writings*, 252.
2. The discourse around the very word "citizen" is deeply contested. I understand this and am intentionally playing on the fact that we as Americans talk about citizenship as if it is a geographical reality that should dominate our discourse. Meanwhile, the language of theology, liturgy, and the scripture understands it in the realm of a universal category. This friction I find interesting.
3. The work of Michael Thomas Hays and Melissa Saul reveals a crisis in formation of citizenship locally and globally. See Michael Thomas Hayes and Melissa Saul, "Educating the Citizens of Empire," *Journal of Curriculum Theorizing* 28, no. 1 (2012).
4. See Wayne Journell, "The Challenges of Political Instruction in a Post-9/11 United States," *High School Journal* 95, no. 1 (2011).

5. Review the Rice Kinder Institute research about change in one of America's largest cities here: https://kinder.rice.edu/houstonsurvey2018. Changing demographics of the state of Texas here: http://worldpopulationreview.com /states/texas-population/. See changing American demography here: http:// www.cnn.com/2008/US/08/13/census.minorities/. Review the death tsunami statistics here: https://www.ministrymatters.com/all/entry/1868/the-coming -death-tsunami.

6. As we dip our toe into the notion of having a global perspective, we need to acknowledge that the very notion of global citizenship is under a great deal of scrutiny at the present. It was one of the hotly debated topics in the campaign season leading up to 2016 and promises to continue to be one in the 2020 presidential election cycle in this country—just as it is playing out to be in other nations around the world. Most conversations about citizenship are locally oriented. On the one hand there is an old maxim that all politics are local. While the pundits have many catch phrases about global politics versus local ones, there is actually some very deep philosophical debate going on here. See the work of James Banks. He believes that citizenship is always located within the nation-state and while one might be informed of the global context it is not of primary concern. He argues that we really are first and foremost a type of tribal member within the wider state, and only then with a minor role in any kind of global society. See J. Banks, *Diversity and Citizenship Education: Global Perspectives* (San Francisco: Jossey-Bass, 2004), 17.

   Jonathan Burack has a stronger opinion and places the nation-state above all else. The concern he has is that citizenship in a democratic form always requires structures. He argues that global structures do not exist and in the end would undermine the local structures and laws. In a society where interdependence between individual and government structures is essential, Burack believes, such interdependence is lost at the global level. In other words, there is already an issue of maintaining healthy relationships between the nation-state and individual; the global will be less responsive. See J. Burack, L. Ellington, and K. Porter, "Students, the World, and the Global Education Ideology," in *Where Did Social Studies Go Wrong?*, ed. J. Leming (Washington, DC: Thomas B. Fordham Foundation, 2003), 40–69.

   What is at stake for these authors and others like them is that the rights of the local may be infringed if global structures are put into place. We don't do even the federal responsiveness to its citizens well . . . what makes us think that global structures would be any better? Yes, there may be some work to do around global human rights, one might argue, but at the end of the day local human rights and traditions may be trampled on. This is the fear many have. Like culture critic Henry Giroux, many believe that at every level the idea of liberal globalization is a threat that will in the end serve only the principalities and powers. Globalization undermines the basic tenets of democracy. H. Giroux, *The Terror of Neoliberalism: Rethinking the Significance of Cultural Politics* (London: Routledge, 2018), 1–19.

7. Their critique of the present context of the western mind and politics is excellent. Leaning heavily on previous work of Aristotle and Henri de Lubac they take up and bring into the contemporary context of politics and capitalism Alasdair MacIntyre's work. John Milbank and Adrian Pabst, *The Politics of Virtue: Post-liberalism and the Human Future* (London: Rowman & Littlefield International, 2016), 69.

8. The Book of Common Prayer (New York: Church Publishing, 2007), 381.

9. See Christopher P. Scheitle, "Race, Diversity, and Membership Duration in Religious Congregations," Baylor University Department of Sociology, July 12, 2010, http://www.baylorisr.org/wp-content/uploads/dougherty_race.pdf. And, see Robert D. Putnam and David E. Campbell, *American Grace: How Religion Divides and Unites Us* (New York: Simon & Schuster, 2012).

10. Milbank and Pabst, *Politics*, 69.

11. See Merriam Webster: https://www.merriam-webster.com/dictionary/politics

12. Ivan Illich, *Tools for Conviviality* (London: Marion Boyars, 2009), §11.

Chapter One: A Birth Narrative

1. William Vincent Wells, *The Life and Public Services of Samuel Adams*, vol. 3 (Boston: Little Brown and Company, 1869), 373.

2. H. Richard Niebuhr, *The Kingdom of God in America* (Middletown, CT: Wesleyan University Press, 1988), 43.

3. David McCullough, *John Adams* (New York: Simon & Schuster, 2001), 39.

4. "The First Virginia Charter 1606," American History 1600–1650, accessed August 4, 2018, http://www.let.rug.nl/usa/documents/1600–1650/the-first -virginia-charter-1606.php.

5. Jon Meacham, *American Gospel: God, the Founding Fathers, and the Making of a Nation* (New York: Random House, 2006), 41.

6. Ibid., 41.

7. H. Richard Niebuhr, *The Kingdom of God in America* (Middletown, CT: Wesleyan University Press, 1988), 34.

8. Ibid., 86–87.

9. Niebuhr wrote, "As the sovereignty of God was institutionalized in laws, the kingdom of Christ in denominations and means of grace, so the string toward the coming kingdom and the hope of its coming were transformed into a moral sanction or into a belief in progress." Ibid. Niebuhr, *Kingdom*, 181–182.

10. Dietrich Bonhoeffer, *Dietrich Bonhoeffer Works: Barcelona, Berlin, New York: 1928–1931*, ed. Clifford J. Green (New York: Fortress Press, 2008), 318.

11. Mark A. Noll, *America's God: From Jonathan Edwards to Abraham Lincoln* (Oxford: Oxford Univ. Press, 2005), 24.

12. Theologians Stanley Hauerwas and Will Willimon in their book *Resident Aliens* wrote, "We have come to believe that few books have been a greater hindrance to an accurate assessment of our situation than *Christ and Culture*." Stanley Hauerwas and William H. Willimon, *Resident Aliens: Life in the Christian Colony* (Nashville: Abingdon, 1989), 40.

13. Stanley Hauerwas, "The End of American Protestantism," *ABC News*, July 2, 2013, accessed August 4, 2018, http://www.abc.net.au/religion /articles/2013/07/02/3794561.htm.

14. Meacham, *Gospel*, 96.

15. See Lynch v. Donnelly, 465 U.S. 668 (1984) U.S. Supreme Court.

16. Derek Heater, *A Brief History of Citizenship* (New York: New York University Press, 2004), 49.

17. Ibid., 63.

18. Ibid., 63–64.

19. Robert R. Palmer, *The Age of Democratic Revolution*, vol. 1 (Princeton: Princeton University Press, 1959), 224.

20. Thomas Hobbes, *Leviathan*, ed. Richard Tuck, Raymond Geuss, and Quentin Skinner (Cambridge: Cambridge University Press, 1996), 9.

21. Ibid., 89.

22. John Locke, *The Second Treatise of Civil Government*, ed. Andrew Bailey (Peterborough, Ontario: Broadview Press, 2015), §59.

23. Heater, *Brief*, 65.

24. Ibid., 66.

25. Jean-Jacques Rousseau, *The Social Contract and Other Later Political Writings* (London: Cambridge University Press, 2016), 41.

26. See Heater, *Brief*, 67–72. All of this was based upon a radical understanding of the individual. The Christian philosopher Abelard had been a prophetic voice of a modern Aristotle. He believed that we must understand in order to believe. It is our reason, yes, but more so it is our understanding that helps us to navigate the world, powers, principalities, and government. Our passions, Abelard wrote, are what motivate us to embrace a life of virtue. Rousseau understood then that these two (reason and virtue) were in conflict. Rousseau, and the rest, would make a shift one more time to a more radical view— reason alone had to dominate. Rousseau believed the individual must train his conscience to take control. See Arthur Herman, *The Cave and the Light: Plato*

versus Aristotle, and the Struggle for the Soul of Western Civilization (New York: Random House, 2013), 394. The scientific study of the mind and psychology teaches today that emotions drive action and reason and not the other way around. This idea plays an important role much later in our conversation. See Jonathan Haidt, *The Righteous Mind: Why Good People Are Divided by Politics and Religion* (London: Penguin Books, 2013).

27. E. Brooks Holifield, *Theology in America Christian Thought from the Age of the Puritans to the Civil War* (New Haven: Yale University Press, 2008), 176.

28. Heater, *Brief*, 70.

29. British political scientist Graham Wallas wrote, "No citizen can imagine his state or make it the object of his political affection unless he believes in the existence of a national type to which the individual inhabitants of the state are assimilated; and he cannot continue to believe in the existence of such a type unless in fact his fellow citizens are like each other and like himself in certain important respects." See Graham Wallas, *Human Nature in Politics* (Boston: Houghton Mifflin, 1919), 274.

30. Meacham, *Gospel*, 85.

31. Thomas Jefferson, *The Writings of Thomas Jefferson*, ed. Henry Augustine Washington (New York: Riker, 1854), 400.

32. Thomas Jefferson, *The Writings of Thomas Jefferson*, ed. Paul Leicester Ford (New York: Putnam, 1894), 263.

33. James Madison, Religious Freedom (Boston: Printed and Sold by Lincoln & Edmands, 1819), 7. I think that Jon Meacham's book *American Gospel* does an excellent job of revealing the battle that was waged in the founding of our nation.

34. Interestingly, it would be years later before American congregations made the weekly collection of money part of worship because they had to. That's right—we have not always had a collection! (We have always had an offering—of bread and wine.) The reason is because congregations did not depend upon voluntary giving by its membership. Most American churches were still established by governmental authorities like their counterparts in Europe at this time period. The congregational churches and the Anglican churches alike were dependent on funds from home and then from the state. The Church was seen as more than just a societal norm; it was seen as necessary if you want good citizens. Church was a public good, so taxes and fees were collected from the people to support its work. Even after the American Revolution, and the writing of the Establishment Clause in the First Amendment, churches were still by and large supported by the state. This would last until 1833 when Massachusetts revoked the religious tax and every other state soon followed.

This changed everything. The separation of church and state was not normative until 1833. The Constitution is referring to a national church, but at the time it was assumed that local churches would be supported by the government for their charity work.

35. "Letter to the Jews of Newport," letter from George Washington, August 18, 1790, Washington Papers, 6:284–85, University of Virginia, Charlottesville, Virginia.

36. We should make note that the French Revolution often is seen as our counterpart. We must be careful not to conflate the French Revolution and the American Revolution. The French Revolution resulted in mass chaos, guillotines in the streets, political pogroms, and eventually Napoleon Bonaparte, who exported French revolutionary violence across Europe until his final defeat at Waterloo. The founding fathers were disquieted and uneasy about what they saw unfolding in France during the 1790s. The only founding father to remain decidedly Francophile and optimistic about the Revolution during its bloodiest stage was Jefferson. Also, because of the inseparable links between the Bourbons and French Catholicism, French republicans have always taken a more oppressive and contemptuous approach to religious expression, and France has never really represented the kind of positive stance towards religious pluralism that is articulated here as central to the American project. For a contemporary example of this, see the French laws banning the wearing of religious items at work, like burqas and crosses.

37. John O'Sullivan, "The Great Nation of Futurity," *United States Democratic Review* 6, no. 23 (1839): 426–430.

38. Ibid.

39. John O'Sullivan, "Annexation," *United States Magazine and Democratic Review* 17 (1845): 5–10.

40. James Polk, "Inaugural Addresses of the Presidents of the United States: From George Washington 1789 to George Bush 1989," Avalon Project—Documents in Law, History and Diplomacy, March 4, 1845, accessed August 5, 2018, http://avalon.law.yale.edu/19th_century/polk.asp.

41. David E. Stannard, *American Holocaust: The Conquest of the New World* (New York: Oxford University Press, 1992). Stannard is arguing for the use of the term "genocide" based upon the population contact with the westward expansion and colonialism.

42. Charles Taylor, *A Secular Age* (Cambridge: Belknap Press of Harvard University Press, 2007), 504.

43. Stanley Hauerwas, *War and the American Difference: Theological Reflections on Violence and National Identity* (Grand Rapids, MI: Baker Academic, 2011), 5–6.

44. Meacham, *Gospel*, 5.

Chapter Two: Our Beloved Civil Religion

1. "A Concise Creed," Benjamin Franklin to Ezra Stiles, March 9, 1790, Philadelphia, Pennsylvania.
2. Robert Neelly Bellah, *Beyond Belief: Essays on Religion in a Post-traditional World* (Berkeley, CA: University of California Press, 1991), 168.
3. See Émile Durkheim, *The Elementary Forms of the Religious Life: A Study in Religious Sociology* (London: Andesite Press, 2017).
4. Robert N. Bellah, "Civil Religion in America," Daedalus, Journal of the American Academy of Arts and Sciences 96, no. 4 (1967): 1–21.
5. John F. Kennedy's inaugural address of January 20, 1961 begins: "We observe today not a victory of party but a celebration of freedom—symbolizing an end as well as a beginning—signifying renewal as well as change. For I have sworn before you and Almighty God the same solemn oath our forebears prescribed nearly a century and three quarters ago . . . The world is very different now. For man holds in his mortal hands the power to abolish all forms of human poverty and to abolish all forms of human life. And yet the same revolutionary beliefs for which our forbears fought are still at issue around the globe—the belief that the rights of man come not from the generosity of the state but from the hand of God." And concludes with: "Finally, whether you are citizens of America or of the world, ask of us the same high standards of strength and sacrifice that we shall ask of you. With a good conscience our only sure reward, with history the final judge of our deeds, let us go forth to lead the land we love, asking His blessing and His help, but knowing that here on earth God's work must truly be our own." Ibid.
6. Bellah reminds us that God is mentioned or referred to in all inaugural addresses but Washington's second, which is a very brief (two paragraphs) and a perfunctory acknowledgment. It is not without interest that the actual word "God" does not appear until Monroe's second inaugural, March 5, 1821. In his first inaugural, Washington refers to God as "that Almighty Being who rules the universe," "Great Author of every public and private good," "Invisible Hand," and "benign Parent of the Human Race." John Adams refers to God as "Providence," "Being who is supreme over all," "Patron of Order," "Fountain of Justice," and "Protector in all ages of the world of virtuous liberty." Jefferson speaks of "that Infinite Power which rules the destinies of the universe," and "that Being in whose hands we are." Madison speaks of "that Almighty Being whose power regulates the destiny of nations," and "Heaven." Monroe uses "Providence" and "the Almighty" in his first inaugural and finally "Almighty God" in his second. See Inaugural Addresses of the Presidents of the United States from George Washington 1789 to Harry S. Truman 1949, 82d Congress, 2d Session, House Document No. 540, 1952.

7. Stanley Hauerwas had a conversation while reviewing the book and he reminded me of his piece on the Gettysburg Address in that he believes it commits Americans to war in perpetuity. You can review his argument here in this shorter piece: https://www.abc.net.au/religion/the-end-of-just-war-why-christian-realism-requires-nonviolence/10097052

8. Dwight D. Eisenhower, in Will Herberg, *Protestant-Catholic-Jew* (Garden City, NY: Doubleday & Co., 1955), 97.

9. Bellah, *Civil*, 4.

10. Ibid.

11. Ibid.

12. Ibid.

13. Abraham Lincoln, in Allan Nevins, ed., *Lincoln and the Gettysburg Address* (Urbana, IL: Univ. of Ill. Press, 1964), 39.

14. Meacham, *Gospel*, 244.

15. Bellah, *Civil*, 18.

16. András Máté-Tóth and Gábor Attila Feleky, "Civil Religion in Central and Eastern Europe: An Application of an American Model," Americana E Journal, June 27, 2016.

17. Ibid.

18. See the following reports: Ronald C. Wimberley, "Testing the Civil Religion Hypothesis." *Sociological Analysis* 37 (1976): 341–352; Ronald C. Wimberley and James A. Christenson, "Civil Religion and Church and State." *Sociological Quarterly* 21 (1980): 35–40; and Ronald C. Wimberley, et al. "The Civil Religious Dimension. Is It There?" *Social Forces* 54 (1978): 890–900 for the data.

19. Máté-Tóth, "Civil Religion."

20. Ibid.

21. Christian Smith and Melinda Lundquist Denton, *Soul Searching: The Religious and Spiritual Lives of American Teenagers* (Oxford: Oxford University Press, 2009).

22. Stephanie McCrummen, "God, Trump and the Meaning of Morality," *Washington Post*, July 21, 2018, accessed August 9, 2018, https://www.washingtonpost.com/news/national/wp/2018/07/21/feature/god-trump-and-the-meaning-of-morality/?utm_term=.2f6fab13910a.

23. Mark Lilla, *The Stillborn God: Religion, Politics, and the Modern West* (New York: Vintage Books, A Division of Random House, 2008), 42–45.

24. Ibid., 308–309.

25. Alexis De Tocqueville, *Democracy in America*, ed. Arthur Goldhammer and Olivier Zunz (New York: Library of America Paperback Classics, 2012), 338.

26. Mark A. Noll, *America's God: From Jonathan Edwards to Abraham Lincoln* (Oxford: Oxford University Press, 2005), 194.

27. Hauerwas, *War*, 17.
28. Hauerwas, "The End."
29. Ibid.
30. Hauerwas, *War*, 17.
31. G. K. Chesterton and James J. Thompson, "What I Saw in America. The Resurrection of Rome. Sidelights," in *The Collected Works of G. K. Chesterton*, vol. 21 (San Francisco: Ignatius Press, 1990), 45. See also Jon Meacham's treatment in *American Gospel*, 242.
32. Meacham, *Gospel*, 243.
33. Ibid., 245.
34. Ibid., 245–246.

Chapter Three: A Frame for Christian Citizenship

1. Alasdair C. MacIntyre, *After Virtue: A Study in Moral Theory* (Notre Dame, IN: University of Notre Dame Press, 1981), 255.
2. Stanley Hauerwas, "A Sanctuary Politics: Being the Church in the Time of Trump," *ABC News*, March 30, 2017, accessed July 20, 2018, http://www.abc.net.au/religion/articles/2017/03/30/4645538.htm.
3. Joseph Henrich, Steven J. Heine, and Ara Norenzayan, "The Weirdest People in the World?" *Behavioral and Brain Sciences* 33, no. 2–3 (2010).
4. Haidt, 113.
5. Ibid.
6. Ibid. Haidt also mentions philosopher John Stuart Mill (1806–1873) here. I think he is wrong in doing so. Mill actually does not fit historically within the same trajectory. The difference between Kant and Mill is that Kant very much depended upon Rousseau. Both believed that political structures were best when a general will demanded individual submission. Mill, on the other hand, believed that such sharing with the rest of society had to be a free sharing of goods. The individual was always to be independent. Here we see clearly that Mill is a student of Aristotle while Kant is a student of Plato, as is Rousseau and Hegel. I suggest reading the difference between Marx and Mill in Herman's, *Cave*, 441–449.
7. Haidt, *Righteous*, 114.
8. R. B. Zojanc, "Attitudinal Effects of Mere Exposure," University of Michigan, September 1965, https://www.psc.isr.umich.edu/dis/infoserv/isrpub/pdf/The attitudinaleffects_2360_.PDF. See also, R. B. Zajonc, "Feeling and Thinking: Preferences Need No Inferences," *American Psychologist* 35, no. 2 (1980): 151–175.
9. Haidt, *Righteous*, 64–73.

10. Charles Taylor, *Sources of the Self* (Cambridge, MA: Harvard University Press, 1992), 324.

11. Ibid.

12. Ibid., 327.

13. Ibid., 331.

14. See his chapter on "Our Victorian Contemporaries" beginning on page 393. Charles Taylor, *Sources of the Self* (Cambridge, MA: Harvard University Press, 1992).

15. Brigette Nerlich, "Imagining Imaginaries," *Making Science Public*, 31 July 2017, blogs.nottingham.ac.uk/makingsciencepublic/2015/04/23/imagining -imaginaries/.

16. Ibid.

17. See inaugural address of Donald Trump as only one example of a humano-centric view that is both subjective and nihilistic. Donald Trump, "The Inaugural Address," The White House, January 2017, accessed July 19, 2018, https://www. whitehouse.gov/briefings-statements/the-inaugural-address/. See also the article on how this address marks a departure from American civil religion here: "Requiem for Civil Religion," editorial, *The Christian Century*, March 1, 2017.

18. MacIntyre, *After Virtue*, 216.

19. Ibid., 212.

20. Ibid., 204.

21. Ibid., 204.

22. In *After Virtue* MacIntyre takes on Jennifer Michael Hecht's argument that the unity of life is a fiction imposed and invented after death, never lived as reality. He takes on Louis O. Mink's thought that "life has no beginnings, middles, or ends; there are meetings, but the start of an affair belongs to the story we tell ourselves later, and there are partings, but final partings only in the story." See Louis O. Mink, quoted in MacIntyre, 212. He reminds us that in Jean Paul Sartre's *La Nausée* (Nausea), the character Antoine Roquentin attempts to write a biography, but surrenders because it is a fool's errand to present one's life as a narrative. MacIntyre agrees "that it is only retrospec-tively that hopes can be characterized as unfulfilled or battles as decisive and so on . . . But we so characterize them in life as much as in art." See MacIntyre, 212. "Narrative is not the work of poets, dramatists and novelists reflecting upon events which had no narrative order before one was imposed by the singer or the writer; narrative form is neither disguise nor decoration," he declares. MacIntyre, 211.

23. Ibid., 210.

24. MacIntyre has a great image for this—the recipe. He writes, "In the reci-pes of a cookery book actions are individuated the way that some analytical

philosophers have supposed to be possible of all actions . . . If in the middle of a lecture on Kant's ethics I suddenly broke six eggs into a bowl and added flour and sugar, proceeding all the while with my Kantian exegesis, I have not, simply in virtue of the fact that I was following a sequence . . . performed an intelligible action," MacIntyre argues action as part of the narrative of the recipe only makes sense in the context of cooking. MacIntyre, 209.

25. Ibid.
26. See Terry Eagleton on the 1980s avant-garde. Eagleton writes "history was scattered . . . adjacency eclipsed sequentiality." See Daniel T. Rodgers, *Age of Fracture* (Cambridge, MA: Harvard University Press, 2011), 230.
27. MacIntyre, 218, 221.
28. Ibid., 221.
29. Ibid., 206–207.
30. Stanley Hauerwas adapts the work of MacIntyre in his opening to *The Peaceable Kingdom*. In this book Hauerwas frames Christian ethics as part of the Christian narrative. I have done the same thing here. I have adapted Christian citizenship with MacIntyre's principles in one hand and Hauerwas's ethics in another. See Stanley M. Hauerwas, *The Peaceable Kingdom: A Primer for Christian Ethics* (Notre Dame, IN: University of Notre Dame Press, 2011), 61–62.
31. George A. Lindbeck, *The Nature of Doctrine: Religion and Theology in a Postliberal Age* (Louisville, KY: Westminster John Knox Press, 2009), 68.
32. Ibid., 81.
33. Hauerwas, "The End."

Chapter Four: A Garden Social Imaginary

1. Cornel West, "On Constructed Rights" (lecture, New Haven, February 28, 2013).
2. We know there are two stories because the language is different in each story. Most every seminarian had to memorize this and knows this by heart. I also think most people in the pew do not know it because we do not teach it very often in congregations. Here is the short version. Over time scholars realized that throughout the Old Testament there are different forms of Hebrew used. These can be historically traced. In other words this was not written by one person. Instead it is an assemblage of texts over time. Popularly this is referred to at the JEDP model. The history of the texts was developed by Jewish and Christian scholars dating from the seventeenth century. By the nineteenth century scholars had a good handle on this. J documents were written around 900–850 BCE. And refer to God as Jehovah. E documents were written around

750–700 BCE. and refer to God as *Elohim*. D is for Deuteronomy, and these were written during King Josiah's reforms around 620 BCE. P stands for the priests who wrote somewhere in the vicinity of 586 BCE, maybe from Babylon and after Israel's return. Here is a great chart by John Gabel and Charles Wheeler from *The Bible as Literature: An Introduction* that helps you see the differences between the stories. (New York: Oxford University Press, 1986), 90.

Genesis 1–2:4a	Genesis 2:4b–3:24
Creation is divided into days.	No days or other periods of time are mentioned.
Creation has a cosmic scope.	Creation has to do with the earth only.
Animals are created before man.	Man created before animals.
Animals are part of a cosmic design (along with plants and everything else)	Animals are created for a limited purpose: to keep man company or be "a helper"—though they turn out to be unsuitable for Adam, forcing God to make Eve instead.
Man is to rule the world.	Man is to have charge of Eden only and, presumably, is never to leave it.
Woman is created simultaneously with man.	Woman is created after (and from) the body of man.
No names are given to creatures.	All creatures, including humanity, are given names
Only the deity speaks.	Four speakers engage in dialogue, one of them an animal.
The deity makes a day of the week holy.	The deity forbids eating the fruit of a tree.

3. Darrin W. Snyder Belousek has an excellent treatment of this topic along with the topic of non-violence in his article entitled, "God, Evil, and (Non) Violence: Creation Theology, Creativity Theology, and Christian Ethics," Conrad Grebel University College, August 26, 2016, accessed August 10, 2018, https://uwaterloo.ca/grebel/publications/conrad-grebel-review/issues/

spring-2016/god-evil-and-nonviolence-creation-theology-creativity. For a deeper engagement of creation and traditional theology around its doctrine Belousek suggests these texts: Bernhard W. Anderson, *From Creation to New Creation: Old Testament Perspectives* (Minneapolis: Fortress Press, 1994); Richard Bauckham, *The Bible and Ecology: Rediscovering the Community of Creation* (Waco, TX: Baylor University Press, 2010); William P. Brown, *The Seven Pillars of Creation: The Bible, Science, and the Ecology of Wonder* (Oxford: Oxford University Press, 2010); Terence E. Fretheim, *God and World: A Relational Theology of Creation* (Nashville, TN: Abingdon Press, 2005); Karl Löning and Erich Zenger, *To Begin with, God Created . . . : Biblical Theologies of Creation,* trans. Omar Kaste (Collegeville, MN: Michael Glazier, 2000); Ben C. Ollenburger, "Isaiah's Creation Theology," *Ex Auditu* 3 (1987): 54–71; "Peace and God's Action against Chaos in the Old Testament," *The Church's Peace Witness,* ed. Marlin E. Miller and Barbara Gingerich Nelson (Grand Rapids, MI: W.B. Eerdmans, 1994), 70–88; "Creation and Peace: Creator and Creature in Genesis 1–11," *The Old Testament in the Life of God's People: Essays in Honor of Elmer A. Martens,* ed. Jon Isaak (Winona Lake, IN: Eisenbrauns, 2009); "Creation and Violence," *Struggles for Shalom: Peace and Violence across the Testaments,* ed. Laura L. Brenneman and Brad D. Schantz (Eugene, OR: Pickwick Publications, 2014), 26–36.

4. In this theological idea offered by Gregory of Nazianzus, there is an ontological discontinuity between God and world; God is differentiated from the creation. See Gregory of Nazianzus, *Festal Orations* (Crestwood, NY: St. Vladimir's Seminary Press, 2008), Oration 45.3–4. See also, Gregory of Nazianzus, *On God and Christ: The Five Theological Orations and Two Letters to Cledonius* (New York: St. Vladimir's Seminary Press, 2002) Oration 29.4 and Oration 30.18.

5. Walter Brueggemann and Carolyn J. Sharp, *Disruptive Grace: Reflections on God, Scripture, and the Church* (Minneapolis, MN: Fortress Press, 2011), xx.

6. Brueggemann, *Grace,* xx.

7. Jonathan Sacks, "The Genesis of Justice," The Office of Rabbi Sacks (blog), October 13, 2014, accessed November 21, 2017, http://rabbisacks.org/genesis -justice-bereishit/.

8. Ibid.

9. We had to learn this in seminary too! Here are some more recent and interesting books if you want to learn more about this connection: Stephanie Dalley's *Myths from Mesopotamia: Creation, the Flood, Gilgamesh, and Others* (New York: Oxford University Press, 2000); Frank Moore Cross's "The Priestly Work" found in *Canaanite Myth and Hebrew Epic: Essays in the History of the Religion of Israel* (Cambridge: Harvard University Press, 1979); Michael Fishbane's

Biblical Myth and Rabbinic Mythmaking (New York: Oxford University Press, 2003) and Richard Elliott Friedman's *The Bible with Sources Revealed* (HarperCollins, 2003).

10. I believe that I have made the case that any system that abstracts the "other" and creates levels of powers and authorities is inherently going to be violent. There is a universal human nature that leans toward domination. This tendency for violence, oppression, and domination is called sin in the church. Our desire to create codes will always bring into both a rejection of sin and a participation in an ever new system of domination. It is the work of the church, though, to continually throw off this domination and seek the ecclesia and community for which Jesus speaks. Simply because we live in sinful world and can name our sin does not mean we are given permission to live in it and throw up our hands. Rather, we are continually invited to be reformed and changed. The thought here is the work of *ecclesia reformata, semper reformanda* (the church reformed, always reforming)—courtesy of Karl Barth and other theologians post World War II. Here, then, is the idea that when scripture clearly speaks to us, we should reform our institutional/structural church practices.

Regarding the organizational question before us, I rely here on the work of Arthur Koestler, author and journalist; Kenneth Earl "Ken" Wilber II, an American writer whose work on "integral theory" is known; and Rolf Sattler, professor, plant biologist specializing in plant morphology, and student of Wilber's. Here the new science offers organizational thinking around the gospel thinking.

The first thing to understand is the nature of hierarchies as an observed reality and not necessarily a domination system. I have been talking in this chapter about dominating hierarchies. I am here rejecting this idea but holding on to the nature of hierarchy as a system or organizing principle. Wilber adopts the word "holarchy" in order to differentiate between observable ordering of organisms and dominating and violent hierarchies. Holarchy was a term first used by Arthur Koestler in his work where "holon" (the basis for a holarchy) is a piece and part of the levels around it. In this way, a divided top-down power structure is divided. Koestler offers this as an example of holarchic relationship: subatomic particles ↔ atoms ↔ molecules ↔ macromolecules ↔ organelles ↔ cells ↔ tissues ↔ organs ↔ organisms ↔ communities ↔ societies. See Arthur Koestler, *The Ghost in the Machine* (New York: Macmillan, 1968); Ken Wilber, *The Collected Works of Ken Wilber* (Boston: Shambhala, 2000), 29. Sattler helps to understand this, "A holarchy or hierarchy is a system of holons at different levels. In this system lower level holons compose a higher level holon, and a higher level holon comprises lower level holons. Any holon is a part with regard to the higher level holon it composes, and at the same time a whole with regard to the lower level holon(s) it comprises. Therefore, a holon is a part/whole. For example, an organ is a part of an organism, but a whole with regard to the cells of which it is comprised" (Rolf Sattler. "Wilber's AQAL Map and Beyond," *Beyond Wilber*, accessed July 21, 2016, http://www.beyondwilber.ca/AQALmap /bookdwl/files/WAQALMB_1.pdf).

Wilber uses the ideas of Chinese boxes and baskets. Barbara Cawthorne Crafton uses this metaphor in her book *The Also Life*. What Wilber helps us to understand is that while we may categorize through holarchy, the reality is that holons are "interpenetrating" (Ken Wilber, *The Collected Works of Ken Wilber* [Boston: Shambhala, 1998], 61). Stattler takes this and expands it based upon Wilber's work to say that if interpenetrating, then what we see "is a whole, a continuum, a unity, because processes by their very nature are interconnecting, and a network of processes is an undivided whole" (Stattler). While reality is homogenous, there is differentiation and because of this differentiation there can be some sense of the holons. We see this in the way we talk about the color of light or the organs of plants. While we can see the other, to make the other a separate entity from ourselves is to reintroduce hierarchy. There is no "radically separate and isolated and bounded entity" (Ken Wilber, *The Collected Works of Ken Wilber* [Boston: Shambhala, 1999], 469).

11. Some three hundred or more years after our Genesis stories were written, Plato (one of the founding fathers of politics) would suggest that people were made of gold, silver, and bronze. Aristotle was more accurate when he surmised that through our very creation humanity is by nature a political animal. See Aristotle, *Politics*, trans. H.W.C. Davis and Benjamin Jowett (Cosimo Classics, 2008), 28. This is simply to say that two of the founding fathers of political philosophy don't have anything as radical as our story. Sacks, "Genesis."

12. Sacks, "Genesis."

13. Ibid.

14. Ibid.

15. Margaret Kean, *John Milton's Paradise Lost: A Sourcebook* (London: Routledge, 2005), 153.

16. Sacks, "Genesis."

17. Charles L. Campbell, *The Word before the Powers: An Ethic of Preaching* (Louisville, KY: Westminster John Knox, 2002), 49.

18. Walter Wink, *Engaging the Powers: Discernment and Resistance in a World of Domination* (Minneapolis, MN: Fortress Press, 1999), 112.

19. Sacks, "Genesis."

20. John F. Kennedy, "Inaugural Address" (speech, Washington, DC, January 20, 1961).
21. United States Constitutional Convention, "Constitution of the United States," World Digital Library, September 17, 1787, accessed July 23, 2018, https://www.wdl.org/en/item/2708/.

Chapter Five: A Rejection of Dominion Politics

1. Philip E. Tetlock et al., "The Psychology of the Unthinkable: Taboo Trade-offs, Forbidden Base Rates, and Heretical Counterfactuals," *Journal of Personality and Social Psychology* 78, no. 5 (2000): 433.
2. Jonathan Sacks, "Taking Responsibility," Office of Rabbi Sacks, September 28, 2013, accessed July 22, 2018, http://rabbisacks.org/bereishit-5774-taking-responsibility/.
3. Ibid.
4. René Girard, "Interview with René Girard," interview by Markus Müller, Anthropoetics.ucla.edu, Spring 1996, accessed July 24, 2016, http://anthropoetics.ucla.edu/ap0201/interv/.
5. Phillip Tabb, *Serene Urbanism: A Biophilic Theory and Practice of Sustainable Placemaking* (London: Routledge, Taylor & Francis Group, 2017), 59.
6. Paul Nuechterlein, "Nuechterlein on the Bible and Sacrifice," Girardian Lectionary, 2006, accessed July 24, 2018, http://girardianlectionary.net/learn/nuechterlein-bible-sacrifice/.
7. Martin Luther King Jr., "Remaining Awake Through a Great Revolution" (sermon at Washington National Cathedral, Washington, DC, March 31, 1968).
8. See Dr. King's sermon at the Lincoln Memorial for the notion of our founder's promissory note. Martin Luther King Jr., "I Have A Dream" (speech at the Lincoln Memorial, Washington, DC, August 28, 1963). See his sermon at the National Cathedral for his idea of a sacred heritage. King, *Awake.*
9. A full treatment of this idea of "wilderness" transformation can be found in *The Jesus Heist.*
10. Walter Brueggemann, "Evangelism and Discipleship: The God Who Calls, the God Who Sends," *Word and World* 24, no. 2 (2004): 122.
11. Ibid., 125.
12. Gil Bailie, *Violence Unveiled: Humanity at the Crossroads* (New York: Crossroad, 2004), 140.
13. Paul J. Nuechterlein, "Passing the Test" (sermon at Prince of Peace Lutheran, Portage, MI, June 26, 2011).
14. When we make the substitutionary theory of the atonement synonymous with a god that demands that the son sacrifice himself, this understanding

of atonement can be used to sanction the commission of religious violence against others in many varying and inhumane forms for the sake of peace. By contrast, the gospel of peace reveals God as both a victim of human violence and as a human whose dignity was violated by the shame of the cross. As such, I do not advocate for throwing out the substitutionary model of atonement altogether, but only that we hold this particular model in conversation alongside other models of atonement and always in the context of a Trinitarian theology. Outside of a Trinitarian theology, penal substitution becomes a god demanding the sacrifice of his son. However, an orthodox perspective always sees God in Christ acting together to save the world. Our belief in the Trinity will always lead to a mature understanding of any theory of atonement. To illustrate, let us turn to Paul's letter to the Philippians, chapter 2. Here we see that the second person of the Trinity, the Christ, the Incarnation, becomes lower than the angels in the unique person of Jesus. It is not enough to leave Jesus as a victim. This is not the whole of the story. God becomes fully incarnate in Jesus. The very God who in the form of Jesus is willing to set the power of God aside to become a victim on the cross is revealed. It is not that a better version of a Greek god requires his demigod son to sacrifice himself, but that God himself makes the substitutionary sacrifice. Paul writes, Christ "emptied himself, taking the form of a slave, being born in human likeness. And being found in human form, he humbled himself and became obedient to the point of death—even death on a cross." The God through whom all things, all flesh, was made is the one who voluntarily becomes powerless even unto death. All of our sinfulness, brokenness, victimhood, violence, and scapegoating hang on the cross with Christ, in Christ, and for Christ. Thus, the atonement reveals that we are connected to the Incarnation itself, in our innermost parts. We stand in the middle of God's narrative, and thus we find fresh power to make our life a substitutionary sacrifice for others so that the borders of God's Garden expand in and through our life and the quality of our community.

15. The theologian Gregory Nazianzus has a similar take on the sacrifice of Isaac and its relationship to Jesus: "Why would the blood of his only Son be agreeable to the Father who did not wish to accept Isaac offered as a burnt offering by Abraham, but replaced that human sacrifice by that of a ram? Is it not obvious that the Father accepts the sacrifice not because he insists upon it or has some need of it, but to carry out his plan: it was necessary for man to be sanctified by the humanity of God, it was necessary for he himself to free us by triumphing over the tyrant through his force, and for him to call us back to him through his Son . . . Let us pass over the rest in reverent silence." Quoted by Olivier Clement, '«Dionysus et le ressuscite,» *Evangile et*

revolution, 93. Original text in *Patrologiae Graecae* XXXVI, Oratio XLV, 22, 654. See also René Girard, *Things Hidden since the Foundation of the World*, trans. Jean-Michel Oughourlian and Guy Lefort (Stanford, CA: Stanford University Press, 1987), 143. René Girard writes, "Before announcing the end of sacrifice, with Christ, the Bible shows his gradually moving away from it in the story of Isaac. When Isaac asks his father: 'The fire and wood are here, but where is the lamb for the burnt offering?' Abraham's answer is extraordinary, and one of the most significant points in the whole of the Bible: 'God himself will provide the lamb for the burnt offering' (Genesis 22.1–8). This sentence announces the finding of the ram that will replace Isaac, but Christians have always seen a prophetic allusion to Christ as well. God, in this sense, will give the one who will sacrifice himself in order to do away with all sacrificial violence. It is not ridiculous, it is marvelous. The great scene of Abraham's sacrifice is the renunciation of the sacrifice of infants (which is latent in the Biblical beginning) and its replacement with animal sacrifice. However, in the prophetic texts, we are a step further: it is the moment in which animal sacrifices will not work any more, as expressed, for instance, in Psalm 40: 'Sacrifice and offering you did not desire, but my ears you have pierced; burnt offerings and sin offerings you did not require.' In other words, the Bible provides not merely a replacement of the object to be sacrificed, but the end of the sacrificial order in its entirety, thanks to the consenting victim who is Jesus Christ . . . In order to free oneself from sacrifice, someone has to set the example, and renounce all mimetic retaliations: 'turn the other cheek,' as Jesus says. To learn about the role of mimetism in human violence helps us to understand why Jesus' teachings in the Sermon of the Mount are what they are. They are not masochistic; they are not excessive. They are simply realistic, taking into account our almost irresistible tendency to retaliate. The Bible conceives the history of the elected people as constant relapsing into mimetic violence and its sacrificial consequences." René Girard, *Evolution and Conversion: Dialogues on the Origins of Culture* (Bloomsbury USA Academic, 2007), 203–204.

16. René Girard, *Violence and the Sacred*, trans. Patrick Gregory (London: Bloomsbury, 2013), 8.

17. Michelle Alexander writes: "Votes cast in opposition to open housing, busing, the Civil Rights Act, and other measures time and again showed the same divisions as votes for amendments to crime bills. . . . Members of Congress who voted against civil rights measures proactively designed crime legislation and actively fought for their proposals." See page 43. "The vastly different sentences afforded drunk drivers and drug offenders speaks volumes regarding who is viewed as disposable—someone to be purged from the body

politic—and who is not." See page 206. "It is far more convenient to imagine that a majority of young African American men in urban areas freely chose a life of crime than to accept the real possibility that their lives were structured in a way that virtually guaranteed their early admission into a system from which they can never escape." See page 184. Michelle Alexander, *New Jim Crow: Mass Incarceration in the Age of Colorblindness* (New York: New Press, 2016).

18. Jonathan Sacks, "Bereishit (5769)—Violence in the Name of G-d," Office of Rabbi Sacks, October 25, 2008, http://rabbisacks.org/covenant-conversation -5769-bereishit-violence-in-the-name-of-g-d/.

19. Brueggemann, "Evangelism," 125. This is how Gideon experiences God, as pure peace, shalom. Gideon was one of Israel's judges and built an altar and called it, "The Lord is peace" (Judg. 6:24). God's work is this shalom, and God calls upon God's people to enact it by going.

Chapter Six: Prophetic Citizenship

1. John Milton, *The Tenure of Kings and Magistrates* (1650), 8.
2. Stanley Hauerwas, "Naming God," *ABC Religion & Ethics* (Australian Broadcasting Corporation), September 24, 2010, http://www.abc.net.au/ religion/articles/2010/09/24/3021305.htm.
3. Brueggemann, *Prophecy*, 3.
4. Ibid.
5. Walter Brueggemann, "Evangelism and Discipleship: The God Who Calls, the God Who Sends," *Word and World* 24, no. 2 (2004), 123.
6. The Roman Catholic document the *Lineamenta*, n15, defines vocation in this way: "Vocation is broader than mission because it is composed of both a call to *communio* and a call to mission. *Communio* is the fundamental aspect destined to endure forever. Mission, on the other hand, is a consequence of this call and is limited to an earthly existence." Kenyan B. Osborne, *Ministry: Lay Ministry in the Roman Catholic Church, Its History and Theology* (Eugene, OR: Wipf & Stock, 2003), 597.
7. Brueggemann, *Prophetic*, 5.
8. Jonathan Sacks, "Freewill (Vaera 5775)." The Office of Rabbi Sacks, January 12, 2015, http://rabbisacks.org/freewill-vaera-5775/.
9. Sacks, "Freewill."
10. Brueggemann, "Evangelism," 125.
11. Ibid., 126.
12. Brueggemann, *Prophetic*, 7–9.
13. Ibid., 13.

14. Ibid., 15.
15. James H. Cone, *God of the Oppressed* (Maryknoll, NY: Orbis Books, 1997), 108.
16. Thomas Jefferson, *The Works of Thomas Jefferson: Collected and Edited by Paul Leicester Ford*, vol. 2 (New York & London: G. P. Putnam's Sons, 1904), 200.
17. Brueggeman, *Prophetic*, 18–19.
18. Stanley Hauerwas and Travis Reed, "What Is A Christian?" The Work of the People, 2012, accessed July 20, 2017, http://www.theworkofthepeople.com /what-is-a-christian.
19. I am adapting here Hauerwas's theology of community as the underlying work of God in the shalom community. Just as Hauerwas repeatedly reminds us that the raising of you and me is linked to Jesus and then Israel's freedom, so too then is our community of shalom today rooted deeply in the call of the people of Israel paradigmatically seen in the lives of Abraham and Sarah, Esther, Isaiah, and Jonah.
20. Hauerwas, *Community*, 3.
21. Ibid., 2.
22. Ibid., 3.
23. Brueggemann, "Evangelism," 126.
24. See Jonathan Sacks, *Not in God's Name: Confronting Religious Violence* (New York: Schocken, 2017). See Emily McNeill's "Rabbi Jonathan Sacks Explores Roots of Religious Violence," *Cornell Chronicle,* April 21, 2016, http://news .cornell.edu/stories/2016/04/rabbi-jonathan-sacks-explores-roots-religious -violence. See also Brian McDonald, "Violence & the Lamb Slain," *Touchstone Archives: Violence & the Lamb Slain,* December 2003, http://www.touchstone mag.com/archives/article.php?id=16-10-040-i.
25. Hauerwas, *Community,* 2.
26. The prosperity gospel is a theology held by some Christians that financial blessings and health for the individual are the will of God for those who believe, speak nicely, demonstrate the positive thinking and speech, and give generously to religious causes. It is an exchange gospel that suggests people get things from God for being good.
27. James H. Cone, *Risks of Faith: The Emergence of a Black Theology of Liberation, 1968–1998* (Boston: Beacon Press, 1999), 109.
28. Brueggemann, "Evangelism," 121.

Chapter Seven: A Differentiated Wilderness Society

1. Vincent Bacote, *The Political Disciple: A Theology of Public Life* (Grand Rapids, MI: Zondervan, 2015), 41.

2. Martin Luther King Jr., "Where Do We Go from Here?" (speech, 11th Annual SCLC Convention, Georgia, Atlanta, August 16, 1967). You can read the whole speech here: https://kinginstitute.stanford.edu/king-papers/documents/where -do-we-go-here-address-delivered-eleventh-annual-sclc-convention.

3. Yes there are quotes about the Ten Commandments by John Adams and James Madison. And, presidents over the years have used them as a way of engendering support from conservative evangelicals. However, the founding father's were very clear as they hashed out the Constitution—no religious sect would have center stage. The reason? Because the framers believed to do so infringed on local authority. Meacham, *Gospel*, 87.

4. See *American Grace* by Robert D. Putnam and David E. Campbell.

5. Jonathan Sacks, "The Ten Utterances (extract from the Koren-Sacks Shavuot Machzor)," The Office of Rabbi Sacks, May 16, 2018, accessed July 28, 2018, http://rabbisacks.org/ten-utterances-extract-koren-sacks-shavuot-machzor/.

6. These treaties were believed to be common among kings and tribal lords. The *Mari Tablets* and in the *Amarna Texts* reveal two examples of these. These are always organized as a covenant between a greater and lesser person in the hierarchy of relationships. When familial or friendly, sometimes language for the parties was described as "father" and "son."

7. See Jon D. Levenson, *Sinai & Zion: An Entry Into The Jewish Bible*, first ed. (San Francisco: Harper, 1985), 26–36.

8. Stanley Hauerwas, *The Peaceable Kingdom: A Primer for Christian Ethics* (Notre Dame, IN: University of Notre Dame Press, 2011), 78.

9. Stanley Hauerwas as quoted in Jeffrey S. Siker, *Scripture and Ethics: Twentieth-century Portraits* (New York: Oxford University Press, 1997), 111.

10. Again, Hauerwas, "The problem of revelation aside, however, the view that the Bible contains a revealed morality that can be applied directly by the individual agent, perhaps with some help from the biblical critic, flounders when considering the status of individual commands." Hauerwas, *Peaceable*, 71.

11. Hauerwas, *Peaceable*, 72.

12. Sacks, *Ten*.

13. Humanity's tendency to kill one another was a central theme in the origin story of Cain and Abel, as well as the story of Lamech. In both stories death is seen as central to sibling rivalry. The multiplication of taking human life was the reason God had to start over with a flood in the Genesis account.

14. Sacks, *Ten*.

15. Ibid.

16. See Miroslav Volf, *The End of Memory: Remembering Rightly in a Violent World* (Grand Rapids, MI: Eerdmans, 2006).

17. Sacks, *Ten*.

18. Ibid.
19. Richard B. Hays, *Echoes of the Scripture in the Gospels* (Waco: Baylor University Press, 2018), 62.
20. Ibid., 209.
21. Ibid., 269 and 282.
22. Sacks wrote, "A contract is about advantage, a covenant is about loyalty . . . A contract is about interests, a covenant is about identity, about belonging to something bigger than me. From a contract, I gain, but from a covenant, I am transformed. I am no longer the person I once was, but am part of something larger than I once was. Thus, a social contract creates a State, but a covenant creates society." Jonathan Sacks, "Biblical Insights into the Good Society (Ebor Lecture 2011)," The Office of Rabbi Sacks, October 2, 2013, accessed July 29, 2018, http://rabbisacks.org /biblical-insights-into-the-good-society-ebor-lecture-2012/.
23. I discovered this interpretation in an article by Rabbi Josh Gerstein, who also quoted Rabbi J. B. Soloveitchik, one of the great twentieth-century Jewish thinkers, who wrote:
    "They felt that they themselves did not have access to the Almighty. Only somebody of great charisma and ability could have access to him. The people sinned because they were perplexed. Moses has been gone for a long time. . . . They did not understand that, while Moses was the greatest of all prophets and the greatest of all men, every Jew has access to God. . . . Sometimes it is a sense of one's greatness that causes sin; sometimes it is a sense of one's smallness." It is possible that the story of the golden calf actually is a reference to a dispute between the later northern and southern kingdoms. See 1 Kings 12:28–30. More than revealing that Israel has one God, the story might reveal that Israel has one place of worship and one kingdom versus a divided one. The theology here is good even if it is a historic controversy in narrative form. See Josh Gerstein, "Revisiting the Sin of the Golden Calf," Algemeiner.com, March 16, 2017, https://www.algemeiner.com/2017/03/16 /revisiting-the-sin-of-the-golden-calf/. See also Joseph B. Soltoveitchik's *Vision and Leadership* (Brooklyn, NY: KTAV Publishing House, 2012), 131.
24. Jonathan Sacks, *Radical Then, Radical Now: On Being Jewish* (Bloomsbury, 2013), 129.
25. Drawing on the work of Rabbi Jonathan Sacks in his book *The Politics of Hope*, we understand that there are always two ideas floating around when we speak about citizenship in the wider community (town, city, nation, globally).
26. Jonathan Sacks, *The Politics of Hope* (London: Vintage, 2000), 64.
27. Ibid., 63.

28. Daniel Elazar, a leading political scientist and specialist in the study of federalism, political culture, and the Jewish political tradition, writes that such a life "expresses the idea that people can freely create communities and polities, peoples and publics, and civil society itself through such morally grounded and sustained compacts (whether religious or otherwise in impetus), establishing thereby enduring partnerships." Daniel Judah Elazar, *People and Polity: The Organizational Dynamics of World Jewry* (Detroit: Wayne State University Press, 1989), 19.

29. Sacks, *Hope*, 63–64.

Chapter Eight: The Rise of King and Prophet

1. Harry S. Truman, *Where the Buck Stops: The Personal and Private Writings of Harry S. Truman*, ed. Margaret Truman (New York: New Word City, 2016), 139.

2. See Hobbes, *Leviathan*, 89. Jonathan Sacks writes, "The best analysis of the subject was given by one of the great rabbis of the 19th century, R. Zvi Hirsch Chajes, in his Torat Nevi'im. His thesis is that the institution of monarchy in the days of Samuel took the form of a social contract—as set out in the writings of Locke and Rousseau, and especially Hobbes. The people recognise that they cannot function as individuals without someone having the power to ensure the rule of law and the defence of the nation. Without this, they are in what Hobbes calls a "state of nature." Sacks, *Consent*.

3. Ibid.

4. Jonathan Sacks, "On the Limits of Power," The Office of Rabbi Sacks, August 16, 2007, http://rabbisacks.org/shoftim-5767-on-the-limits-of-power/.

5. Ibid.

6. See my book entitled *Vocātiō: Imaging a Visible Church*. It is about just this topic.

7. René Girard, *I See Satan Fall Like Lightning*, trans. by James G. Williams (Maryknoll: Orbis Books, 2001), 10.

8. Levenson, *Sinai & Zion*, 191. Deuteronomy 18:15–19 reads: The LORD your God will raise up for you a prophet like me from among your own people; you shall heed such a prophet. This is what you requested of the LORD your God at Horeb on the day of the assembly when you said: "If I hear the voice of the LORD my God any more, or ever again see this great fire, I will die." Then the LORD replied to me: "They are right in what they have said. I will raise up for them a prophet like you from among their own people; I will put my words in the mouth of the prophet, who shall speak to them everything that I

command. Anyone who does not heed the words that the prophet shall speak in my name, I myself will hold accountable."

9. Ibid., 191.
10. Ibid.
11. Ibid., 195.
12. Ibid., 23.
13. While the Sinai tradition could never be completely rooted out of the Old Testament and the Tanahk by the Deuteronimists, this essential biblical voice was, unfortunately, displaced in the Christian tradition by the second generation of Jesus followers. The New Testament and the emerging church of the late first century relocates the ministry of Jesus to the temple. Removing traces of Moses and the Sinai prophets, the Gospel and Epistle authors recast Jesus as the Messiah of the temple faith. Moreover, the second and third generation of followers accepted him as such. This squarely placed Jesus, and consequently the writers themselves, as inheritors of the temple religion.
14. Wilda C. Gafney, *Daughters of Miriam: Women Prophets in Israel* (Minneapolis: Fortress Press, 2008), 111–12.
15. Walter Brueggemann, "Walter Brueggemann: Jesus Acted Out the Alternative to Empire," *Sojourners*, June 22, 2018, accessed August 5, 2018, https://sojo.net/articles/walter-brueggemann-jesus-acted-out-alternative-empire.
16. Ibid.

Chapter Nine: A Step Into God's Story

1. Howard Thurman, *Jesus and the Disinherited* (Boston, MA: Beacon Press, 1996), 29.
2. I typically use NRSV in the texts from scripture. Here I am translating and using my own word study.
3. René Girard, *Things Hidden Since the Foundation of the World* (Stanford, CA: Stanford University Press, 1987), 215–23.
4. Ibid., 221.
5. The complete absence of any sexual element has nothing to do with repression—an explanation thought up at the end of the nineteenth century and worthy of the degraded puritanism that produced it. The fact that sexuality is not part of the picture corresponds to the absence of the violent mimesis with which myth acquaints us in the form of rape by the gods. This idol—what we have called the model-obstacle—is completely absent.
6. Jason Porterfield, "The Subversive Magnificat: What Mary Expected the Messiah to Be Like," *Enemy Love*, January 19, 2013, http://enemylove.com/subversive-magnificat-mary-expected-messiah-to-be-like/.

7. Dietrich Bonhoeffer, *The Mystery of the Holy Night*, ed. Manfred Webber (New York: Crossroad, 1996), 6. The text was translated originally by Peter Heinegg from Bonhoeffer, *Werke*, vol. 9.
8. Charles Taylor, *A Secular Age* (Cambridge, MA: Belknap Press of Harvard University Press, 2007), 775.
9. Richard A. Horsley and John S. Hanson, *Bandits, Prophets, and Messiahs; Popular Movements in the Time of Jesus* (New York: Harper, 1988), 127.
10. Flavius Josephus, *Josephus: The Antiquities of the Jews*, trans. William Whiston (London: Aeterna Press, 2015), 18.116–119.
11. The passage is taken from Matthew 4:1ff. The connections are taken from Daniel Harrington, *The Gospel of Matthew* (Collegeville, MN: Liturgical Press, 1991), 68.
12. Ibid., 70.
13. Walter Wink, Henry F. French ed., *Walter Wink: Collected Readings* (Minneapolis: Fortress Press, 2013) 106.
14. Ibid.
15. Ibid.
16. Ibid.

Chapter Ten: A Different Destiny

1. Criss Jami, *Killosophy: Killing Knowledge. Loving Wisdom* (United States: Criss Jami, 2015), 63.
2. Taken from an excerpt from René Girard's *Things Hidden since the Foundation of the World*. Research undertaken in collaboration with Jean-Michel Oughourlian and Guy Lefort (Stanford, CA: Stanford University Press, 1987), 215–223.
3. Ibid.
4. Walter Brueggemann, "Walter Brueggemann: Jesus Acted Out the Alternative to Empire," *Sojourners*, June 22, 2018, accessed August 5, 2018, https://sojo.net/articles/walter-brueggemann-jesus-acted-out-alternative-empire.
5. The Rev. Sam Wells is the first person I know of who used the term "Nazareth Manifesto" in his essay by the same name. Wells offers that Jesus did not simply offer a word of release for the captives and food for the poor, Jesus seeks to be with the people in their hunger and imprisonment. Sam Wells, "Nazareth Manifesto," *Vagt Lecture: The Nazareth Manifesto*, April 27, 2008, https://web.duke.edu/kenanethics/NazarethManifesto_SamWells.pdf.
6. Walter Brueggemann writes that the prophetic task is twofold: "The first prophetic task is to be clear on the force and illegitimacy of the totalism. And what we have to recognize is that almost all of us, conservative and

liberals—almost all of us, clergy and laity—are to some extent inured in the totalism. We take it as normative. And to take that as normative is a great narcotic that makes us passive and apathetic. Becoming clear and unambiguous about the force of the totalism is a teaching point that we really have to work at. . . . The second task of prophetic imagination that I could identify is that we have to pronounce the truth about the force of the totalism that contradicts the purpose of God. That's called prophetic judgment. And my sense is that in the institutional church we are very quiet about prophetic judgment, because we and most of our parishioners are too deeply committed to totalism, and you really are not able to talk that way." Walter Brueggemann, "Walter Brueggemann: Jesus Acted Out the Alternative to Empire," *Sojourners*, June 22, 2018, accessed August 5, 2018, https://sojo.net /articles/walter-brueggemann-jesus-acted-out-alternative-empire.

7. Stanley Hauerwas, *Matthew: Brazos Theological Commentary on the Bible*, comp. R. R. Reno (Grand Rapids, MI: Brazos Press, 2006), 67.

8. Charles L. Campbell, *The Word before the Powers: An Ethic of Preaching* (Louisville, KY: Westminster John Knox, 2002), 49.

9. Walter Wink, *Engaging the Powers: Discernment and Resistance in a World of Domination* (Minneapolis, MN: Fortress Press, 1999), 112.

10. See also John Kavanaugh's discussion of the link between violence and the commodity form of life in John F. Kavanaugh, *Following Christ in a Consumer Society: The Spirituality of Cultural Resistance* (Maryknoll, NY: Orbis Books, 2006), 43–53.

11. Jesus was killed by humanity as a re-enactment of ancient religious sacrifice. He participated totally in the mimetic sacrifice. If that were the end of it, then we would be invested in just another community with a scapegoat theology that repeated the violence of mythic gods. But God took our violence and broke it open. Jesus was raised from the dead by God and in so doing, Girard says, God "refutes the whole principle of violence and sacrifice. God is revealed as the 'arch-scapegoat', the completely innocent one who dies in order to give life. And his way of giving life is to overthrow the religion of scapegoating and sacrifice—which is the essence of myth." The Old Testament narrative reveals God to be the maker of shalom that undoes the endless sibling rivalries and repeated sacrifices that bend humankind towards vengeance. The story of Jesus lines up with the stories of Cain and Abel, Joseph, Job, and the Psalms, as well as the experience of Moses and the Israelites in Egypt. The story of the people of shalom is a story that reverses all scapegoat typologies. Christ is innocent and reveals the violence and scapegoating of the world. Only in the shalom community's innocence can people strive for peace and reveal the violence that dominates every age. God in Christ Jesus, the incarnation

made flesh in history, enables an anthropological reading of the scripture that reverses human violence and reveals the community of peace. We begin to understand that inside our shared monstrosity, there is a fragment of humanity in perfect communion with God. Wink says we are "fleetingly human, brokenly human." We are created in the very image of the Incarnation: "Only God is human, and we are made in God's image and likeness—which is to say, we are capable of becoming human." Jesus the Prince of Peace helps us glimpse our true humanity by revealing a capacity for peace-building that has been deep within us since our creation.

Jesus turns our inherited notions about God upside down. We discover that we have been a part of religious systems of domination. We believed that God requires Jesus's death, making God a mythic monster. We believed that we should be grateful for this sacrifice because of our monstrous flesh. We attended church and give generously in order to undo our fleshly sin, make recompense for our evil, and gain eternal life. The medieval church innovated a theory of atonement that remains popular today encouraging such maxims. This theology built cathedrals and lined the purses of many clerics. However, substitutionary atonement theory does not line up with the story of the sacrifice of Isaac, where God made clear that no human sacrifices were required. It does not line up with the idea that humans are modeled on the eternal Incarnation. Moreover, this theory of the atonement sanctions the commission of violence against others in many varying and inhumane forms for the sake of peace. By contrast, the gospel of peace reveals God as a victim of violence, and as a human worth saving. This gospel reveals that we are connected to the Incarnation itself, in our innermost parts. Living and following Jesus is about embracing the Incarnation and rejecting the old mimetic tendencies that inevitably find their way back into religion—even Christianity. By the grace of God, the Incarnation is our hope and our potential. The world is truly turned upside down by the resurrection of God in Christ Jesus. See Walter Wink, *Engaging the Powers Discernment and Resistance in a World of Domination* (Minneapolis, MN: Fortress Press, 1999), 102.

12. American soldiers have seen action in the following engagements: The Barbary Wars (1783–1812), War of 1812, War with Mexico (1846–48), American Civil War (1861–65), Indian Wars (1865–91), Spanish-American War (1898), Philippine-American War (1899–1902), Banana Wars (1898–1935), Boxer Rebellion (1899–1901), Moro Rebellion (1899–1913), Mexico (1910–19), World War I (1917–18), Russian Revolution (1918–19), World War II (1941–45), Korean War (1950–53), Lebanon crisis of 1958, Vietnam War (1964–75), Grenada, Beirut, Libya, Panama, Post-Cold War era (1991–2001), Persian Gulf War (1990–91), Somalia, Haiti, Yugoslavia, War on

Terrorism (2001–present) and includes forces on the ground in Afghanistan, Philippines, Iraq, and Syria.

13. Hauerwas, *Unleashing*, 120.

Chapter Eleven: A Decolonized Citizenship

1. Ekemini Uwan, "Decolonized Discipleship," blog, February 8, 2018, accessed August 16, 2018, http://www.sistamatictheology.com/blog.

2. Ched Myers, *Binding the Strong Man: A Political Reading of Mark's Story of Jesus* (Maryknoll, NY: Orbis Books, 1994), 190.

3. Ched Myers, "Confronting Legion," *Radical Discipleship*, June 11, 2016, accessed August 7, 2018, https://radicaldiscipleship.net/2016/06/16/confronting-legion/.

4. Ibid.

5. Ibid.

6. "The famous and feared Tenth Legion was often symbolized by a pig mascot (left, countermark coin symbolizes 'Legio X Fretensis,' the Tenth Legion, showing a boar). These veteran imperial soldiers saw action in Judea in the revolt of 6 CE, again during the counterinsurgency of 68–70, and were also responsible for the siege of Masada, after which they were based in Jerusalem." Ibid.

7. Ibid.

8. See also J. Duncan M. Derrett, "Contributions to the Study of the Gerasene Demoniac," *Journal for the Study of the New Testament* 2, no. 3 (1979): 5.

9. See research conducted by University of Chicago's Project on Security and Terrorism by Robert Pape and James Feldman. Robert Anthony Pape and James K. Feldman, *Cutting the Fuse: The Explosion of Global Suicide Terrorism and How to Stop It* (Chicago: University of Chicago Press, 2012).

10. Frantz Fanon, *The Wretched Earth*, trans. Richard Philcox (Grove Press: New York, 1963), 19.

11. Fanon writes, "Sometimes people hold a core belief that is very strong. When they are presented with evidence that works against that belief, the new evidence cannot be accepted. It would create a feeling that is extremely uncomfortable, called cognitive dissonance. And because it is so important to protect the core belief, they will rationalize, ignore and even deny anything that doesn't fit in with the core belief." Frantz Fanon, ed., *Black Skins, White Masks*, trans. Richard Philcox (New York: Grove Press, 1952), 146.

12. Friedrich Wilhelm Nietzsche, *Beyond Good and Evil; On the Genealogy of Morality*, trans. R. J. Hollingdale (New York & London: Penguin, 1973), 146.

13. "Onward, Christian Soldiers" is a nineteenth-century English hymn. The words were written by Sabine Baring-Gould in 1865, and the music was

composed by Arthur Sullivan in 1871. Marcus Tullius, *Cicero: Cicero's Select Orations*, trans. Duncan William (New Haven: Sidney's Press, for Evert Duyckinck, 1811), 33.

14. I am using the research and work of Ched Myers here in the discourse on the feedings. Myers, *Binding*, 206–210.

15. Vincent Taylor, *The Gospel According to St. Mark: The Greek Text with Introduction, Notes and Indexes* (London: Macmillan, 1963), 323.

16. Maximilian Zerwick and Mary Grosvenor, *A Grammatical Analysis of the Greek New Testament* (Rome: Biblical Institute Press, 1974), 124.

17. Haidt, *Righteous*, 212–213.

18. Cornel West, *Prophesy Deliverance!: An Afro-American Revolutionary Christianity* (Louisville, KY: Westminster John Knox Press, 2002), 113.

Chapter Twelve: The Story of the Disinherited

1. Dietrich Bonhoeffer, *The Cost of Discipleship* (New York: Scribner, 1963), 118.

2. Bruce J. Malina, *The New Testament World Insights from Cultural Anthropology* (Louisville, KY: Westminster John Knox Press, 1981), 47.

3. Ibid.

4. Joel Marcus, *Mark 1–8: A New Translation with Introduction and Commentary*, vol. 1 (New Haven: Yale University Press, 2010), 366.

5. Susan E. Miller, *Women in Mark's Gospel* (London: T&T Clark, 2002), 59–60.

6. Marcus, *Mark*, 372.

7. Haidt, *Righteous*, 172–179.

8. Ibid., 174.

9. In a brilliant article on the unspoken class system in America, Clive Crook describes how our own language in America supports a class system most of us would just like to pretend is nonexistent. Clive Crook, "American Snobbery," *The Atlantic*, July 17, 2013, accessed August 11, 2018, https://www.theatlantic .com/national/archive/2012/05/american-snobbery/256931/.

10. Robert N. Bellah, *Habits of the Heart: Individualism and Commitment in American Life* (Berkeley: University of California Press, 1996), 2.

11. Dan E. Beauchamp, "Public Health as Social Justice," *Inquiry* 13, no. 1 (March 1, 1976): 12:3–14.

12. Ann Robertson, "Health Promotion and the Common Good: Theoretical Considerations," *Critical Public Health* 9, no. 2 (1999): 117–133.

13. Mary Ann Glendon, *Rights Talk: The Impoverishment of Political Discourse* (New York, NY: Free Press, 1993), 12.

14. George Lakoff, *Moral Politics: What Conservatives Know That Liberals Don't* (Chicago: University of Chicago Press, 1996), 113 and 295.

15. Robert Runcie, *The Truth Shall Make You Free: The Lambeth Conference 1988* (Church House Publishing, 1988), 16.

Chapter Thirteen: The Hive Lens

1. Amy Gutmann and Dennis Thompson, "The Mindsets of Political Compromise," *Perspectives on Politics* 8, no. 4 (2010): 1125. See also online version here: https://president.upenn.edu/meet-president/mindsets-political -compromise.
2. Haidt, *Righteous*, 358–359.
3. Adam Smith, *The Theory of Moral Sentiments* (Oxford: Oxford University Press, 1976), part VI, sec ii, ch 2.
4. Nassim Nicholas Taleb, *Antifragile: Things That Gain from Disorder* (New York: Random House, 2012), 151.
5. Durkheim, *Elementary*, 219–220; 271–272.
6. Jonathan Haidt, J. Patrick Seder, and Selin Kesebir, "Hive Psychology, Happiness, and Public Policy," *Journal of Legal Studies* 37 (2008): 133–156.
7. Robert D. Putnam and David E. Campbell, *American Grace: How Religion Divides and Unites Us* (New York: Simon & Schuster, 2012), 471–492.
8. Putnam, *Grace*, 526–534.
9. Haidt, *Righteous*, 360.
10. See Marc Dunkelman's work *The Vanishing Neighbor: The Transformation of American Community* (New York: W. W. Norton, 2014).
11. Capon, *Kingdom*, 204.
12. Ibid., 203.
13. Ibid., 203.
14. Ibid., 205.
15. Ibid., 206.
16. Ibid., 201.
17. I was introduced to Ivan Illich's work through the reading of Charles Taylor's *A Secular Age*. I am using Taylor's treatment of Illich. Ivan Illich's work entitled *The Rivers of the North of the Future* is worth a read. See Taylor, *Secular*, 714–715.
18. Taylor, *Secular*, 714
19. Charles Taylor agrees with Illich here that what happens to the Samaritan story is that it is corrupted. A friend of mine, the Right Reverend Sean Rowe, remarked to me recently, "Every movement must organize." When the movement falls into something more "normal" in worldly terms, says Taylor, it automatically begins to form rules and boundaries. It forms a new tribe and community. With this new normal there is a new set of tribal insiders

and tribal outsiders. The church, Illich and Taylor argue, "develops into a need to shore up and institutionalize them, introduce rules, divide responsibilities" (715). We create a new modern bureaucracy. Illich argues that the Reformation really does something important to humanism by institutionalizing it. Taylor writes, "Rules then become modern bureaucracies based upon rationality and rules prescribe treatments for categories of people; so we fit into categories; our rights, entitlements, burdens depend on the shape of life these rules give us" (716). Taylor clearly see this as "a corruption of the original" (716). What happens, Taylor explains, is that the organization of daily life is constantly creating a system of ins and outs and in so doing, undermines "a sense of mutual belonging" that is the intent of the parable. Jesus is not creating a system of morality, but a way of being in the world with one another. The randomness of our encounters invites us to continuously break the code and system in which we are formed (718).

20. Capon, *Kingdom*, 202.
21. Fleming Rutledge, "Who Is the Good Samaritan?" *Generous Orthodoxy*, May 1, 2005, http://generousorthodoxy.org/sermons/who-is-the-good-samaritan.aspx
22. Ibid.
23. Glenn Greenwald is a liberal author who often writes for the *Guardian* newspaper. He coined the term in his highly critical book of the George H. W. Bush White House years, entitled *A Tragic Legacy*. See Glenn Greenwald, *A Tragic Legacy: How a Good vs. Evil Mentality Destroyed the Bush Presidency* (New York: Three Rivers Press, 2008), 48 and 52.
24. Religion and the Cold War specialist Dianne Kirby, in the article entitled *The Cold War and American Religion*, says, "The process of designating communism a religion has a long provenance. It was used by Martin Dies, creator and first chairman of the House Un-American Activities Committee, originally known as the Dies Committee, to argue that Americans had to fight faith with faith, in *The Trojan Horse in America* (New York: Dodd, Mead, 1940). Dies posited an irreconcilable conflict between Christ and Marx, stating the future of Western civilization necessitated the restoration of Christian influence in America." Religious ideas were enshrined in the crucial 1950 Cold War document NSC 68, which referred to defeating the fanatic faith of communism by mobilizing a "spiritual counter-force." (Ernest R. May, ed., *American Cold War Strategy: Interpreting NSC 68* [Boston: Bedford, 1993], 29–30.) Dulles was convinced that a universal values-based creed was essential for world order. Soon after Eisenhower's first inauguration, Dulles spoke with the president about the need for a comprehensive education program that would assure popular understanding "of the 'American mission' and its problems." Shortly afterwards, *Reader's Digest*, in language resonant with

Dulles's own sentiments, reported that Eisenhower wanted to use his influence and his presidency to encourage "a spiritual turning point in America, and thereby to recover the strengths, the values, and the conduct which a vital faith produces in a people." (Stanley High, "What the President Wants," *Reader's Digest* [April 1953]: 2–4.) The book *The Cold War and American Religion* by Dianne Kirby is a fascinating historical account. For full article see Dianne Kirby, "Cold War and American Religion," *Oxford Research Encyclopedia of Religion*, August 14, 2017, http://religion.oxfordre.com/view/10.1093/acrefore/9780199340378.001.0001/acrefore-9780199340378-e-398.

25. Putnam, *Grace*, 471–489.

Chapter Fourteen: Vineyard, Sword, and Cross

1. Katie G. Cannon, *Teaching Preaching: Isaac Rufus Clark and Black Sacred Rhetoric* (London: Continuum, 2007), 181.
2. Joachim Jeremias, *The Parables of Jesus* (London: Xpress Reprints, 1995), 70.
3. Ibid.
4. Myers, *Binding*, 308–309.
5. Stanley Hauerwas, "The Politics of the Church and the Humanity of God," *ABC News*, June 18, 2012, accessed August 14, 2018, http://www.abc.net.au/religion/articles/2012/06/19/3528056.htm.
6. S. G. F. Brandon, *Jesus and the Zealots: Aftermath* (Manchester: John Rylands Library, 1971), 45.
7. Robert C. Tannehill, *The Sword of His Mouth: Forceful and Imaginative Language in Synoptic Sayings* (Philadelphia: Fortress Press, 1975), 173.
8. Daniel L. Dreisbach, *Thomas Jefferson and the Wall of Separation between Church and State* (New York: New York University Press, 2003), 77.
9. William Stringfellow, *An Ethic for Christians and Other Aliens in a Strange Land* (Waco, TX: Word Books, 1973), 111.
10. Wink, *Powers*, 82.
11. Stanley Hauerwas writes in his exposition of Matthew's version of the story: "Jesus's command that the sword be put away is not a conclusive text, committing his followers to some version of pacifism. Arguments for Christian non-violence, just as arguments for the Christian justification of violence, depend on how the story is told and the kind of community that exists to tell the story. Jesus's command that the sword be put away is but one expression that testifies to his willingness to be given over to sinners and crucified so that we might be made part of the new age inaugurated by his birth, death, and resurrection. Therefore, Christian non-violence cannot be a position separable

from what it means to be a disciple. Rather, Christian non-violence is, in the words of John Howard Yoder, the pacifism of the messianic community. Such pacifism would 'lose its substance if Jesus were not Christ and would lose its foundation if Jesus Christ were not Lord.'" Stanley Hauerwas, *Matthew* (Grand Rapids, MI: Brazos Press, 2006), 224.

12. Myers, 380.

13. Hauerwas, 235.

14. Brian McDonald, "Violence & the Lamb Slain: An Interview with René Girard," Touchstone Archives: Violence & the Lamb Slain. December 2003. Accessed July 24, 2017. http://www.touchstonemag.com/archives/article .php?id=16-10-040-i.

15. Wink, *Powers*, 82.

16. Stanley Hauerwas, *The Peaceable Kingdom: A Primer for Christian Ethics* (Notre Dame, IN: University of Notre Dame Press, 2011), 118.

17. The theological gloss that the shared meal is a remembrance of Christ's sacrifice for atonement was not established until the third century, nevertheless the common understanding about the atonement by most Christians is informed by this late development. Many Christians do not have a breadth of understanding about the multiple Christian and orthodox theories of the atonement. There are actually seven theories of atonement: the moral influence theory, ransom theory, Christus Victor, the satisfaction theory, the penal substitution theory, the governmental theory, and the scapegoat theory. People may call these by different names. It points to the reality that while most people live their Christian lives within one theory there are multiple theologies of atonement that are accepted within orthodox Christianity. Most people are familiar with the one where God requires Jesus to be a blood sacrifice—substitutionary atonement. If you are interested in the many theologies of the Christian Church I suggest reading *Crucifixion* by Fleming Rutledge. This is an excellent text on the subject. Fleming Rutledge, *Crucifixion: Understanding the Death of Jesus Christ* (Grand Rapids, MI: W.B. Eerdmans, 2017), 635.

Chapter Fifteen: The State's Accountability to God

1. James H. Cone, *The Cross and the Lynching Tree* (Maryknoll, NY: Orbis Books, 2016), 155.

2. I first understood this concept when I read scholar and activist Ched Myers's commentary on Mark entitled *Binding the Strong Man*. In it, Myers claims the term "fishers of men" is not about "saving souls" but about "overturn(ing) the existing order of powers, and privilege." The problem I have with Myers's

reading is that at times it devolves into a humanistic justice argument will-ing to accept violence. I also think that it is too focused on social action and does not take into account the overarching theme of the cross, resurrection, and salvation as a cosmic undoing and redoing. I am offering here a differ-ent version—one with a critical eye to Myers's reading, though clearly I am indebted to it. Ched Myers, *Binding the Strong Man: A Political Reading of Mark's Story of Jesus* (Maryknoll, NY: Orbis Books, 2008), 132.

3. Robert Farrar Capon, *Kingdom, Grace, Judgment: Paradox, Outrage, and Vindication in the Parables of Jesus* (Grand Rapids, MI: W.B. Eerdmans, 2002), 113–15.

4. Ibid., 113.

5. Herman, *Cave*, 171.

6. Ibid., 170.

7. Tertullian, *On Idolatry*, trans. Sydney Thelwall (New York: Kissinger, 2004), 18–19.

8. Ched Myers, "Mark: Invitation to Discipleship," in *The New Testament: Introducing the Way of Discipleship*, ed. Sharon Ringe and Wes Howard-Brook (Maryknoll, NY: Orbis Books, 2002), 9.

9. Ibid.

10. Karl Barth, *The Church and State*, trans. Ronald Howe (Toronto: Macmillan Company, 1939), 35.

11. See Jeff Sessions's statement: "I would cite you to the Apostle Paul and his clear and wise command in Romans 13, to obey the laws of the government because God has ordained the government for his purposes . . . Orderly and lawful processes are good in themselves. Consistent and fair application of the law is in itself a good and moral thing, and that protects the weak and protects the lawful." Further comments by Jeff Sessions can be found in, "Attorney General Sessions Addresses Recent Criticisms of Zero Tolerance By Church Leaders" (speech, Fort Wayne Rotary Club: Rotarians, Religious Leaders, Lawyers, and Law Enforcement Gathering, Fort Wayne, IN, June 14, 2018).

12. See *Time* magazine article from June 12, 1933. "Berlin's vast Sportpalast rumbled one night last week with a great gathering of the 'German Christians,' Nazi Wing of the Evangelical Church (*Time*, June 12, et seq.). Joachim Hessenfelder was on deck to demand the super-Nazification of the Church. Their presiding officer was brisk, sleek, pomaded young Rev. Joachim Hossenfelder, Bishop of Berlin and Brandenburg. Their prime hot-head was one Dr. Reinhold Krause. Meeting a few days after the 450th birthday of their Church's founder, Martin Luther, they proceeded to juggle ecclesiastical dynamite. According to Nazi Pastor Krause, German Protestantism needed a 'second Reformation.'" "Germany: New Heathenism," *Time*, November

27, 1933, accessed August 15, 2018, http://content.time.com/time/magazine /article/0,9171,746354,00.html.

13. See interview with Doris Bergen, a professor of holocaust studies at the University of Toronto. She believes there was never a need "to exhort Germans to be obedient to the regime, because it never occurred to most of them to do otherwise." She reminds us that German Protestantism at the time was enmeshed with the idea that the nation's rule was supreme. Bergen, author of *Twisted Cross: The German Christian Movement in the Third Reich*, explains "The whole Nazi system rested on approval of the Christian population, which was 98 percent of the population . . . The idea some Americans have that there was a faction of Christians opposing Nazis—it was not like that," Bergen notes. "Most Christians were Nazis and Nazis were Christians, and that's just the way it was." See Dina Kraft, "The Real Story behind the Nazi Establishment's Use of 'Romans 13,'" Haaretz.com, June 20, 2018, https://www.haaretz.com /us-news/.premium-the-real-story-behind-the-nazi-establishment-s-use -of-romans-13-1.6194455.

14. Barth, *The Church and State*, 35.

15. Ibid., 66.

16. Romans 13—Stanley Hauerwas, YouTube, October 14, 2014, accessed August 15, 2018, https://www.youtube.com/watch?v=PSw3tL-VkuI.

17. Martin Luther King Jr., "Paul's Letter to American Christians," Stanford, November 4, 1956, http://okra.stanford.edu/transcription/document_images /Vol03Scans/414_4-Nov-1956_Pauls Letter to American Christians.pdf.

Chapter Sixteen: A Tabling Christian Citizenship

1. William J. Barber II, *Forward Together: A Moral Message for the Nation* (St. Louis, MO: Chalice Press, 2014), 21.

2. Walter Wink, *The Powers That Be: Theology for a New Millennium* (New York: Doubleday, 1998), 98–111.

3. Ibid.

4. Ibid.

5. Hauerwas, *Unleashing*, 15, 16, 17.

6. Stanley Hauerwas, "A Sanctuary Politics: Being the Church in the Time of Trump," *ABC News*, March 30, 2017, accessed July 20, 2018, http://www.abc .net.au/religion/articles/2017/03/30/4645538.htm.

7. Karl Barth, *Church Dogmatics: The Doctrine of God*, vol. II/1, trans G. W. Bromiley and Thomas F. Torrance (Edinburgh: T. & T. Clark, 1975), 168.

8. Karl Barth, *Church Dogmatics: The Doctrine of God*, vol. IV/4.3.1, trans G. W. Bromiley and Thomas F. Torrance (Edinburgh: T. & T. Clark, 1975), 146–147.

9. See Cornel West's book *The American Evasion of Philosophy* (Madison, WI: University of Wisconsin Press, 1989).

10. West, *Prophecy*, 146.

11. Barth, *Dogmatics*, vol. IV/4.3.1, 146–147.

12. Hauerwas, "A Sanctuary Politics."

13. Hauerwas, "A Sanctuary Politics."

14. Putnam and Campbell, *Grace*, 418.

15. Ibid., 442.

16. Ibid., 472–474.

17. Ibid., 491.

18. Jon Meacham, *Soul of America: The Battle for Our Better Angels* (New York: Random House Large Print, 2018), 266–271.

19. Talal Asad, *Formations of the Secular: Christianity, Islam, Modernism* (Stanford: Stanford University Press, 2003), 178.

20. Willis Jenkins, *The Future of Ethics: Sustainability, Social Justice, and Religious Creativity* (Washington, DC: Georgetown, 2013), 100.

21. Brueggemann, *Prophecy*, 3.

22. See Milbank on Lubac's rejection of *grace* as a mere *extraneum*, or change in status. Instead, Milbank argues that "wherever self-transcending love and mercy are shown, there divine charity is present." John Milbank, *The Suspended Middle: Henri De Lubac and the Renewed Split in Modern Catholic Theology* (Grand Rapids, MI: W. B. Eerdmans, 2014), 22.

23. Stanley Hauerwas and Romand Coles, ""Long Live The Weeds And The Wilderness Yet": Reflections On A Secular Age," *Modern Theology* 26, no. 3 (2010), 349–62.

24. See Hauerwas and Coles, *Christianity*, 112.

25. Stanley Hauerwas, *After Christendom: How the Church Is to Behave If Freedom, Justice, and a Christian Nation Are Bad Ideas* (Nashville: Abingdon Press, 1999), 91.

26. Coles, *Beyond*, 121.

27. Jeremy Neill, "Political Involvement and Religious Compromises," *Political Theology* 14, no. 1 (April 21, 2015): 47–51.

28. Hauerwas and Coles, *Christianity*, 195–207. See also Hauerwas and Jena Vanier's book *Living Gently in a Violent World: The Prophetic Witness of Weakness (Resources for Reconciliation)* (Downers Grove, IL: InterVarsity Press, 2008).

29. This list is created from a long list of ideas on the internet.

30. Coles, *Gated*, 213–237.

Conclusion: No Pleasant Valley Sunday

1. Pauli Murray, *Dark Testament: And Other Poems* (Norwalk, CT: Silvermine Publishing, 1970), 27.
2. See Milbank and Pabst critique. *Politics*, 87.
3. Ibid., 122.
4. Ibid., 275–276.
5. Ibid., 276.
6. MacIntyre, *After*, 50–51.
7. Ibid., 10–11.
8. Ibid.

Bibliography

Alexander, Michelle. *New Jim Crow: Mass Incarceration in the Age of Colorblindness*. New Press, 2016.

Anderson, Benedict R. O'G. *Imagined Communities: Reflections on the Origin and Spread of Nationalism*. Verso, 2016.

Apple, Michael W. *Ideology and Curriculum*. Routledge, 1979.

Aristotle. *Politics*. Translated by H. W. C. Davis and Benjamin Jowett. Cosimo Classics, 2008.

Asad, Talal. *Formations of the Secular: Christianity, Islam, Modernism*. Stanford University Press, 2003.

Athanasius. *The Incarnation of the Word of God*. Translated by Religious C.S.M.B. The Macmillan Company, 1946.

Bacote, Vincent. *The Political Disciple: A Theology of Public Life*. Zondervan, 2015.

Bailie, Gil. *Violence Unveiled: Humanity at the Crossroads*. Crossroad, 2004.

Banks, J. *Diversity and Citizenship Education: Global Perspectives*. Jossey-Bass, 2004.

Barber, William J. *Forward Together: A Moral Message for the Nation*. Chalice Press, 2014.

Barth, Karl. *The Church and State*. Translated by Ronald Howe. The Macmillan Company, 1939.

Beauchamp, Dan E. "Public Health as Social Justice." *Inquiry* 13, no. 1 (1 Mar. 1976): 3–14.

Beiner, Ronald, and J. G. A. Pocock. "The Ideal of Citizenship since Classical Times." *Theorizing Citizenship*. State University of New York Press, Albany, 1995.

Beiner, Ronald. *Civil Religion: A Dialogue in the History of Political Philosophy*. Cambridge University Press, 2011.

Bellah, Robert N. "Civil Religion in America." *Daedalus, Journal of the American Academy of Arts and Sciences* 96, no. 4 (1967): 1–21.

Bellah, Robert N. *Habits of the Heart: Individualism and Commitment in American Life*. University of California Press, 1996.

Bellah, Robert Neelly. *Beyond Belief: Essays on Religion in a Post-traditional World*. University of California Press, 1991.

Bilder, Mary Sarah. *Madison's Hand: Revising the Constitutional Convention*. Harvard University Press, 2017.

Bonhoeffer, Dietrich. *The Cost of Discipleship*. Scribner, 1963.

Bonhoeffer, Dietrich. *Dietrich Bonhoeffer Works. Barcelona, Berlin, New York: 1928–1931*. Edited by Clifford J. Green. Fortress Press, 2008.

The Book of Common Prayer: And Administration of the Sacraments and Other Rites and Ceremonies of the Church: Together with the Psalter or Psalms of David. Church Publishing, 2007.

Brandon, S. G. F. *Jesus and the Zealots: Aftermath*. John Rylands Library, 1971.

Brueggemann, Walter. *The Prophetic Imagination*. Fortress Press, 2001.

Brueggemann, Walter. "Evangelism and Discipleship: The God Who Calls, the God Who Sends." *Word and World* 24, no. 2 (2004): 121–135.

Brueggemann, Walter. *Sabbath as Resistance: Saying No to the Culture of Now*. Westminster John Knox Press, 2017.

Brueggemann, Walter. "Walter Brueggemann: Jesus Acted Out the Alternative to Empire." *Sojourners*, 22 June 2018, sojo.net/articles/walter-brueggemann-jesus-acted-out-alternative-empire. Accessed 5 Aug. 2018.

Brueggemann, Walter, and Carolyn J. Sharp. *Disruptive Grace: Reflections on God, Scripture, and the Church*. Fortress Press, 2011.

Burack, J., et al. "Students, the World, and the Global Education Ideology." *Where Did Social Studies Go Wrong?* Edited by J. Leming, 40–69. Thomas B. Fordham Foundation, Washington, DC, 2003.

Cannon, Katie G. *Teaching Preaching: Isaac Rufus Clark and Black Sacred Rhetoric*. Continuum, 2007.

Cicero, Marcus Tullius. *Cicero's Select Orations*. Translated by Duncan William. Sidney's Press, for Evert Duyckinck, 1811.

Coles, Romand. *Beyond Gated Politics: Reflections for the Possibility of Democracy*. University of Minnesota, 2005.

Cone, James H. *God of the Oppressed*. Orbis Books, 1997.

Cone, James H. *Risks of Faith: The Emergence of a Black Theology of Liberation, 1968–1998*. Beacon Press, 1999.

Cone, James H. *The Cross and the Lynching Tree*. Orbis Books, 2016.

Cornwallis, Charles. "Cornwallis Papers from Yorktown." *Gilder Lehrman Institute of American History*, www.gilderlehrman.org/content/surrender-british-general-cornwallis-americans-october-19-1781. Accessed 27 July 2018.

Cortes, Ernesto. "Open Forum." *The Texas Observer*, 26 Oct. 2012, www.texas observer.org/2348-open-forum-habits-of-democracy/. Accessed 16 Aug. 2018.

Crook, Clive. "American Snobbery." *The Atlantic*, 17 July 2013, www.theatlantic .com/national/archive/2012/05/american-snobbery/256931/. Accessed 11 Aug. 2018.

Cuomo, Gov. Mario. "Religious Belief and Public Morality: A Catholic Governor's Perspective." John A. O'Brien Lecture in the University of Notre Dame's Department of Theology, 13 Sept. 1984, Notre Dame, IN.

Derrett, J. Duncan M. "Contributions to the Study of the Gerasene Demoniac." *Journal for the Study of the New Testament* 2, no. 3 (1979): 2–17.

Dozier, Verna J. *The Dream of God: A Call to Return*. Church Publishing, 2006.

Dreisbach, Daniel L. *Thomas Jefferson and the Wall of Separation between Church and State*. New York University Press, 2003.

Durkheim Émile. *The Elementary Forms of the Religious Life: A Study in Religious Sociology*. Andesite Press, 2017.

Elazar, Daniel Judah. *People and Polity: The Organizational Dynamics of World Jewry*. Wayne State University Press, 1989.

Epps, Garrett. "Constitutional Myth #4: The Constitution Doesn't Separate Church and State." *The Atlantic*, 11 July 2011, www.theatlantic.com/national /archive/2011/06/constitutional-myth-4-the-constitution-doesnt-separate -church-and-state/240481/. Accessed 14 Aug. 2018.

Fanon, Frantz. *Black Skins, White Masks*. Translated by Richard Philcox. Grove Press, 1952.

Fanon, Frantz. *The Wretched Earth*. Translated by Richard Philcox. Grove Press: New York, 1963.

"The First Virginia Charter 1606." *American History 1600–1650*, www.let.rug.nl /usa/documents/1600-1650/the-first-virginia-charter-1606.php. Accessed 4 Aug. 2018.

Franklin, Benjamin. "A Concise Creed." Received by Ezra Stiles, 9 Mar. 1790, Philadelphia, Pennsylvania.

Gabel, John Butler, and Charles B. Wheeler. *The Bible as Literature: An Introduction*. Oxford University Press, 1986.

Gafney, Wilda C. *Daughters of Miriam: Women Prophets in Ancient Israel*. Fortress Press, 2008.

"Germany: New Heathenism." *Time*, 27 Nov. 1933, content.time.com/time/mag-azine/article/0,9171,746354,00.html. Accessed 15 Aug. 2018.

Gerson, Michael. "The Last Temptation." *The Atlantic*, 11 Mar. 2018, www.the atlantic.com/magazine/archive/2018/04/the-last-temptation/554066/. Accessed 19 July 2018.

Gerstein, Josh. "Revisiting the Sin of the Golden Calf." Algemeiner.com, 16 Mar. 2017, www.algemeiner.com/2017/03/16/revisiting-the-sin-of-the-golden -calf/. Accessed 5 Oct. 2017.

Girard, René. *Evolution and Conversion: Dialogues on the Origins of Culture*. Bloomsbury USA Academic, 2007.

Girard, René. *Things Hidden since the Foundation of the World*. Translated by Jean-Michel Oughourlian and Guy Lefort. Stanford University Press, 1987.

Girard, René. *I See Satan Fall like Lightning*. Translated by James G. Williams. Orbis Books, 2001.

Girard, René. *Violence and the Sacred*. Translated by Patrick Gregory. Bloomsbury, 2013.

Giroux, H. *The Terror of Neoliberalism: Rethinking the Significance of Cultural Politics*. Routledge, 2018.

Glendon, Mary Ann. *Rights Talk: The Impoverishment of Political Discourse*. Free Press, 1993.

Gray, John. *Two Faces of Liberalism*. Polity Press, 2004.

Greenwald, Glenn. *A Tragic Legacy: How a Good vs. Evil Mentality Destroyed the Bush Presidency*. Three Rivers Press, 2008.

Gregory of Nazianzus. *On God and Christ: The Five Theological Orations and Two Letters to Cledonius*. St. Vladimir's Seminary Press, 2002.

Gregory of Nazianzus. *Festal Orations*. St. Vladimir's Seminary Press, 2008.

Gutmann, Amy, and Dennis Thompson. "The Mindsets of Political Compromise." *Perspectives on Politics* 8, no. 4 (2010): 1125–1143.

Haidt, Jonathan. *The Righteous Mind: Why Good People Are Divided by Politics and Religion*. Penguin Books, 2013.

Haidt, Jonathan, et al. "Hive Psychology, Happiness, and Public Policy." *Journal of Legal Studies* 37 (2008): S133–S156.

Harrington, Daniel J. *The Gospel of Matthew*. Liturgical Press, 2007.

Hauerwas, Stanley. *Unleashing the Scripture: Freeing the Bible from Captivity to America*. Abingdon, 1993.

Hauerwas, Stanley. *After Christendom: How the Church Is to Behave if Freedom, Justice, and a Christian Nation Are Bad Ideas*. Abingdon Press, 1999.

Hauerwas, Stanley M. *The Peaceable Kingdom: A Primer for Christian Ethics*. University of Notre Dame Press, 2011.

Hauerwas, Stanley. *War and the American Difference: Theological Reflections on Violence and National Identity*. Baker Academic, 2011.

Hauerwas, Stanley. "A Sanctuary Politics: Being the Church in the Time of Trump." *ABC News*, 30 Mar. 2017, www.abc.net.au/religion/articles /2017/03/30/4645538.htm. Accessed 20 July 2018.

Hauerwas, Stanley. "The End of American Protestantism." *ABC News*, 2 July 2013, www.abc.net.au/religion/articles/2013/07/02/3794561.htm. Accessed 4 Aug. 2018.

Hauerwas, Stanley. "The Politics of the Church and the Humanity of God." *ABC News*, 18 June 2012, www.abc.net.au/religion/articles/2012/06/19/3528056.htm. Accessed 14 Aug. 2018.

Hauerwas, Stanley, and Romand Coles. *Christianity, Democracy, and the Radical Ordinary: Conversations between a Radical Democrat and a Christian.* Cascade Books, 2008.

Hauerwas, Stanley, and Romand Coles. " 'Long Live the Weeds and the Wilderness Yet': Reflections On A Secular Age." *Modern Theology* 26, no. 3 (2010): 349–362.

Hauerwas, Stanley, and William H. Willimon. *Resident Aliens: Life in the Christian Colony: A Provocative Christian Assessment of Culture and Ministry for People Who Know That Something Is Wrong.* Abingdon Press, 1989.

Hayes, Michael Thomas, and Melissa Saul. "Educating the Citizens of Empire." *Journal of Curriculum Theorizing* 28, no. 1 (2012): 207–219.

Hays, Richard B. *Echoes of the Scripture in the Gospels.* Baylor University Press, 2017.

Heater, Derek. *A Brief History of Citizenship.* New York University Press, 2004.

Henrich, Joseph, et al. "The Weirdest People in the World?" *Behavioral and Brain Sciences* 33, nos. 2–3 (2010): 61–83., doi:10.1017/s0140525x0999152x.

Herman, Arthur. *The Cave and the Light: Plato versus Aristotle, and the Struggle for the Soul of Western Civilization.* Random House, 2013.

Hobbes, Thomas. *Hobbes: "Leviathan."* Edited by Richard Tuck et al. Cambridge University Press, 1996.

Hoffman, John. *Sovereignty.* University of Minnesota Press, 1998.

Holifield, E. Brooks. *Theology in America: Christian Thought from the Age of the Puritans to the Civil War.* Yale University Press, 2008.

Horsley, Richard A., and John S. Hanson. *Bandits, Prophets, and Messiahs: Popular Movements in the Time of Jesus.* Harper, 1988.

Illich, Ivan. *Tools for Conviviality.* Marion Boyars, 2009.

Illich, Ivan. *Deschooling Society.* Marion Boyars, 2012.

Jami, Criss. *Killosophy: Killing Knowledge. Loving Wisdom.* Criss Jami, 2015.

Jefferson, Thomas. "Jefferson to Charles Yancey." Received by Charles Yancey, In Ford, 10:1–4, Polygraph Copy at the Library of Congress, 6 Jan. 1816, Washington DC.

Jefferson, Thomas. *The Writings of Thomas Jefferson.* Edited by Henry Augustine. Washington, Riker, 1854.

Jefferson, Thomas. *The Writings of Thomas Jefferson*. Edited by Paul Leicester Ford. Putnam, 1894.

Jefferson, Thomas. *The Works of Thomas Jefferson: Collected and Edited by Paul Leicester Ford,* vol. 2. G. P. Putnam's Sons, 1904.

Jeremias, Joachim. *The Parables of Jesus.* Xpress Reprints, 1995.

Josephus, Flavius. *Josephus: The Antiquities of the Jews.* Translated by William Whiston. Aeterna Press, 2015.

Journell, Wayne. "The Challenges of Political Instruction in a Post-9/11 United States." *High School Journal* 95, no. 1 (2011): 3–14.

Kean, Margaret. *John Milton's Paradise Lost: A Sourcebook*. Routledge, 2005.

Kennedy, John F. "Inaugural Address." Inaugural Address, 20 Jan. 1961, Washington, DC.

King, Martin Luther. "Paul's Letter to American Christians." *Stanford*, 4 Nov. 1956, okra.stanford.edu/transcription/document_images/Vol03Scans/414_4 -Nov-1956_Pauls%20Letter%20to%20Amer%20Christians.pdf.

King, Martin Luther. "I Have A Dream." Speech at the Lincoln Memorial, 28 Aug. 1963, Washington, DC.

King, Martin Luther. "Where Do We Go from Here?" 11th Annual SCLC Convention, 16 Aug. 1967, Atlanta, Georgia.

King, Martin Luther. "Remaining Awake Through a Great Revolution." Sermon at Washington National Cathedral, 31 Mar. 1968, Washington, DC.

Kirby, Dianne. "Cold War and American Religion." *Oxford Research Encyclopedia of Religion*, 14 Aug. 2017, religion.oxfordre.com/view/10.1093/acrefore /9780199340378.001.0001/acrefore-9780199340378-e-398. Accessed 25 Aug. 2018.

Kraft, Dina. "The Real Story behind the Nazi Establishment's Use of 'Romans 13.'" *Haaretz.com*, 20 June 2018, www.haaretz.com/us-news/.premium-the -real-story-behind-the-nazi-establishment-s-use-of-romans-13-1.6194455. Accessed 15 Aug. 2018.

Lakoff, George. *Moral Politics: What Conservatives Know That Liberals Don't*. The University of Chicago Press, 1996.

Levenson, Jon D. *Sinai & Zion: An Entry into the Jewish Bible*. 1st ed. Harper, 1985.

Lilla, Mark. *The Stillborn God: Religion, Politics, and the Modern West*. Vintage Books, 2008.

Lindbeck, George A. *The Nature of Doctrine: Religion and Theology in a Postliberal Age*. Westminster John Knox Press, 2009.

Little, Becky. "The Birth of Illegal Immigration." History Channel, 17 Sept. 2017, www.history.com/news/the-birth-of-illegal-immigration. Accessed 25 July 2018.

Locke, John. *The Second Treatise of Civil Government*. Edited by Andrew Bailey. Broadview Press, 2015.

MacIntyre, Alasdair C. *After Virtue: A Study in Moral Theory*. University of Notre Dame Press, 1981.

Madison, James. *Religious Freedom*. Printed and sold by Lincoln & Edmands, 1819.

Malina, Bruce J. *The New Testament World: Insights from Cultural Anthropology*. Westminster John Knox Press, 1981.

Marcus, Joel. *Mark 1–8: A New Translation with Introduction and Commentary*, vol. 1, Yale University Press, 2010.

Marshall, Thurgood. "Who Is Qualified to Be a Judge?" American College of Trial Lawyers, 14 Mar. 1977, Coronado, California.

Máté-Tóth, András, and Gábor Attila Feleky. "Civil Religion in Central and Eastern Europe: An Application of an American Model." *Americana E Journal*, 27 June 2016.

McCrummen, Stephanie. "God, Trump and the Meaning of Morality." *Washington Post*, 21 July 2018, www.washingtonpost.com/news/national/wp/2018/07/21/feature/god-trump-and-the-meaning-of-morality/?utm_term=.2f6fab13910a. Accessed 9 Aug. 2018.

McCullough, David. *John Adams*. Simon & Schuster, 2001.

McNeill, Emily. "Rabbi Jonathan Sacks Explores Roots of Religious Violence." *Cornell Chronicle*, Cornell, 21 Apr. 2016, news.cornell.edu/stories/2016/04/rabbi-jonathan-sacks-explores-roots-religious-violence. Accessed 21 July 2017.

Meacham, Jon. *American Gospel: God, the Founding Fathers, and the Making of a Nation*. Random House, 2006.

Meacham, Jon. *Soul of America: The Battle for Our Better Angels*. Random House Large Print, 2018.

Milbank, John. *Theology and Social Theory: Beyond Secular Reason*. Basil Blackwell, 1990.

Milbank, John. *The Suspended Middle: Henri De Lubac and the Renewed Split in Modern Catholic Theology*. W. B. Eerdmans Publishing Company, 2014.

Milbank, John, and Adrian Pabst. *The Politics of Virtue: Post-liberalism and the Human Future*. Rowman & Littlefield International, 2016.

Miller, Susan E. *Women in Mark's Gospel*. T&T Clark, 2002.

Milton, John. *The Tenure of Kings and Magistrates . . .* 1650.

Mukherjee, Siddhartha. *The Gene: An Intimate History*. Vintage, 2017.

Müller, Markus, and René Girard. "Interview with René Girard." *Anthropoetics*. ucla.edu, 1996, anthropoetics.ucla.edu/ap0201/interv/. Accessed 24 July 2016.

Murray, Pauli. *Dark Testament: And Other Poems*. Silvermine Publishing, 1970.

Myers, Ched. *Binding the Strong Man: A Political Reading of Mark's Story of Jesus.* Orbis Books, 1994.

Myers, Ched. "'Binding the Strong Man': Jesus' Master Metaphor." *Radical Discipleship*, 4 June 2015, radicaldiscipleship.net/2015/06/04/binding-the -strong-man-jesus-master-metaphor/. Accessed 5 Aug. 2018.

Myers, Ched. "Confronting Legion." *Radical Discipleship*, 11 June 2016, radical-discipleship.net/2016/06/16/confronting-legion/. Accessed 7 Aug. 2018.

Neill, Jeremy. "Political Involvement and Religious Compromises." *Political Theology* 14, no. 1 (21 Apr. 2015): 32–57.

Nerlich, Brigette. "Imagining Imaginaries." *Making Science Public*, 31 July 2017, blogs.nottingham.ac.uk/makingsciencepublic/2015/04/23/imagining -imaginaries/.

Niebuhr, H. Richard. *The Kingdom of God in America.* Wesleyan University Press, 1988.

Nietzsche, Friedrich Wilhelm. *Beyond Good and Evil: On the Genealogy of Morality.* Translated by R. J. Hollingdale, Penguin, 1973.

Noll, Mark A. *America's God: From Jonathan Edwards to Abraham Lincoln.* Oxford University Press, 2005.

Nuechterlein, Paul J. "Passing the Test." Sermon delivered at Prince of Peace Lutheran, 26 June 2011, Portage, MI.

Nuechterlein, Paul. "Nuechterlein on the Bible and Sacrifice." *Girardian Lectionary*, 2006, girardianlectionary.net/learn/nuechterlein-bible-sacrifice/. Accessed 24 July 2018.

Original Broadway Cast Recording. *Hamilton the Musical.* Atlantic, New York.

O'Sullivan, John. "The Great Nation of Futurity." *The United States Democratic Review* 6, no. 23 (1839): 426–430.

O'Sullivan, John. "Annexation." *The United States Magazine and Democratic Review* 17 (1845): 5–10.

Palmer, Robert R. *The Age of Democratic Revolution*, vol. 1. Princeton University Press, 1959.

Pape, Robert Anthony, and James K. Feldman. *Cutting the Fuse: The Explosion of Global Suicide Terrorism and How to Stop It.* University of Chicago Press, 2012.

Plato. *Plato's Republic.* Translated by G. M. A. Grube and C. D. C. Reeve. Hackett Publishing Company, 1997.

Polk, James. "Inaugural Addresses of the Presidents of the United States: From George Washington 1789 to George Bush 1989." *Avalon Project—Documents in Law, History and Diplomacy*, 4 Mar. 1845, avalon.law.yale.edu/19th_cen-tury/polk.asp. Accessed 5 Aug. 2018.

Putnam, Robert D., and David E. Campbell. *American Grace: How Religion Divides and Unites Us.* Simon & Schuster, 2012.

R.E.M. "Stand." *Stand*. Scott Litt and Warner Brothers, 1988.

Reno, R. R., and Stanley Hauerwas. *Matthew: Brazos Theological Commentary on the Bible*. Brazos Press, 2006.

"Requiem for Civil Religion." *Christian Century*, 1 Mar. 2017.

Robertson, Ann. "Health Promotion and the Common Good: Theoretical Considerations." *Critical Public Health* 9, no. 2 (1999): 117–133.

"Romans 13—Stanley Hauerwas." *YouTube*, 14 Oct. 2014, www.youtube.com /watch?v=PSw3tL-VkuI. Accessed 15 Aug. 2018.

Rothstein, Richard. *The Color of Law: A Forgotten History of How Our Government Segregated America*. Liveright Publishing, 2017.

Rousseau, Jean-Jacques. *Rousseau: The Social Contract and Other Later Political Writings*. Cambridge University Press, 2016.

Runcie, Robert. *The Truth Shall Make You Free: The Lambeth Conference 1988*. Church House Publishing, 1988.

Rutledge, Fleming. *Crucifixion: Understanding the Death of Jesus Christ*. Eerdmans Publishing Company, 2017.

Sacks, Jonathan. *The Politics of Hope*. Vintage, 2000.

Sacks, Jonathan. "On the Limits of Power." The Office of Rabbi Sacks, 16 Aug. 2007, rabbisacks.org/shoftim-5767-on-the-limits-of-power/.

Sacks, Jonathan. "Taking Responsibility." The Office of Rabbi Sacks, 28 Sept. 2013, rabbisacks.org/bereishit-5774-taking-responsibility/. Accessed 22 July 2018.

Sacks, Jonathan. "Biblical Insights into the Good Society (Ebor Lecture 2011)." The Office of Rabbi Sacks, 2 Oct. 2013, rabbisacks.org/biblical-insights-into -the-good-society-ebor-lecture-2012/. Accessed 29 July 2018.

Sacks, Jonathan. "The Consent of the Governed (Shoftim 5777)." The Office of Rabbi Sacks, 22 Aug. 2017, rabbisacks.org/consent-governed-shoftim-5777/. Accessed 30 July 2018.

Sacks, Jonathan. "The Genesis of Justice." The Office of Rabbi Sacks, 13 Oct. 2014, rabbisacks.org/genesis-justice-bereishit/. Accessed 21 Nov. 2017.

Sacks, Jonathan. "Bereishit (5769)—Violence in the Name of G-d." The Office of Rabbi Sacks, 4 Apr. 2016, rabbisacks.org/covenant-conversation-5769 -bereishit-violence-in-the-name-of-g-d/. Accessed 19 July 2017.

Sacks, Jonathan. *Not in God's Name: Confronting Religious Violence*. Schocken, 2017.

Sacks, Jonathan. "The Ten Utterances (Extract from the Koren-Sacks Shavuot Machzor)." The Office of Rabbi Sacks, 16 May 2018, rabbisacks.org/ten -utterances-extract-koren-sacks-shavuot-machzor/. Accessed 28 July 2018.

Scheitle, Christopher P. "Race, Diversity, and Membership Duration in Religious Congregations." *Baylor University Department of Sociology*, 12 July 2010, www .baylorisr.org/wp-content/uploads/dougherty_race.pdf.

Sessions, Jeff. "Attorney General Sessions Addresses Recent Criticisms of Zero Tolerance by Church Leaders." Fort Wayne Rotary Club: Rotarians, religious leaders, lawyers, and law enforcement gathering, 14 June 2018, Fort Wayne, Indiana.

Siker, Jeffrey S. *Scripture and Ethics: Twentieth-Century Portraits.* Oxford University Press, 1997.

Simon, Paul. *The Glass House: Politics and Morality in the Nation's Capital.* Continuum, 1984.

Smith, Adam. *The Theory of Moral Sentiments.* Oxford University Press, 1976.

Smith, Christian, and Melinda Lundquist Denton. *Soul Searching: The Religious and Spiritual Lives of American Teenagers.* Oxford University Press, 2009.

Smith, Gregory A., and Jessica Martínez. "How the Faithful Voted: A Preliminary 2016 Analysis." *Pew Research Center,* 9 Nov. 2016, www.pewresearch.org/fact -tank/2016/11/09/how-the-faithful-voted-a-preliminary-2016-analysis/. Accessed 19 July 2018.

Snyder Belousek, Darrin W. "God, Evil, and (Non)Violence: Creation Theology, Creativity Theology, and Christian Ethics." *Conrad Grebel University College,* 26 Aug. 2016, uwaterloo.ca/grebel/publications/conrad-grebel-review /issues/spring-2016/god-evil-and-nonviolence-creation-theology-creativity. Accessed 10 Aug. 2018.

Sordi, Marta, and Annabel Bedini. *The Christians and the Roman Empire.* University of Oklahoma Press, 1994.

St. Jerome, and Origen. *Ancient Christian Fathers: St. Jerome: Commentary on Isaiah; Origen Homilies 1–9 on Isaiah.* Translated by Thomas P. Scheck, vol. 68. Paulist Press, 2015.

Stannard, David E. *American Holocaust: The Conquest of the New World.* Oxford University Press, 2006.

Stringfellow, William. *An Ethic for Christians and Other Aliens in a Strange Land.* Word Books, 1973.

"The Subversive Magnificat: Mary's Expectations of the Messiah." *Enemy Love,* 19 Jan. 2013, enemylove.com/subversive-magnificat-mary-expected -messiah-to-be-like/. Accessed 22 July 2017.

Tabb, Phillip. *Serene Urbanism: A Biophilic Theory and Practice of Sustainable Placemaking.* Routledge, Taylor & Francis Group, 2017.

Tannehill, Robert C. *The Sword of His Mouth: Forceful and Imaginative Language in Synoptic Sayings.* Fortress Press, 1975.

Taylor, Charles. *Sources of the Self.* Harvard University Press, 1992.

Taylor, Charles. *A Secular Age.* Belknap Press of Harvard University Press, 2007.

Taylor, Vincent. *The Gospel According to St. Mark: The Greek Text with Introduction, Notes and Indexes.* Macmillan, 1963.

Tertullian. *On Idolatry.* Translated by Sydney Thelwall. Kissinger, 2004.

Tetlock, Philip E., et al. "The Psychology of the Unthinkable: Taboo Trade-Offs, Forbidden Base Rates, and Heretical Counterfactuals." *Journal of Personality and Social Psychology* 78, no. 5 (2000): 853–870.

"Thomas Jefferson's Monticello." *Thomas Jefferson's Monticello,* www.monticello .org/site/plantation-and-slavery/thomas-jefferson-and-sally-hemings-brief -account. Accessed 5 Aug. 2018.

Thurman, Howard. *Jesus and the Disinherited.* Beacon Press, 1996.

Tocqueville, Alexis de. *Democracy in America.* Edited by Arthur Goldhammer and Olivier Zunz. Library of America Paperback Classics, 2012.

Truman, Harry S. *Where the Buck Stops: The Personal and Private Writings of Harry S. Truman.* Edited by Margaret Truman, New Word City, 2016.

Trump, Donald. "The Inaugural Address." The White House, Jan. 2017, www .whitehouse.gov/briefings-statements/the-inaugural-address/. Accessed 19 July 2018.

United States Constitutional Convention. "Constitution of the United States." *World Digital Library,* 17 Sept. 1787, www.wdl.org/en/item/2708/. Accessed 23 July 2018.

Uwan, Ekemini. "Blog." *Ekemini Uwan: Decolonized Discipleship,* 8 Feb. 2018, www.sistamatictheology.com/blog. Accessed 16 Aug. 2018.

Volf, Miroslav. *The End of Memory: Remembering Rightly in a Violent World.* Eerdmans, 2006.

Wallas, Graham. *Human Nature in Politics.* Houghton Mifflin, 1919.

Washington, George. "Letter to the Jews of Newport." Washington Papers, 6:284–85, 18 Aug. 1790, University of Virginia, Charlottesville, Virginia.

Wells, Sam. "Nazareth Manifesto." *Vagt Lecture: The Nazareth Manifesto,* 27 Apr. 2008.

Wells, William Vincent. *The Life and Public Services of Samuel Adams,* vol. 3. Little Brown and Company, 1869.

West, Cornel. *Prophesy Deliverance! An Afro-American Revolutionary Christianity.* Westminster John Knox Press, 2002.

West, Cornel. "On Constructed Rights." 28 Feb. 2013, New Haven.

"What I Saw in America. The Resurrection of Rome. Sidelights." *The Collected Works of G. K. Chesterton,* by G. K. Chesterton and James J. Thompson, vol. 21. Ignatius Press, San Francisco, 1990.

Wink, Walter. *Engaging the Powers: Discernment and Resistance in a World of Domination.* Fortress Press, 1999.

Wink, Walter. *The Powers That Be: Theology for a New Millennium.* Doubleday, 1998.

Zajonc, R. B. "Feeling and Thinking: Preferences Need No Inferences." *American Psychologist* 35, no. 2 (1980): 151–175.

Zauzmer, Julie, and Keith McMillan. "Sessions Cites Bible Passage Used to Defend Slavery in Defense of Separating Immigrant Families." *Washington Post*, 15 June 2018, www.washingtonpost.com/news/acts-of-faith/wp/2018/06/14/jeff -sessions-points-to-the-bible-in-defense-of-separating-immigrant-families /?utm_term=.bb737f8d46b0. Accessed 15 Aug. 2018.

Zerwick, Maximilian, and Mary Grosvenor. *A Grammatical Analysis of the Greek New Testament*. Biblical Institute Press, 1974.

Zojanc, R. B. "Attitudinal Effects of Mere Exposure." University of Michigan, Institute for Social Research Library, Sept. 1965, www.psc.isr.umich.edu/dis /infoserv/isrpub/pdf/Theattitudinaleffects_2360_.PDF.

About the Author

The Rt. Rev. C. Andrew "Andy" Doyle was seated as the ninth bishop of Texas on June 7, 2009, at Christ Church Cathedral, Houston. Born in 1966 in Carbondale, Illinois, and raised in Houston, Bishop Doyle served five years as canon to the ordinary prior to his election. He holds a BFA from the University of North Texas and served at St. Stephen's Episcopal School, Austin, before receiving an M.Div. from Virginia Theological Seminary. He is known today for his work in communications, leadership, vision, mission, and writing.

He is the author of *Unity in Mission*, 2011; *Unabashedly Episcopalian*, 2012, (available in both English and Spanish); *Church: A Generous Community Amplified for the Future*, 2015; *A Generous Community: Being Church in a New Missionary Age*, 2015; *Small Batch: Local, Organic, and Sustainable Church*, 2016; *The Jesus Heist: Reclaiming The Gospel from the Church*, 2017; *Vocātiō: Imaging a Visible Church*, 2018.

He is sought out to participate in innovative conversations about church mission strategy, structures, and communications in an amplified world filled with digital natives. Today he is interested in how our conversations inside the church may contribute to a paralyzed mission, and the nature of the vocation of the church itself and the church's vocations.

His six-word autobiography is "Met Jesus on pilgrimage, still walking."

He enjoys music (and collects classic rock vinyl from the 1960s and 1970s), genealogy, fly fishing and the outdoors, painting and writing. He is married to JoAnne and they have two children.